If you're a curvy sewist looking for in-depth advice on how to fit jeans, *Fit and Sew Custom Jeans* is a fantastic choice. The book covers a comprehensive array of fitting adjustments, using sewing patterns that are available in a wide range of sizes. Achieving a wonderful fit in a pair of jeans is the ultimate confidence booster, and Helen Bartley is here to help you achieve it. — **Jenny Rushmore, founder & creative director, Cashmerette**

I was lucky enough to attend a jeans workshop in Portland some years ago, but this book gives you all the necessary information without having to travel. I can't wait to get my material washed and dried (three times) and to put into practice the techniques that Helen Bartley has worked so hard to explain and demonstrate. Even if you don't wear jeans, the modifications chapter will enable you to expand your variety of pants and trousers. A great reference book to add to your Palmer/Pletsch library. — **Celia Banks, Palmer/Pletsch Certified Sewing Instructor, Sew Fundamental Ltd, Cheshire, England**

Fitting jeans needs a book of its own, and this book is it! In addition to covering fabric, fit (on real people!), construction, and much more, Helen gives complete instructions for many creative adaptations for pockets, hems, and styles. — **Connie Hamilton, Palmer/Pletsch Certified Sewing Instructor, Hartwell, Georgia**

Fit and Sew Custom Jeans covers every aspect and answers every question needed to successfully fit and make the perfect jean for any body. The step-by-step text and clear, concise illustrations make this book easy to follow; and Helen (and Hazel's) light wit put a smile on my face. I enjoyed and learnt from every page. — **Susan Neall, fashion sewing instructor and teacher trainer in Sydney, Australia, and events coordinator for sewinspirationalevents.com.au**

Helen has developed unique techniques for getting the tight jeans fit that had so far eluded me. Her efficient fit-as-you-sew order, clear illustrations, and explanations of techniques make sewing custom-fit jeans a reality. She includes visual examples of the fitting process on "real people" bodies, including men! Inspiring ideas for pockets and design changes will have you planning to make multiple pairs of jeans. Helen's sidekick Hazel pipes in with her wisdom, making the book fun to read. This is a must-have book for anyone wanting to learn how to fit and sew quality jeans that rival the best designers. — **Nancy Seifert, Palmer/Pletsch Certified Sewing Instructor, Sammamish, Washington, and coordinator and workshop instructor for Palmer/Pletsch, Seattle**

FIT AND SEW
• CUSTOM
jeans

**CLASSIC AND CREATIVE
SEWING TECHNIQUES
FOR MODERN PATTERNS**

Fit and Sew Custom J… all things jeans. Auth… of research and testin… sewing techniques to home sewists, showing them how to create their own designer jeans at home. Walking you through the special tools, materials, and techniques needed to sew jeans, Helen is with you every step of the way on your jeans-making journey.

Fit and Sew Custom Jeans is full of case studies, clear photographs, creative ideas, and practical tips. My favorite thing about this book is that it empowers you to make your own jeans without any assumptions about how you want your jeans to fit or look. With this book, Palmer/Pletsch gives you tools to help you sew jeans you'll love. — **Jennifer Wiese, owner, Workroom Social and Camp Workroom Social, Brooklyn, New York**

I strongly feel that once you tackle making your own jeans, you'll develop the confidence to sew absolutely anything. Whether you're a first-time or master jean-maker, I think you'll find this book extremely helpful on your jean-making journey. The jeans-specific fitting advice is extremely helpful, and I love all the ideas and suggestions for hacking and customizing a tried-and-true pattern. A wonderful addition to any sewing library! — **Heather Lou, founder, Closet Core Patterns**

Fit and Sew Custom Jeans is comprehensive, organized, easy to understand, and filled with answers to questions about jeans construction. I was delighted to find so much insight into RTW and options on design ideas. It is very helpful that Helen uses different body shapes in her examples and how this impacts our choice of denim.

After reading this book, I am highly motivated to start another pair of jeans…and try some different options. It's going to make the difference between a pair of jeans that I like and a pair that I love to wear! Great reading and great reference! — **Zeta Fonseca, Palmer/Pletsch workshop attendee and avid sewist**

Helen Bartley's *Fit and Sew Custom Jeans* is a superbly curated collection of jean fitting, design and sewing methods. It's everything you wanted to know about jeans that you didn't know you should ask! With an approach¬able and humorous cadence, this book represents much talent and research by all of its capable contributors. Why wouldn't you invite Helen (and Hazel) to guide you along the path to sew your perfect custom jeans? — **Colleen Baerg, Palmer/Pletsch Certified Sewing Instructor and owner of Sewing by the Sea, Campbell River, BC.**

I have been using the Palmer/Pletsch tissue-fitting method for many decades. Using this technique with jeans is impressive. Another exciting area is sewing jeans for males; the photos are amazing. The section on hems and the "bottom line" is a must-read. (My favorite is the fringed raw edge.) This book will be a requirement for my jean classes, and it is an excellent resource. — *Susie Birden Brown, Palmer/Pletsch Certified Sewing Instructor, Newark, California*

Once again, Palmer/Pletsch has created a fantastic learning guide. *Fit and Sew Custom Jeans* is filled with information on not only how to sew jeans, but also how to fit and modify your favorite jeans pattern. This book is great for novice jean makers and also those that are experienced and wanting to have some fun with pattern modifications. This book is a must for any sewing library! — *Whitney Luckenbill, creator of TomKat Stitchery*

The first pair of jeans I made was 40 years ago—so challenging were they to make, I swore I'd never make another pair. I held that view until *Fit and Sew Custom Jeans* came into my hands. This book is a comprehensive, well-written (and humorous) manual with no jeans-related detail left out. Helen Bartley has done a stellar job documenting the jeans-making process, with illustrations at every step, yet she doesn't gloss over what worked and what didn't in the many pairs she made during the book's progress. Now I'm left wondering why I'd ever want to buy another pair of jeans again. — *Cheryl Lampard, style maven and founder of Style Matters International, educator, passionate sewist, and Palmer/Pletsch Certified Sewing Instructor, Naples, Florida.*

Finally, jeans that fit, look great, and are comfortable! Helen Bartley's encyclopedic knowledge of fitting princi¬ples and construction techniques will guide you through the detailed, yet oh so worth it, effort of creating your dream jeans. The instructions are clear and concise, providing all the fine-tuning techniques needed for any fitting adjustment. Regardless of your size, age or shape, *Fit and Sew Custom Jeans* will help you create jeans that are comfortable and look great not just when you are

standing in front of the mirror, but when you are really wearing them as the comfortable, everyday garment they are intended to be. — *Julie Brady, Palmer/Pletsch Certified Sewing Instructor, Portland, Oregon*

Fit and Sew Custom Jeans leaves no stone (or should I say snap or rivet?) unturned! Helen Bartley breaks the code on the mystery of sewing one's own perfect jeans. "You can do it!" she encourages throughout the book. With her usual clear and understandable style of teaching, Helen explains how to custom fit a variety of jeans styles to any body type, using the Palmer/Pletsch tissue-fitting method. She adeptly details all the tried-and-true, step-by-step construction methods. Going beyond construction, Helen explains how to modify one's jeans for style, flair and individual pizazz. Wonder what equipment you'd need? Helen provides the goods about that as well, in addition to the why and the how.

From skinny to relaxed, custom jeans can be in the home-sewer's closet at last! This is another valuable book from Palmer/Pletsch to add to your sewing library. — *Lois Gase, Palmer/Pletsch Certified Sewing Instructor, Boston, Massachusetts.*

What a joy to have an entire book devoted to the art of fitting and sewing custom jeans! Helen's take on styling, fitting, and sewing jeans is modern, comprehensive and completely thorough. There are charts and help throughout the book, and the "butt fit" technique? Pure genius! This well-organized book will guide you through the jeans making process no matter what the current styles are. Everything you need to make jeans is here. — *Pamela Leggett, owner Pamela's Patterns and Palmer/Pletsch Certified Sewing Instructor, Connecticut*

Helen really figured out how to achieve a very fitted jean, in keeping with today's popular styles. The book includes concise instructions aided by excellent illustrations and photos. They will surely cement in your mind anything you don't already understand. I loved how Helen's personality came through throughout the book, as well as the fun tips from Hazel! — *Marta Alto, Palmer/Pletsch Certified Sewing Instructor, Portland, Oregon*

FIT AND SEW
CUSTOM
jeans

CLASSIC AND CREATIVE SEWING TECHNIQUES FOR MODERN PATTERNS

by Helen Bartley

Pati Palmer, Managing Editor and Publisher

Linda Wisner, Creative Director, Book Designer

Jeannette Schilling, Technical Illustrations

Pati Palmer, Studio Photography

Helen Bartley, Technical Photography

Helen Bartley, Jeans Styling and Sewing

Kaylee Kepple, Cover Photo

Ann Gosch, Technical and Copy Editing

ACKNOWLEDGMENTS

So many people helped with the creation of this book. It makes me misty. I'm still stunned that Pati Palmer actually said yes when I mentioned writing a book on sewing jeans. I have always felt that the Palmer/Pletsch team produced the best, most comprehensive sewing books, and working with them has been the honor of a lifetime. Not only is Pati the editor supreme, but she is also a mentor and friend without whom this book simply would not exist. A big enough "thank you" to Pati for her work, patience, and expertise is just not possible. Marta Alto originally inspired me to sew jeans in a Palmer/Pletsch pants workshop years ago. Her creative influence, ingenious sewing techniques, and savvy edits are laced throughout this book. Graphic artist Jeannette Schilling brought each sewing technique to life with her exquisite illustrations. Her ability to translate my sketches and scribbles is mystifying. Ann Gosch edited the book with kindness and expertise, and because she sews, she filed down the rough edges of my instructions like no one else could. Linda Wisner's oversight and design skills pulled the whole package together and made it the fluid visual pleasure I could only dream of.

Many others are to blame too! My mother, Juanita Rogers, taught me to love sewing as a child. At 96 years old she spent days editing this book. My precious daughters, Ava and Molly Bartley, and my sweetheart, Greg Olson, get huge thanks for providing both unlimited modeling and counseling services. My brother Dale Grummert, a sportswriter, suffered through editing the book as a person who doesn't sew and offered up a fresh perspective. The coolest high school sewing teacher, Phoebe Miletich, who introduced me to my first Palmer/Pletsch sewing book and planted the seed that sewing could be more than a hobby. Coach Rachelle Disbennett Lee conspired with me in all of my harebrained schemes for over 15 years. Thanks to my cat, Hazel, for all her pro tips and for being the sweetest sewing companion ever.

These pages are filled with the images of friends and family who gave hours of their time as fitting subjects and models. Endless thanks to Heather Adams, Ava Bartley, Molly Bartley, Julie Brady, Taylor Flores, Jeff Joyner, Greg Olson, Pati Palmer, and Alli Yahn.

So many teachers, Palmer/Pletsch Certified Sewing Instructors, and workshop attendees read, reviewed, and offered priceless improvements to the book. Thank you to Marta Alto, Colleen Baerg, Celia Banks, Elizabeth Bryant, Zeta Fonseca, Lois Gase, Connie Hamilton, Cheryl Lampard, Whitney Luckenbill, Sue Neall, Nancy Siefert, Diana Stanley, and Deb Wilkinson. I can't even believe all the hours you spent on this.

To sewing industry folks that helped out— Rain Delisle, Stan Gray, Heather Lou, Rhonda Pierce, Gary Rael, Jenny Rushmore, Frank Smyth, and Lori VanMaanen—thank you!

Thank you all for giving so very much to me and to this project. I am humbled and grateful.

In loving memory of Mimi the Sewing Lounge Dog—October 2006 to April 2021—who attended more of my sewing classes than any other creature. RIP, my little friend.

Publisher's Cataloging-In-Publication Data
(Prepared by The Donohue Group, Inc.)

Names: Bartley, Helen, 1961- author, photographer. | Palmer, Pati, editor, publisher, photographer. | Wisner, Linda, designer. | Schilling, Jeannette, illustrator. | Gosch, Ann, editor.
Title: Fit and sew custom jeans : classic and creative sewing techniques for modern patterns / by Helen Bartley ; Pati Palmer, Managing Editor and Publisher ; Linda Wisner, Creative Director, Book Designer ; Jeannette Schilling, technical illustrations ; Pati Palmer, Studio Photography ; Helen Bartley, close-up photography ; Helen Bartley, styling and sewing ; Ann Gosch, technical and copy editing.
Other Titles: Jeans
Description: First edition. | Portland, OR U.S.A. : Palmer/Pletsch Publishing, 2021. | Includes index.
Identifiers: ISBN 9781618471062 | ISBN 9781618471079 (ebook)
Subjects: LCSH: Sewing--Handbooks, manuals, etc. | Jeans (Clothing)--Handbooks, manuals, etc. | Fashion design--Handbooks, manuals, etc.
Classification: LCC TT715 .B37 2021 (print) | LCC TT715 (ebook) | DDC 646.2--dc23

CONTENTS

HELEN BARTLEY

Helen Bartley learned sewing at her mother's knee and has devoted much of her life to it. She studied textiles, fashion design and clothing construction at Eastern Washington University and is now a Palmer/Pletsch Certified Sewing Instructor and corporate educator who teaches pants, knits and fit workshops in Portland, Oregon. She served as technical editor for the Palmer/Pletsch book, *Knits for Real People*, and as contributor, garment maker, and model for both that book and the highly regarded *The Palmer/Pletsch Complete Guide to Fitting*.

In 2008 she opened Seam Divas Sewing Lounge, where hundreds of students of all experience levels have benefited from her knowledge and empathetic teaching style. She has conducted numerous workshops in the the Pacific Northwest and beyond.

Helen is also a guitarist and singer-songwriter who occasionally performs in the Portland area.

FOREWORD BY PATI PALMER

Although I've designed a dozen jeans patterns for McCall's, I have not sewn dozens of pairs to perfect techniques. Helen Bartley has. My colleague Marta Alto and I met Helen when she started taking our workshops to be the best she could be at fitting herself and others. We decided to mentor Helen in her quest to be a jeans expert.

Years of teaching jeans classes and workshops allowed Helen to test techniques to determine the ones that were easiest to do for the most professional results. Students are often our best teachers and Helen listened and made changes along the way.

Helen's construction order includes fitting during the sewing process. We had been using the Palmer/Pletsch Tissue-Fitting Method for jeans, but when the denim had a lot of stretch and a workshop student wanted a tight fit, the jeans ended up too big. It was Helen who devised a blended method using tissue-fitting for the first fitting and formulas for how much narrower and shorter in the crotch to cut the fabric.

Now, after more than five years, the jeans book you hold in your hands will allow you to use any jeans pattern and make a pair that looks like those of the top jeans brands and fits because they are custom-made. You and your friends will be in awe!

Pati Palmer, CEO, Palmer/Pletsch

Throughout this book, you will encounter Hazel, and learn from her wisdom.

WHY SEW JEANS?

THE CASE FOR SEWING JEANS

Jeans are the great, elusive garment. The one garment that everyone loves, theoretically, but that gives us the most grief when trying to find our perfect pair. We love the idea of wearing jeans but hate shopping for them. We love the memory of that one great pair that got away, is worn out or long gone.

What do you remember about that pair? Were they your favorite pair you wore when you learned horseback riding? Did you wear them out dancing in college and remember the compliments you got? The pair that was so comfy and made you feel so good that you wore them over and over? Most everyone I talk to says they love jeans but hate shopping for them. They are always: too long, too short, too high in rise, too low in rise, too loose here, too tight there, perfect here, not perfect there.

Don't we even expect more from our jeans fit than we do most other garments? They need to fit perfectly *and* be comfortable too, even in a thick and sometimes rigid fabric. That's a pretty tall order for ready-to-wear (RTW) jeans manufacturers, considering the gazillion different body shapes out there. Think of all the potential body types and our desire for a "perfect" fit, which is also a very individual thing.

We as sewists struggle with fit for any garment. We know if we want something to fit perfectly, we need to make it ourselves. We must learn techniques for altering patterns, and then master fitting as we sew. It's no different with jeans. A perfectly fitting pair of jeans will be different for each wearer, and only that wearer can tell you how they need to fit, look and perform. They don't happen by accident. When we choose to sew our own jeans we take control away from ready-to-wear limitations and put it in our own hands. In this book we will break down the jeans-making process step-by-step, from materials selection to hammering in the last rivet. With care and practice you can make the jeans you'll dub as your new faves.

A BIT OF HISTORY

The real focus of this book is making jeans for the home sewist, but a little history is a fun place to begin.

In the late 1800s the miners and construction workers in the United States needed sturdy work pants. A Nevada tailor named Jacob Davis added rivets to the pockets and the bottom of the button fly of his work pants, created with the fabric he ordered from dry-goods supplier Levi Strauss in San Francisco. Voila, the "amazing riveted pants" were born.

Davis could barely keep up production for the demand. He feared that his trademark rivet idea would be stolen, so he sought a patent. When finances proved that patent out of his reach, he turned to Strauss and offered a partnership if he could cover the $68 U.S. patent fee. Strauss began production of Davis' pants and the now-famed Levi's brand was born.

The first Levi's jeans were called waist or waist-high overalls. They had buttons on the waistband front and back to attach suspenders. A button fly was featured because zippers had not yet been invented. Lee jeans would begin sporting zippers or "hookless fasteners" in its cowboy pants in 1926.

JEANS BRANDING

Branding is an integral part of jeans history and marketing. Pocket stitching, tag, rivet and button designs make a manufacturer stand out in a giant sea of denim blue.

For a deeper dive into jeans history and denim love, check out the websites and books we list in Resources, page 235. A metric conversion chart can be found on page 237. (The measurements in this book are mostly in inches.)

This book is devoted to making jeans that can be sewn by anyone using readily available materials, a home sewing machine and ideally a home serger. A serger is not required, but it significantly speeds construction. Construction methods, with or without a serger, will be addressed in Chapter 7.

Get ready to make jeans that are yours alone!

CHAPTER 2

TOOLS

ALL THE THINGS

I resisted writing this bit because I always look at the tools section of sewing books and think, *duh*. Of course you need all of those things! Now, while in the thick of it, I understand why this chapter is necessary. To have a good sewing experience and turn out your best product, you need the proper tools. And a certain part of me appreciates a sexy sewing notions photo collage.

Your most important tools are your heart and mind. When tempted by the latest gadget, remember that it won't get up and cut, fit, and sew your jeans for you. Less is more.

THE MACHINES

Sewing Machines

You should be able to make jeans with any sewing machine that can sew through multiple layers of denim. Some will do it better than others.

Brand-specific recommendations are unreliable in today's manufacturing world. Even from the beginning of the industrial era, design, engineering, raw materials, and cosmic energy have come together intermittently to make the "perfect" machine of any kind—sewing machines and cars alike. As with any appliance, certain sewing machine models have proven more precise and/or more durable than models made before or after by the same companies.

When shopping for a sewing machine, do your research first. Scour the sewing education sites and blogs. Don't trust all the reviews on shopping sites. You don't know the intention or the skill level of the writer. Ask people who sew jeans what they prefer and why. Speak to the sewing machine technician at your local dealer in addition to the salesperson. Techs know which machines come back for problems and those that they never see until it's time for a cleaning. Consider also a good used or refurbished machine. If you buy from a reputable dealer it will have a warranty and will often include lessons on operation.

Gary Rael, sewing machine technician extraordinaire at House of Sewing, always gives me the best advice about machines from vintage to new. Find yourself a good machine dealer. It beats all the online machine reviews for truth and transparency.

If your dealer offers jeans sewing classes, take a class and use a store machine to see if it really works for you.

Sergers

A serger is not mandatory for sewing jeans but it makes the job quicker and easier without sacrificing durability. In this book most of the seams are finished with a serger. Details and options for seaming are covered in Chapter 6 starting on page 114. The same suggestions for choosing a sewing machine apply for sergers. People have favorites. Try before you buy!

A PRO'S VIEW

Frank Smyth, owner of House of Sewing in Vancouver, Washington—my local go-to dealer

I have relied on this gem of a local sewing resource for many years. I asked Frank his pro view on what kind of sewing machine would be best for sewing jeans. As suspected, I didn't get a make and model recommendation from Frank. Yeesh. Here's what he said:

Industrial machines are built to do one thing only and do it really well: straight stitch or bartack or overlock, etc. Most people want a machine that will do multiple stitches. Household machines will often have more bells and whistles (embroidery stitches, etc.), but may not have the power you want to consistently sew through heavy denim.

When choosing a household machine that "does it all," you're always going to give a little bit up in each step of your sewing

process (as compared to an industrial that does just one thing really well), but if you're only going to sew a couple of pairs of jeans, you probably don't want to spend $10,000 on multiple commercial machines. I encourage my customers to bring in what they're having trouble with and I ask them what their current machine's not doing that they want it to do, and we'll attempt to duplicate the problem in the shop and find them something that works better. You really have to try out each machine regardless of the brand.

Frank also specifically stressed the importance of using both the correct type and quality of needles and thread in the successful operation of any sewing machine. Oh, yes, I'll tell you all about those in Chapter 3. Wink.

If your sewing machine has been sitting idle for years, have it serviced or consider a refurbished machine from your trusted local dealer. If you want a new machine, ask that dealer to make a recommendation. Then sew on the machine in the store to make sure it will sew through many layers of fabrics.

PRESSING EQUIPMENT

Irons

You'll want a good steam iron for all of your sewing. Important features: a quality soleplate (stainless steel or nonstick, each style has merits), adjustable steam (including steam off), shot-of-steam button for extra steam, water vessel with a window to the water level, and a fill spout that is easy to open/close and fill. A pipe dream would be the ability to cancel the auto-off feature so the iron stays hot between pressing sessions. It's rare. Some don't have auto-off at all. Others have a longer time limit and give a little alarm warning before turning off.

Like many products, the models change frequently and quality can vary. For this reason, we don't recommend brands or models. Buy from a source that will accept your return if the iron doesn't meet your standards.

Pressing Surfaces

An ironing board works just fine, but we love a large, sturdy pressing surface.

Illustrated instructions for making an excellent padded pressboard are found in the Palmer/Pletsch book *Pants for Real People*. Set atop a cabinet with casters, your pressing space can double as a mobile storage area too. Here are two examples from my studio.

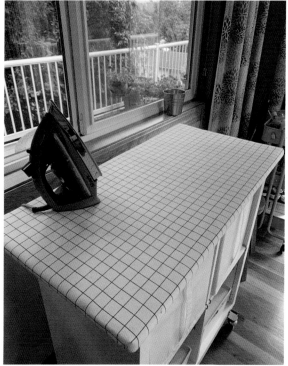

Pressing Tools

Seam roll or seam stick—These make pressing the long seams of pant legs much easier. Mine is made from half of a 2½" dowel and 24" long. Sand well before using.

Clapper—A good clapper is a pounding block and point presser combined. It's great for flattening pocket hems, belt loops, waistband ends, and seam intersections, making them much easier to stitch. I will often leave jeans pockets under a clapper overnight or while assembling other parts.

Ham—Used for pressing curved seams such as in the hip area. I love the old sawdust-filled hams. You can make your own with pretty fabrics or order a custom-made ham and seam roll. The beauties pictured here are by Stitch Nerd Custom Shop (stitchnerdcustomshop.com).

Press cloth—For use with fusible interfacings to protect iron and board. You can make one from plain muslin or cotton organza by pinking the edges. Label "for fusibles only" so you don't accidently use it for regular pressing. Change out often, since they tend to build up adhesive residue.

SEWING NOTIONS

You'll want all of your basic sewing supplies as well:

Scissors—Sharp fabric shears and paper scissors.

Rotary cutter and ruler—I use both. Nothing like a blade and ruler for cutting belt-loop strips.

Pins—

- **Straight pins.** 1⅜" long, 0.5mm gauge pins with glass heads work great for both tissue and fabric and for pinning into cardboard surfaces while altering your pattern.
- **Flower head quilting pins.** 2⅛" long, 0.7mm gauge. The longer, heavier pin goes through multiple layers of denim beautifully.

Seam gauge—Small and handy for quick measurements.

Seam ripper—Because ripping of basting stitches is an intentional part of making jeans that fit, find one that is comfortable to hold and work with.

Marking tools—The marker that shows up best on your fabric is the one to go with. I like chalk wheels and chalk pencils best.

Buttonhole cutter—A chisel-style cutter with a mat or board is most precise. You can also use small, sharp scissors or a seam ripper to open buttonholes.

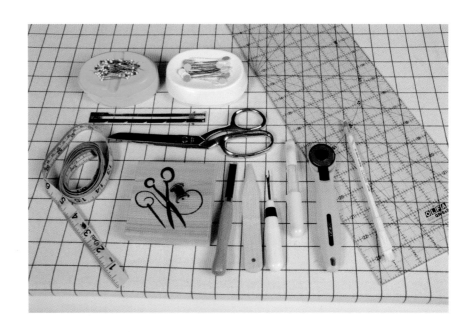

ALTERATION SUPPLIES

Gridded cardboard—You want a surface large enough that no part of your tissue hangs off while altering. It must also be pinnable. A gridded folding cardboard cutting board or cutting table is ideal. The grid makes altering easier.

Gridded pattern alteration tissue—Perfect Pattern Paper from McCall's (available at palmerpletsch.com) was developed at the suggestion of our students. It is the same weight and strength as pattern tissue. It has a 1/8" grid that makes alterations easy and accurate. Heavier papers overpower the pattern. Regular gift tissue can tear too easily, and moisture can cause the dye on colored paper to run.

Tape—1/2" Scotch Magic tape is the best tape to use on patterns and pattern paper. It performs far better than any tape we've found. It will not scrunch up with the heat of the iron and is the right width to avoid stiffening the pattern. No substitutions! Bossy. A weighted dispenser is handy.

Soft lead pencil—Since the ink from some pens can penetrate the tissue and make a mess of your cutting board, we recommend using a pencil. Or protect your cutting board with paper under the tissue.

6" clear plastic ruler—Mark a common seam allowance width on each end.

Waistline fitting elastic—Most jeans waistbands are about 1½" wide. We use the 1½" Pamela's Fantastic Elastic (see Resources, page 235) and sew Velcro to each end to make an adjustable "fitting" elastic. See page 36.

Pins—1³/₈" long extra-fine (.5mm gauge) glass-head pins. These work best on pattern tissue. See preceding page for more pin info.

Mirrors—For accurate tissue-fitting you shouldn't bend or twist to see your alterations. All you need is a full-length mirror and a handheld mirror for a good rear view.

HARDWARE SETTING TOOLS

You'll need a hammer, awl, wire cutters and/or needle-nosed pliers with cutter, and small piece of metal or anvil to use as a surface for hand setting rivets and tack buttons. A piece of wood or a magazine will protect your work surface.

Some rivet setting systems come with all the tools you need to set their rivets except the hammer. This one from Tandy Leather has a setting post that is concave on one end, so it perfectly fits the rivet head, and a little round anvil to use as a hammering surface.

Prym makes a clever little kit that includes the setting tool as well.

Oops!

If you have an unfortunate rivet experience you can use this handy-dandy rivet removal tool. You can also use good wire cutters like those pictured above to remove an errant rivet, but this little gem makes it a little easier. You just push the top of your rivet or snap into the same size hole on the resin tray, place the metal post on top of the back of the rivet, point down, and strike with your hammer. If a rivet doesn't come completely out, it will loosen it enough to easily cut the shank with your wire cutters. See Resources page 235.

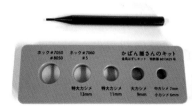

Investment Reality Check

You can also install rivets and buttons with a tabletop press. This one installs rivets, tack buttons, grommets, and snaps. I have it because I teach sewing classes and install lots of different types of hardware, in addition to that used on jeans. My students love the ease of using this machine and it's fun too. But let it be known: **You don't need an industrial press!**

HAZEL SAYS

It's helpful to place a rivet press on a sturdy surface that is about stool height (19") so you can stand above it and use your body weight and gravity to help with operation.

An industrial press requires a unique die for each type of fastener you use. This can be a significant investment, but it makes proper installation a breeze. I label my top and bottom die pieces with matching, colored tapes for organization. I'm just geeky that way.

CHAPTER 3

MATERIALS

INGREDIENTS FOR JEANS

Sure, you want to read the materials chapter, silly! Knowing a bit about denim will help you find the one that is best suited for your project. I will give you some guidelines, and your job is to learn when and where you can break the rules. Every good maker knows: The rules are not just going to break themselves! I'll also talk about the notions that go into making jeans.

Hazel seasons some denim.

DENIM

Denim is a twill weave fabric made from 100% cotton, classically with a yarn-dyed blue thread in the warp (lengthwise yarn) and white in the weft (crosswise yarn). It is traditionally colored deep blue with a dye made from indigo leaves, a plant derived originally from Asia. Synthetic indigo dye is less expensive and widely used in manufacturing. If it's important to you to have fabrics made only from organic cotton and natural indigo dye, that will become part of your search.

A Bit About Weaves

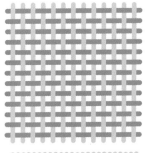

Plain weave – The weft and warp yarns interlace alternately, one over the other.

Twill weave – In its simplest form, the weft yarn passes over one warp yarn and then under two warp yarns and so on, with a "step," or offset, between rows to create the characteristic diagonal pattern.

The twill weave is strong yet has enough give to mold and shape to the body with extended wear. The cotton fiber helps with this feature as well.

Twill weaves for denim include right-hand warp, left-hand warp, ring-spun twill, and broken twill. There are plenty of resources explaining the details of twill weaves. You may have heard of selvedge denim, which is woven on shuttle looms, making a strong finished selvedge that won't ravel. Side seams cut using the selvedge add prestige to a turned-up hem. You can learn as much as your heart desires. I dare you!

Labeling Denim

Denim is described by both fiber and weight. The weight is the number of ounces that one square yard of denim weighs. Most high-quality RTW jeans and work pants are made with a minimum 13.5 oz. denim. Many jeans are made with up to 21 oz. denim, which are very rigid. It would be difficult to sew all the jeans details on 21 oz. denim with a standard household machine, but I haven't tried it, so you go do it and let me know how it goes!

Sometimes the label doesn't say the weight of the denim. Often you aren't sure of the true fiber content, either.

Weights below 9-10 oz. are generally better for shorts, skirts and work shirts. Many of the stretch denims found in fabric stores are too light-weight to make a comfortably snug jean without showing every lump and bump on the body.

A PRO'S VIEW ON DENIM

Denim Sourcing

As I learned from Stan Gray, president of EE Schenck—a Portland, Oregon, fabric and notions distributor and fabric converter—ready-to-wear trends determine what denim is manufactured. Most of the denim that consumers can buy, what we see in fabric stores, is the surplus from what textile manufacturers make to sell to fabric suppliers, or it's leftover from apparel manufacturing. This surplus stock is bought up by fabric stores to sell to their customers. When it's gone, it's gone.

To get yardage that is exactly to your specifications, you would need to order like a RTW company, in large quantity. Large fabric distributors like EE Schenck order as much as they can of just a few of these denims so they can have consistency in what they sell for a couple of years at a time. But again, when it's gone, it's gone, and the replacement might be slightly different in color or feel based on what the market dictates at the time. Weight and basic construction may be different. For this reason, consistency is difficult to maintain long-term. The product just keeps changing as RTW demands change.

How do you choose? **By knowing what kind of jeans you want to make** and then by touch and feel, as with any fabric. Simply put, for looser jeans, nonstretch and heavier denim will be comfortable and wear well. For tighter jeans, especially skinny-legged styles, lighter weight and stretchy denims will feel great. A blend of cotton and 1-2% spandex provides nice give. For super-skinny jeans and jeggings, a blend of cotton, poly, and spandex will be most comfy and give the skintight look of this style. Keep in mind that the weight of the fabric affects the perceived stretch. A 12 oz. denim with 1% spandex will seem more rigid than a 10 oz. denim with 1% spandex.

Touch is your best indicator of a good denim. It should have some substance and a good hand. It will soften after washing, but should not be too rough or stiff beforehand. Check for give in both crosswise and lengthwise directions. If it has an elastic fiber, check the percentage. High elastic content can make denim nice and stretchy but shortens its life as the elastic tends to fail with repeated washings long before the cotton. Bubbles will form in stress areas where the elastic degrades. Cold-water washings and hanging to dry are essential.

What? No fabric stores in your area? Luckily, we live in times when sewists and merchants can gather virtually and share their finds through social media. See sewing blogs too. We makers can't wait to share our finds with each other.

If you can't find what you want locally and don't know what to order online, reach out and ask a pro. A good online fabric store will have a detailed description of the fabric and several photos. I recommend ordering swatches of several options before purchasing. Most good vendors have swatch options. Shop at sites that give really good descriptions and list the weight and fiber content specific to each selection. Email them with your questions. They expect it! Most of them are fabric geeks just like you.

Many shops and pattern companies sell kits with everything you need to make jeans. A quick look at their websites and social media will give you lots of user reviews and oftentimes much more help to make your best jeans. See Resources, page 235.

FABRIC FOR POCKET BAGS

I like to use a cute cotton print for my pocket bags. It satisfies my urge to buy up fat quarters when I have no intention of making a quilt. It's also fun to see a colorful something while I get dressed. You can use any light- to medium-weight cotton fabric you choose.

HARDWARE

Rivets and tack buttons give jeans their unique look. They are also functional, adding strength to the areas where they are applied. There are many kinds to choose from.

RIVETS

Rivet sets have two components, the top (public side) and the bottom, also called a stud with a post.

Rivet Styles

Cap rivets have a smooth rounded top and a flat back.

Double cap rivets are smooth and look the same top and bottom. The top side will often be engraved with a brand name.

Nipple rivets have a raised center. They are the favorite style of many RTW brands including Levi's. I don't use them because the raised center tends to scratch the back of my guitar when I'm playing. I like smooth rivets for this reason only!

Ring rivets have a defined sphere or tiny ball inside the larger rivet with a lower profile than a nipple rivet.

Rivet Sizes

The top of the rivet for jeans, the part that shows, averages 9mm to 10mm in width, but you will see different sizes too.

The length of the post or stud depends on its intended use and installation method. It usually measures about 9-10mm so it can be installed through several layers of denim.

On a coin pocket corner, for example, the rivet goes through six layers of denim. If the post is longer than 10mm, it may not compress tightly enough to the fabric, leaving a sharp edge that sticks up. Experimenting with the same layers as your jeans will tell you for sure.

Rivet Posts

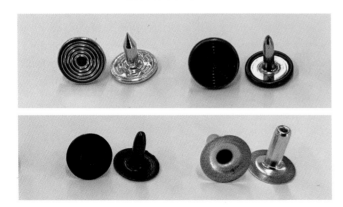

There are **solid posts** and **hollow posts**. Here are back and side views of posts. First row left to right—one-piece solid post and two-piece solid post. Second row left to right—pointed hollow post and tubular hollow post.

Solid posts are harder metal and easier to install manually because they don't bend as much, but they must be shortened with wire cutters so the rivet doesn't protrude from the denim surface.

The metal in the hollow studs compresses more easily, but also may need shortening. Hollow posts also bend more easily sometimes, making your rivet go in crooked. Metal quality can differ too. But they all can be made to work! For best results follow the manufacturer instructions along with some of the many YouTube videos online. I'll give you the basics in Chapter 7 pages 155-156.

Hammer-on rivets are available in limited selection at fabric stores, but you can find many colors and styles online. Some vendors sell kits with zippers and hardware for different styles of jeans. We've listed several in our Resources on page 235.

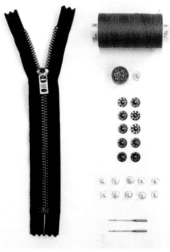

courtesy Cashmerette Patterns

JEANS METAL BUTTONS

Traditionally a jeans button is pressed or hammered on with a raised shank button piece and flat post or nail piece on the underside. The button diameter for the waistband is 17mm, and 14mm for a button fly, typically. You can find larger tack buttons too. You see all sizes in RTW.

Side and bottom view of tack button with post.

Not all tack buttons are created equal.

The one on the *left* has a metal front and shank with a small plastic insert inside to grip the post. This type is the strongest because it has less plastic to become brittle and break over time. The metal lip at the top also grips the post.

The *middle* one has a metal front and shank with plastic inside and on the top of the shank.

And the one on the *right* has a metal front, all plastic back and shank.

THAT'S A SNAP!

Cobrax press buttons, often found in higher-end RTW, have a strong snap connection and do not need a buttonhole. This can be an advantage if your sewing machine has difficulty making a good buttonhole through the unlevel surface of a denim waistband.

SEW-ON BUTTONS

Traditional buttons may also be used. The A. Smile jeans of the 1970s had two large navy blue buttons and an extended front overlap.

Rhonda Pierce, spokesperson for SCHMETZ Needles North America (SCHMETZneedles.com) loves to sew and quilt. Every day she is inspired by others who create with needle and thread. I asked Rhonda for her pro view about sewing machine needles for jeans:

Use a quality sewing machine needle designed for sewing denim or jeans in size 90/14 or larger. These needles have a medium ballpoint and a reinforced blade that makes them work well for penetrating extra-thick fabrics like denim with less skipping of stitches, needle deflection, and needle breakage.

A heavy microtex or stretch needle (sizes 90/14 or 100/16) can work well for stretch denims with a high synthetic or elastic content.

If you choose to use a heavy topstitching thread, use a topstitch needle. The topstitch needle has an elongated eye to accommodate thicker threads.

NEEDLES

I recommend getting at least one pack each of needles sizes 90/14 and 100/16 and larger if you're working with heavier denim.

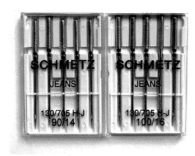

With all needle/fabric/thread combinations, you'll always want to make test samples. No exceptions. None. Yes, I'm watching.

THREAD

GETTING TECHNICAL

Thread weight: Refers to how many meters equals 1 gram. For 40 wt., 40 meters of the thread weighs 1 gram. So, the higher the number, the finer or lighter the thread.

Thread Tex: Refers to the weight in grams of 1,000 meters of thread. So, the higher the Tex number, the thicker the thread.

Many thread spool labels don't tell you the "weight" or the "Tex" number. They just describe the type of thread and the fiber content—all-purpose polyester thread, heavy-duty nylon upholstery thread, cotton topstitching thread, and so on.

My favorite thread sizes for jeans:

Seams: Polyester Tex 30—A regular all-purpose sewing thread. A quality polyester thread will be durable and run smoothly through most sewing machines.

Serge finishing: Polyester Tex 27—Slightly lighter weight than regular sewing thread, to minimize the bulk of three or four threads used at once. Usually sold in large cone-shaped spools and labeled as serger thread.

Topstitching: Polyester Tex 40—It's slightly heavier weight than all-purpose thread, so the topstitching has more visual impact. It is easier to sew with than thicker threads, while maintaining good tension. It's sometimes called topstitching and/or buttonhole thread.

And yeah, it's a big deal because jeans are all about the topstitching. Thread manufacturer websites offer more product information than they can print on the spool. Find lots of tips for topstitching success in Chapter 6, but you will find your *own* solutions by experimenting before you start sewing your jeans.

INTERFACING

Palmer/Pletsch PerfectFuse interfacings are ideal for jeans. I recommend PerfectFuse Sheer for the fly areas and pocket tops. It stretches crosswise, and in the lengthwise direction it is stable.

PerfectFuse Medium works well for waistbands. It is stable in both directions but remains soft and fuses well. See page 240.

Both interfacings weights come in 1-yard and 3-yard packages with complete use and care instructions printed on the front and back of the insert. Store in the packages so you will be able to refer to the instructions.

ZIPPERS

Both metal and polyester coil zippers work well for jeans. It's a personal preference. Zippers are sold in different lengths and also by the width of the teeth in millimeters. I prefer 4.5mm metal zippers for most jeans. A heavier weight or construction-worker pant uses a 5mm or larger. In synthetic coil zippers I use a 3mm pant or skirt zipper. Today's synthetic coil zippers are as strong as metal.

For either type of zipper, buy a length 2-4" longer than you need. It's easier to cut the excess off above the waistband than to guess where the zipper stop should be placed. At the point you are sewing your zipper, you can't be sure exactly where your waistband seam will be since it is fine-tuned later in the fitting process. Better safe than sorry!

OTHER LITTLE HELPERS

I'm a fan of sticky helpers for sewing. Zipper installation is a breeze with 1/8"-wide basting or craft tape, and I love a good glue pen for temporary tacks here and there while sewing jeans. You'll see these items show up throughout Chapter 7 to help with construction.

Glue holds ends of belt loop in place with help of flower pin as an anchor for bartacking ends. (See exposed button fly page 203.)

CHAPTER 4

PATTERNS, FIT & ALTERATIONS

This chapter holds the key to achieving your very best jeans fit starting with choosing the right size, followed by a step-by-step tutorial on tissue-fitting and how-tos for all the alterations you may need. In Chapter 5, Fitting Real People, you'll see it all put into action.

JEANS PATTERNS

Jeans are just pants with a few drafting changes—convert the back darts to a shaped yoke; reshape the front pockets; tighten up the fit, and voila! Jeans! Large and small pattern companies have jeans patterns. They may all size differently, so you must read what each says about its pattern sizes. My goal is to help you select the right size pattern from any maker.

OUR JOB AS SEWISTS

No matter how well a pattern is drafted it's still our job as sewists to make sure the garment will fit our own bodies. It's *impossible* to draft a pattern that will fit all body types.

PATTERN SIZE

Why Can't I Find My Size? A current hot topic on social media and elsewhere in Sewingland is size inclusivity. It would be nice if patterns were available to fit any size. The sizes included in most patterns are the most common sizes purchased. Adding more sizes might require a larger envelope, more paper, and more grading and therefore more cost.

Cost is a real factor as big and small pattern companies alike struggle to stay viable. Consumers hesitate to pay $20-$30 for sewing patterns, but when you consider the ton of work involved in creating a good one, it's worth it.

Larger pattern companies draft to their size standards maintaining the hourglass shape. This gives other pattern companies an opportunity to target a specific body shape.

For example, the Cashmerette "Ames" jean has sizes up to a 62" hip. It is targeted to curvy bodies and has two separate pelvis shapes (apple or pear) and two leg shapes (straight or skinny) that you can interchange for personal fit and styling.

Fit student Heather models her new Cashmerette Ames Jeans.

23

As a teacher of both sewing and pattern fitting, I have had many students who are smaller or larger than the sizes available. When this is the case, we pick the size closest to the student and grade from there.

Refer to the Palmer/Pletsch *Pants for Real People* book for tips on how to grade a pattern up or down and then use the Palmer/Pletsch Tissue-Fitting Method and alter the tissue to fit. *Results are nearly always excellent.*

HOW DO YOU WANT *YOUR* JEANS TO FIT?

Fit...to be Worn

Jeans fit is tricky—often we are trying to accomplish a snug fit over uneven terrain. The more a body differs from a simple cylinder shape, the more challenging the fit. It's simpler with a stretch denim that gives and molds to the body, but it can be done in nonstretch denim using many of the tissue-fitting concepts that we use in fitting other pant styles.

But *you*, the wearer, define great fit. It's as individual as your taste and can change depending on your activity. Dress-up jeans and real working jeans are equally important in a wardrobe, but you may want a completely different fit based on the fabric you are using. Create your Personal Jeans Profile.

A PRO'S VIEW ON PATTERNS

HEATHER LOU, CLOSET CORE PATTERNS

So, what makes a great jeans pattern? I asked Heather Lou, founder of Closet Core Patterns and creator of the popular "Ginger" and "Morgan" jeans patterns, her pro view on what elements are most important:

All the details should act as a cohesive whole and should be scaled appropriately, such as where the rise sits on your body, the size and shape of the yoke, and the shape and proportions of the pockets.

Since jeans are a complicated garment to sew, you should also look for thorough and well-developed instructions, and perhaps additional online resources like tutorials and sew-alongs. While no pattern can fit everyone perfectly straight out of the package, a good pattern will fit most people without major modifications. My advice if you are looking for a jeans pattern is to check the pattern hashtag on Instagram. Seeing how it looks on a wide variety of body types (and reading what everyone has to say about fit and construction!) can save you from investing in a pattern that may not work for you.

Closet Core offers patterns, denim, and jeans hardware. See Resources, page 235.

PERSONAL JEANS PROFILE

Think for a moment about what you really want in a pair of jeans, then answer the following for each different pair you want to make. This will help the fitting process go more smoothly.

TYPE OF JEAN FIT

☐ **Relaxed style** – Smooth fit through the hip, seat, thigh, but not tight anywhere. "I want my jeans to fit like a comfortable pair of pants with jean details."

☐ **Riding style** – Snug to tight through the seat and upper thigh. "I want my jeans pretty bun-hugging, but not skintight."

☐ **Skinny** – Super snug (tight!) often all the way to the ankle, but at least to the knee. Negative ease. "I want my jeans like a second skin." (You must choose a stretch denim for this style!)

RISE

☐ Hi rise—above the waist (navel)

☐ At or just below the waist

☐ About 2" below the waist or_____ (You choose.)

☐ Low-rise—point to where! (Determine in tissue.)

TYPE OF DENIM

☐ Rigid 100% cotton denim

☐ Rigid 100% cotton selvedge denim

☐ Stretch denim (cotton/spandex blend)

☐ Super-stretchy denim (cotton/poly/ spandex blend)

LEG WIDTH

☐ Straight

☐ Tapered

☐ Bootcut or flared

☐ '70s wide-leg flares

LAYOUT

☐ Straight of grain

☐ Bias cut (See *Pants for Real People* for bias-cut jeans.)

ZIPPER

☐ Poly coil

☐ Metal

NOTES:

Palmer/Pletsch
SYSTEM OF SEWING

YOUR PERSONAL JEANS PROFILE

Begin each jeans project with a clear goal in mind by completing (or at least thinking really hard about) a jeans profile. The questions you answer as you move through the form on the preceding page (which I originally created for my students) may trigger some ideas about fit, performance, and comfort that you might not have thought about previously. Copy this form and use it every time you make jeans. If you're like me, jeans are your pant wardrobe. It's okay to have several pairs and why not have them custom-made to order?

By the way, teachers are welcome to make the form on the previous page their own, by adding their name, logo, website or other contact info.

IT'S YOUR THANG— DO WHAT YOU WANNA DO

Which statement below describes you?

- I just want to learn to sew jeans and I don't care if the fit is perfect for the first pair. I will make changes on the next pair.

- I want to learn to make jeans fit my body in any fabric including stretch and in any leg shape. I want tools to use to make decisions.

Neither of these goals is better than the other. The second one is more comprehensive, and yes, more time-consuming, but it builds fit into the sewing process. It is the one we are teaching.

OUR JEANS-MAKING ORDER INCLUDES FIT

Many jeans patterns start with an explanation of good fit and show some alterations to achieve it. Others have you sew all of the details and crotch seam, and do lots of topstitching before trying them on. That would entail a lot of ripping if an area didn't fit right.

We emphasize the **order in which we alter the pattern, fabric-fit, and sew**. It differs from most sewing instructions for jeans. It also differs from RTW's assembly line order, which works for RTW because it doesn't deal with fitting. The Palmer/Pletsch sewing method has forever preached fitting-as-you-sew to ultimately get the results you really want. Here's when being picky will pay off.

This order includes several fitting stages where you can still make changes, and it will allow you to avoid ripping out topstitching.

If you follow it every time you sew a pair of jeans you cannot fail. It involves some intentional ripping of basting stitches because we've determined, after self-inflicted straight pin injuries, that we no longer use pin-fitting in fabric for jeans.

Snap-VIEW
JEANS-MAKING ORDER

- [ ] **Tissue-fit and alter pattern.**
- [ ] **Cut fabric.**
- [ ] **Sew the front pockets, part of the front crotch, and zipper.**
- [ ] **Baste yoke/back, vertical seams.**
- [ ] **Try on; adjust.**
- [ ] **Remove basting.**
- [ ] **Sew yoke, inseams, crotch, and side seams.**
- [ ] **Try on again for a final check, fit the waistband, mark the hem.**
- [ ] **Finish sewing the jeans.**

EASE

Whether sewing a regular fashion pant or jeans, you can choose the amount of ease based on personal preference, style, and fabric. For guides to ease in hip width and crotch depth for different fabrics see pages 30 and 31.

HIP EASE

At the hip, most jeans have:

No ease: The finished jean hip measurement equals the body hip measurement.

OR

Negative ease: The finished jean hip measurement is *smaller* than the body hip measurement.

Hip vs. Leg Ease

Think through hip ease vs. leg ease as well. For jeans in a stretch fabric I sometimes like negative ease all over. When I decided to make a cold-weather jean using a heavy, nonstretch denim lined with cotton flannel for warmth, I made them fitted from waist to the crotch. The legs, however, could not be a tight fit or I would not be able to bend down to sit around the campfire.

Ease Depends on Body Size

A 1/4" side seam adjustment = 1" change in circumference (four seam allowances times 1/4"). Seam allowance adjustments on a larger size have less impact than on a smaller size. A 1/8" adjustment would be barely noticed on a large size but could make a big difference on a small size.

Ease and Personal Preference

We find that many of our students don't know their own personal ease preference, plus they may not be familiar with how much denim can stretch whether it is rigid or has spandex in the blend. They often start out saying they don't want a tight jean, but they nearly always end up saying, "Well, not *that loose...*" when we get to the inseams and side seams. We laugh and they return to their machines and re-baste. A little ripping is a small price for great fit.

Ease and Fabric + the Case for 1" Seam Allowances

Misjudging the amount your denim will stretch can make the jeans too big or too small around, or too long or too short in the crotch. How can you hedge your bet? If too long, you can recut. If too short you can sew the waistband higher, but not much if you have only a 5/8" or 3/8" seam allowance. **That is why we love 1" seam allowances at the waist, side, and inseams.** They provide insurance and options.

Don't worry! We are going to give you all the tools you need to start with the best pattern size based on your style preferences and your denim. Then we'll show you how to make that pattern fit you.

a skinny jean with negative ease waist to ankle

straight leg jean

CROTCH DEPTH AND CROTCH LENGTH

Take some time to study and understand the following concepts regarding fitting body shapes and learn the "cause and effect" of one alteration as it relates to the next. Step-by-step alterations for each example are found at the end of this chapter. First, a little homework. Yep, you should keep reading.

Before 1974, the terms *crotch length* and *crotch depth* were used interchangeably until Pati Palmer assigned each to an area of the pant in her first book, *Pants for Any Body.*

Crotch Depth is the distance from the waist to the crotch.

Crotch Length is the distance from the center front waist to the center back waist through the legs.

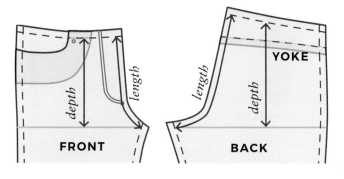

Crotch Depth is altered equally on the front and back pattern pieces by lengthening or shortening above the crotch curve. True seamlines if necessary, page 46.

Lengthen:

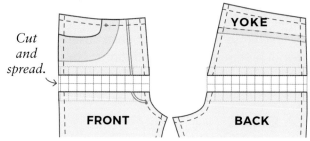

Cut and spread.

FRONT   BACK

OR Shorten:

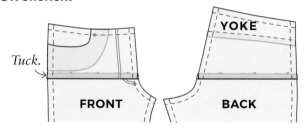

Tuck.

FRONT   BACK

Crotch Length is shortened or lengthened at the front itself and/or back waist and/or inseams.

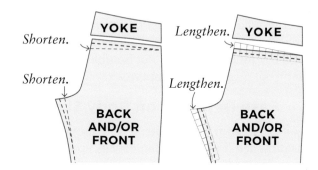

Shorten.   YOKE   Lengthen.   YOKE

Shorten.   Lengthen.

BACK AND/OR FRONT   BACK AND/OR FRONT

NOTE: Changes to back crotch are ONLY on the back and not the yoke. You want to retain the size and shape of your yoke.

CROTCH DEPTH AND LENGTH ARE INTERRELATED

Adjusting one affects the other.

Adjusting crotch **depth** affects crotch **length**. When you add crotch depth you *may* now need to take inseams in if thighs are too loose.

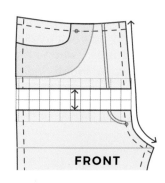

FRONT

Study this. It shows how one affects the other.

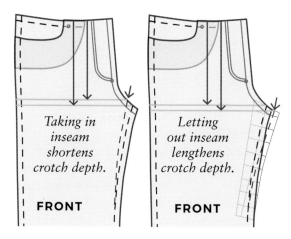

Taking in inseam shortens crotch depth.

FRONT

Letting out inseam lengthens crotch depth.

FRONT

(For more in-depth information, see the Palmer/Pletsch book *Pants for Real People* Chapter 6.)

TISSUE-FITTING

WHY TISSUE-FIT?

Tissue-fitting means trying on the tissue so you can see where you need to alter. In the Palmer/Pletsch Tissue-Fitting Method you first reinforce the tissue by taping the front and back crotch just inside the seamlines to prevent tearing.

For jeans, tissue-fitting is a way to check areas that would be more difficult to change in fabric such as:

- Crotch depth (rise)
- Crotch shape
- Leg width
- Yoke shaping
- Waistband shape—straight or curved

Trust your eyes, because what you see is what you get. I have come up with a way to tissue-fit jeans even if the pattern has negative ease.

The tissue becomes your "muslin," eliminating the need to sew one. More fitting will be done in fabric and, as we mentioned earlier, our order gives you opportunities to see and correct fitting issues throughout the construction process.

FINDING YOUR BEST SIZE

STEP ONE: Measure around the fullest part of the hip and above the crotch curve, about 7"-9" from waist. The tape measure is snug against the body and level to the floor. Write this in your size chart on page 31.

STEP TWO: Compare your hip measurement with the pattern's. Using your hip measurement find the size on your pattern envelope that is closest. Write it in your size chart on page 31. This will be the pattern size you start with.

SIZE	8	10	12	14
HIP	33.5	34.5	36	38

Sample section of a pattern size chart.

Based on your fabric and the finished hip measurement of the pattern you are using, you may decide to go smaller or larger. But start here!

STEP THREE: Find the pattern's hip FGM (finished garment measurement). Some, but not all, patterns tell you the finished garment measurements. We suggest you place a tape measure on the pattern hip and measure it for yourself. This eliminates any guesswork.

Measure your pattern at the hipline front and back above the crotch curve, seamline to seamline. You are measuring half the actual jean, so double this number and write it on your chart.

The hipline on the pattern is about 3" above the inseam as shown. It's often the widest part of the side seam.

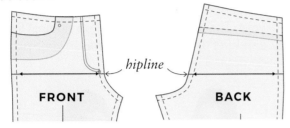

STEP FOUR: **Consider your fabric.** Knowing the denim you will use for your jeans before you start will affect final size choice. A rigid nonstretch denim will need more ease than a super-stretchy cotton/poly/spandex blend. Also, consider your personal preference for each pair based on how you plan to wear them.

The fabric wrap test may help. If your hip measures 40" and the finished hip measurement on the pattern is 37", will 37" of your fabric stretch to fit your hips?

Or do the opposite and just stretch the fabric around your hips and then measure the amount of fabric needed to fit snugly. Choose the size that has the closest finished hip measurement.

Negative Ease

In general, we have found that for a nonstretch denim you are safe with the FGM equal to or 1" smaller than your hips, because all cotton twill grows a bit on the body and will snugly conform to your hips. For a stretchy denim you are safe with the FGM 1"-2" smaller than your hips. Use the wrap test to verify the amount. If you then use 1" seam allowances on sides, inseams, and waist, you'll never have a fit disaster! See page 111 for creating 1" seam allowances.

NOTE: The wrap test can be used with any fabric, from ultra-stretchy fabric to extra-thick nonstretch as in Helen's cold-weather jeans (page 85), but it is especially helpful and your best bet for stretch denim.

WRAP-TEST YOUR DENIM

Use the fabric wrap test to help decide what size pattern to use based on your hip measurement and the amount of stretch in your fabric. You'll need two pins and your fabric. Fold your denim on the grain that is going around your body, usually the crosswise grain, so that it's double. (We double the fabric to reduce the stretch a little to accommodate for seams, topstitching, and pockets.) Put one pin in your fabric a few inches from one edge.

Wrap around your body at hip level and pull it just taut enough to feel like comfortable jeans. If you are using a stretchy fabric and want negative ease, you can stretch as you pull. Put the other pin in the fabric where it meets at your center. Measure between the pins and write the number on the chart. Choose the pattern size that has the hip FGM closest to your fabric measurement.

Pati shows how fabric stretches.

Pati wraps the doubled fabric around her hips snugly.

Pati measures between the pins. 39" of fabric comfortably stretched around her hip. The size 12 pattern's FGM is 39".

PATTERN SIZE CALCULATION CHART

FIND YOUR BEST PATTERN SIZE WITH EASE OR NEGATIVE EASE

*Below is an example of finished garment measurements (FGM) from two different patterns—
one that allows for ease and one that has negative ease.*

SIZE	8	10	12	14	16	18	20	22	24
HIP	33.5	34.5	36	38	40	42	44	46	48
FGM design with Ease	37	38	39.5	41.5	43.5	46	48	50	52
FGM design with Negative Ease	32.5	33.5	35	37	39	41	43	45	47

**This is a sample chart we used to make Pati's stretch jeans shown in Chapter 5, Fitting
Real People, from the book** *Fit and Sew Custom Jeans.*

Pati's Hip Measurement	Pati's Pattern's Size for a 40" Hip	FGM: For size 16 in this design	Wrap Test Results
40"	16	43.5"— This will be too big for how Pati wants her stretchy fabric to fit.	39" of Pati's fabric stretched to easily fit her 40" hip. The size of the pattern with the closest FGM is size 12. We will use a size 12, which has 39.5" FGM.

Here is a blank chart you can complete. It can be used for rigid or stretchy fabric.

My Hip Measurement	Pattern Size for This Hip Measurement	Finished Garment Measurement of pattern in this size	Wrap Doubled Fabric Snugly Around Hip and Measure
			_____" fits around me. _____ size with closest FGM

Use these tools and you will find the best pattern size for your fabric. Start
with an accurate hip measurement and select a size closest to it. Then use
the fabric wrap test to choose the size based on the closest FGM. You will feel
confident from the very outset.

Now you are ready to prep your pattern for tissue-fitting!

Palmer/Pletsch
SYSTEM OF SEWING

www.palmerpletsch.com

PREPARE YOUR PATTERN FOR TISSUE-FITTING

Now that you have chosen your pattern size and your fabric, prepare the pattern for tissue-fitting. If you are using a PDF pattern, go to page 60.

Neatness counts! As teachers doing hands-on classes, we've seen it all and we know for certain that mistakes multiply.

1. **Remove your pieces from the large sheet of tissue** by "rough cutting" outside the largest size in the grouping. If you have a single-size pattern, cut the pieces outside the solid line. If you have a PDF pattern printed on heavy paper, see page 60 for how to trace your pattern onto Perfect Pattern Paper for tissue-fitting.

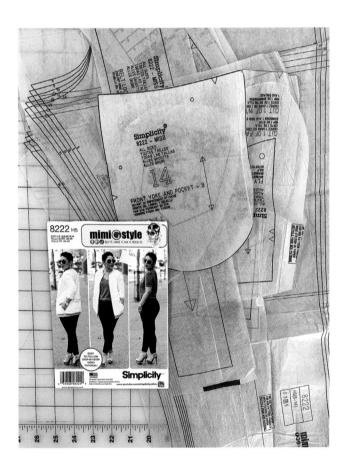

HAZEL SAYS...

Whether you're tissue-fitting or not, always trim your pattern pieces to the cutting line before cutting from fabric. It improves accuracy by keeping the tissue from moving during cutting.

Snap-VIEW PATTERN PREP ORDER

- ☐ Rough-cut pieces to remove from big sheet.
- ☐ Press tissue.
- ☐ Trim to your size.
- ☐ Mark stitching lines.
- ☐ Reinforce crotch seam with tape.
- ☐ Clip to the curves.
- ☐ Tape or pin side front to front.
- ☐ If you have negative ease, add tissue to sides of front, back, and yoke.
- ☐ Pin yoke to back.
- ☐ Pin side seams and inseams together.

2. **Press the tissue.** Using a DRY iron set at the wool setting, carefully press your tissue. A *warm* iron will not be hot enough. Drips and steam can spoil your pattern. If your pattern gets wet set it aside and allow it to air dry.

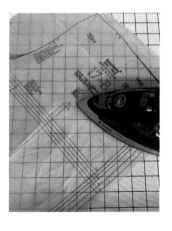

3. **Trim the tissue** using scissors or a rotary cutter. Trim so that you can see your size line, but don't leave extra tissue outside it.

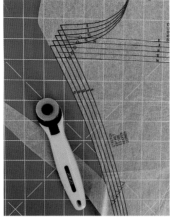

4. **Mark stitching lines.** Multisize patterns don't have the stitching lines printed on the tissue. Mark the stitching lines with a pencil or waterproof pen. Use the measuring tool of your choice.

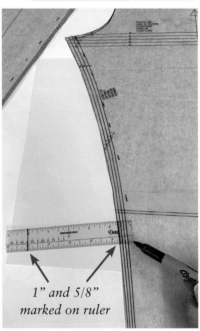

1" and 5/8" marked on ruler

5. **Reinforce the pattern.** Taping the crotch reinforces the pattern tissue so it won't tear when trying on the tissue. Here's how—

With tissue **right side up**, pin the front, back, and yoke to a cardboard cutting board to keep the tissue from moving. Even the electricity in the air can cause your pattern to jump to the tape and crinkle up!

Tape the entire crotch, front and back, *inside* the stitching line. Use 1/2" Scotch Magic tape. It handles pressing best and doesn't overpower the tissue like 3/4" tape. Use short lengths of tape, lapping ends about 1/4" as you go.

Tape the yoke piece at center back.

6. **Clip to the curves.** To get the tissue seamline right up to your body, clip crotch curves to the tape, front and back. Tug lightly on the tissue to make sure it's taped securely.

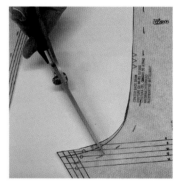

ASSEMBLE THE TISSUE

1. **Pin WRONG SIDES TOGETHER**, for fitting the right side of your body. If your left side is much larger than your right, pin tissue right sides together and fit your left side.

2. **Pin** or **tape** side front to front. If you tape, use small pieces so it's easy to take apart later. I prefer using tape here because pins tend to fall out.

3. **For negative ease add tissue to sides.** If the pattern hip is equal to or smaller than your hip, add tissue to the sides for tissue-fitting. Denim will stretch to fit, but the tissue won't. Therefore, add a 3"x 18" strip of pattern tissue to the sides of the pattern starting at the waist. Palmer/Pletsch Perfect Pattern Paper is the same weight as most pattern tissue.

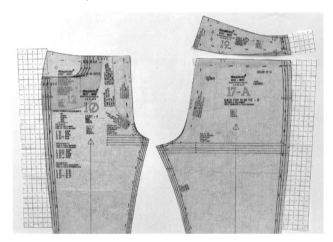

Now we can tissue-fit for the areas we can't easily change in fabric. If you need more width at the waist, some of this added tissue will remain, otherwise this "chunk" will be removed before you cut fabric. This will be determined during the tissue-fitting process.

It helps to have 1" inseams, side seams, and waist seam allowances as insurance. You can add them before cutting fabric, see Chapter 6, page 111.

4. **Pin** the yoke to back, wrong sides together.

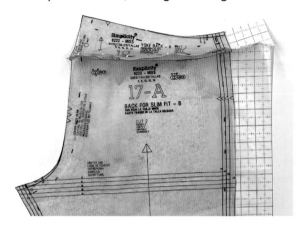

5. Start with the **side seam** and match front and back hemlines, pinning vertically into the cardboard. Smooth the layers together to the top. Pin the side seams on the seamline starting at the waist/side seam intersection with pins pointing down so they won't fall out.

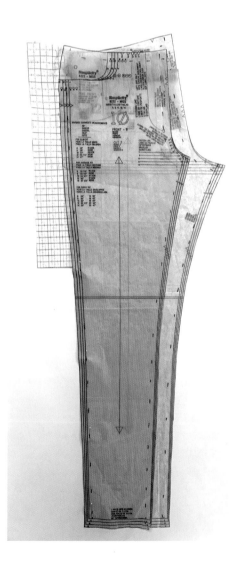

If you've added the "chunk" of tissue, match the cut edges of pattern front and back and pin on the cut lines from waist to hip. (With negative ease, we know that the tissue will not fit if pinned on the actual stitching line.)

6. Now bring the inseams together matching the hemline. Pin. Smooth tissue to knee and pin from the knee to the hem on the seamline with pins pointing down. Lift the tissue and match the outer edges of the curved parts.

7. Turn up the bottom hem to avoid stepping on the tissue.

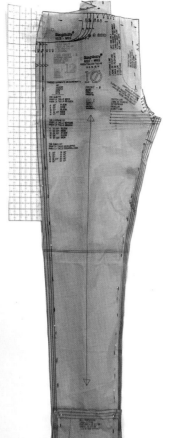

When you try on the tissue, you will pull it up until the crotch seamline touches your body.

The top inseam pin goes into the tissue at the inseam/crotch seam intersection and points down. Continue pinning on the inseam seamline with pins

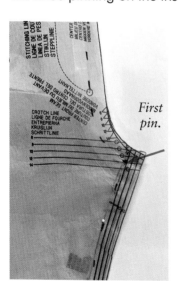

First pin.

a few inches apart and pointing down. If you follow this order you will have more success. The side seams are the last seams to fit because everything you alter before may affect the width and shape. See pages 39-50 to learn how to make the common tissue alterations.

Snap-VIEW TISSUE-FITTING ORDER

- [ ] **Put elastic at your preferred waist level.**
- [ ] **Try on the tissue.**
- [ ] **Match pattern centers (front and back) to yours.**
- [ ] **Determine crotch depth.**
- [ ] **Back. Yoke.**
- [ ] **Inseams. Side seams.**
- [ ] **Waistband.**

Find your preferred waistband level. Place 1½" -wide elastic around your waist. Move it to where you want your 1½"-wide waistband to sit. If you want it lower in the front than in the back, that is okay.

Below Natural Waist   *At Natural Waist*

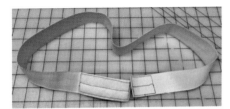

HAZEL SAYS...

Sew Velcro to each end to make a permanent "fitting" elastic.

Most jeans waistbands are about 1½" wide. We use the 1½" Pamela's Fantastic Elastic (available at pamelaspatterns. com) with Velcro sewn to the ends to make it adjustable.

Try on the tissue—properly! Stand with legs apart so you can pull the tissue up to your crotch and center it between the legs. Pretend the tissue is an elevator and pull up the front and back evenly.

Start at the back. If you pull the front up to the waist first, you won't be able to get the back up to the waist, and the side seam won't be perpendicular to the floor.

For a very slim leg jean you may need to unpin the tissue below the knee to get it on, as Ava (to the right) has done.

Wrong   **Right**

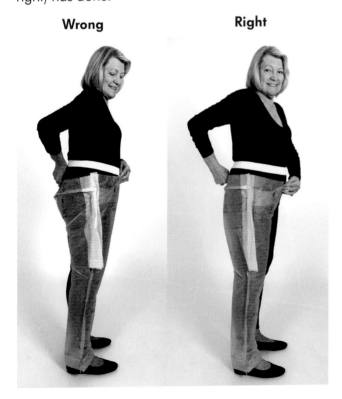

Bring pattern center front and center back to body center front and center back. Unpin or let out the sides if necessary.

If you're fitting tissue for a snug stretch jean, it may be hard to get the tissue up without tearing. Place the palms of your hands on your thigh, front and back, and gently work the pattern tissue up evenly until the crotch seam touches your body.

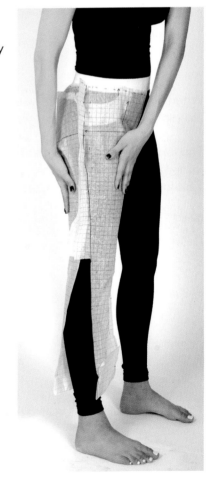

36

Crotch Depth

- Check that the pattern crotch stitching line touches your body.

- For proper shaping, your tissue's waist needs to come to wherever you've chosen to wear your waistband.

crotch stitching line touching body

- During your actual fitting you may add tissue as Ava has in this photo. Later, before cutting from fabric, you can reduce the amount added to accommodate for **negative ease**. See page 110.

The Back

Using your handheld mirror and standing with your back toward a full-length mirror, check the back. If you see puddles in back, pull the tissue up at the center back until the wrinkles are gone. See page 14.

If your seat is preventing you from pulling the tissue up, you may need to lower the back crotch stitching line first. See page 42.

Seat pushing down on tissue causes puddles.

HAZEL SAYS...

For a great rear view while fitting, find a hand mirror big enough to get a good look at your backside.

Stand in front of a full-length mirror with your back side facing the mirror. Hold the mirror over your shoulder until you see the back.

Now you can see well enough to get that purrrr-fect fit. Meow.

Workshop attendee Wendy McIntyre from Sydney, Australia.

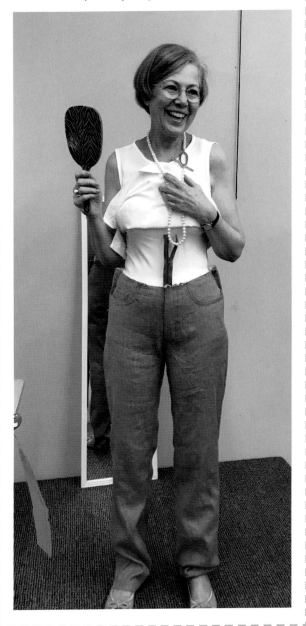

The Yoke

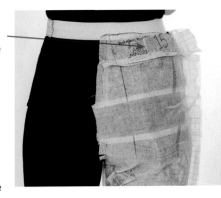

Shape the yoke to the body as this model has done. Tape small darts in the yoke until the tissue shapes to your body. See page 42 for more.

Inseams

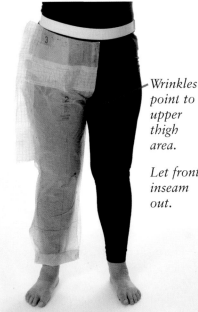

If wrinkles or diagonal smile lines point to the inseams, you need to let the inseams out where you see wrinkles, which may be the back and/or the front. For this model, it is the front. See page 43 for more.

Wrinkles point to upper thigh area.

Let front inseam out.

Side Seams

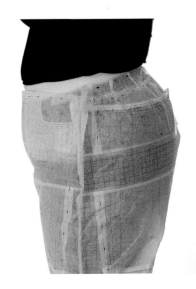

Pin the tissue to your shape at side seams. Even if you won't be adding width because you wrap-tested your fabric for stretch, having the shape marked on the rectangle of tissue added to the side seam gives you a template for your side seam shape. See page 45 for more.

Fit the Waistband

Cut the largest size and wrap the full length around your waist. Cut the size that is 6" longer (3" on each side of center front) than your waist.

ALTER YOUR PATTERN

On pages 35 through 39 in this chapter we walked you through the best order for tissue-fitting jeans. Now let's look at the how-tos for the pattern alterations. It's important to work in this order because many adjustments affect other areas of fit. Your goal is to be very close to great fit after you alter your tissue so that perfecting the fit in fabric is easy.

Because of negative ease in tight jeans and the limitations it poses in the tissue, fewer pattern alterations are done in tissue and more are done in the fabric-fitting phase. What we've learned from fitting tight jeans will help when fitting any tight pant. This book will be a great companion to the comprehensive pant fitting and sewing book, *Pants for Real People.*

With the tissue and your elastic in place, follow this order of altering your pattern.

WAIST WIDTH

There are two options and you can use both.

Let out side seams—If the pattern centers front and back don't reach yours, you can let out the side seams.

Straighten center front—If you've let out the side seams and the center back reaches your center back, but the front doesn't, you may need to straighten the center front by adding tissue.

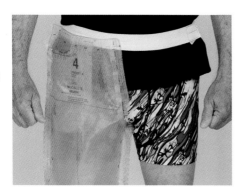

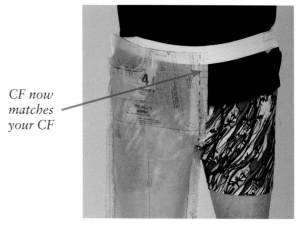

CF now matches your CF

If the center front reaches yours but you see this wrinkle pointing from thigh to waist, straighten the center front.

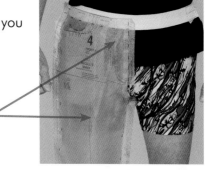

Or you will end up with these wrinkles in the front.

Alter the Pattern

To straighten center front, add tissue as shown above. Or cut on center front from waist edge to crotch seam stop (the mark on the pattern indicating the fly opening). Cut from edge to the mark to create a hinge. Move the seam allowance to the right 3/8" to 3/4". Insert tissue and tape in place.

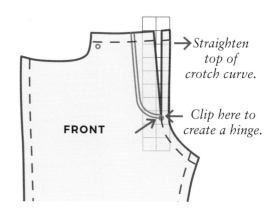

Straighten top of crotch curve.

FRONT

Clip here to create a hinge.

CROTCH DEPTH TOO SHORT

Before on Body   **After on Body**

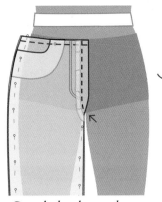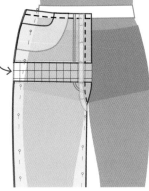

Crotch depth too short.

If the crotch seamline is touching your body and the tissue doesn't come up to your waist at the sides, then lengthen the crotch depth. Remember, *you* define where your waist is!

Measure from pattern waist stitching line to bottom of elastic at the side for the amount needed.

Alter Pattern Front and Back

To lengthen pattern, add tissue to back and front evenly. There should be only a 1/4"-1/2" lap of pattern over alteration tissue.

1. Draw alteration line about 1" above bottom of zipper mark.

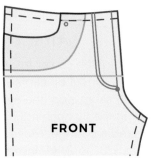

2. Cut on your alteration line. Anchor one section of the pattern tissue to the alteration tissue along one line on the grid.

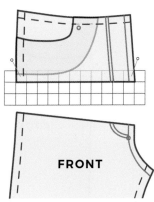

3. Spread the pattern the desired amount. Use the lines on Perfect Pattern Paper as your ruler and line up cut pattern pieces. Pin in place.

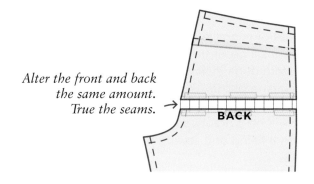

Horizontal lines align with cut edge.

Vertical lines align with cut edges.

4. Tape in place. Trim away excess tissue. True crotch seams if necessary. See page 46.

Alter the front and back the same amount. True the seams.

HAZEL SAYS...

If the pattern's lengthen-and-shorten line is in the crotch curve, don't use it. Draw another line above the curve on both front and back.

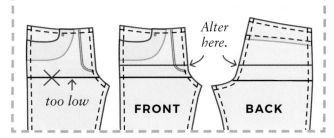

Alter here.

too low

FRONT   BACK

40

CROTCH DEPTH TOO LONG

If the crotch seam does not touch your body when the waist stitching line is matched to the bottom of the elastic, you will need to make a tuck to shorten the crotch depth.

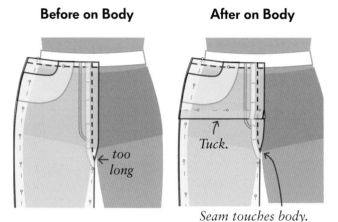

Before on Body   **After on Body**

too long

Tuck.

Seam touches body.

Alter Pattern Front and Back

To shorten pattern, tuck front and back the same amount. This example removes 1". Draw one line above the curve perpendicular to the grainline. Draw another line above it 1" away and bring the two lines together.

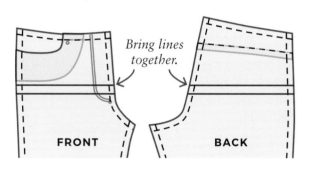

Bring lines together.

FRONT   BACK

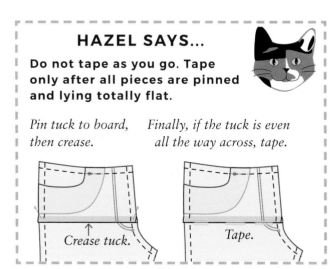

HAZEL SAYS...

Do not tape as you go. Tape only after all pieces are pinned and lying totally flat.

Pin tuck to board, then crease.   *Finally, if the tuck is even all the way across, tape.*

Crease tuck.   *Tape.*

BACK PUDDLES

Puddles are caused by a sway or flat back and/or a low derriere. If you have a flat rear, you need less length in the back crotch. Pull up the center of the back until the puddles go away.

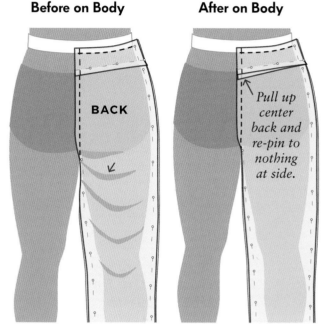

Before on Body   **After on Body**

BACK

Pull up center back and re-pin to nothing at side.

If you are also low, the seat can push down on the back crotch seam, causing puddles; and after you pull the back up, the crotch may feel tight. See "Sitting Room" on page 42.

Alter the Back

For the yoke to remain the same shape, alter the back only. Draw a new lower stitching line from the center back to nothing at the side. Pin the yoke to the new seamline.

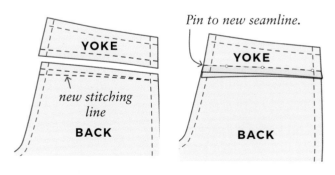

Pin to new seamline.

YOKE   YOKE

new stitching line

BACK   BACK

More Sitting Room

If the crotch seam goes into your back cleavage you need more "sitting" room. This usually happens when you pull up the back to get rid of the puddles. Lower the back crotch stitching line. The amount you lower will be similar to the amount pulled up.

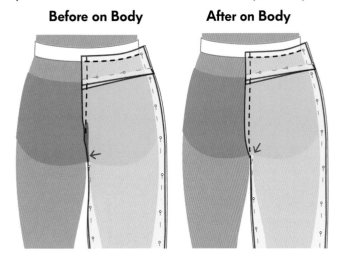

Before on Body   **After on Body**

Alter—Lower the Back Crotch Curve

Lower the back crotch curve **up to 3/4".** (I prefer to wait until I see the jeans in fabric before lowering it more.) Mark the amount and blend with center back seam and inseam.

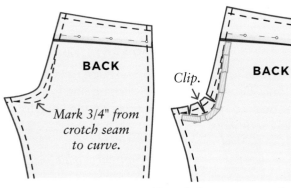

BACK

Mark 3/4" from crotch seam to curve.

Clip.

BACK

Tape below your new, lower seamline and clip to the tape. (Only new tape is shown.)

Try on to see if the center back is now a little long after lowering the back crotch seam. If so, pull up the back even more.

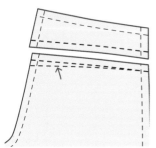

SHAPE THE YOKE

If the top of your yoke is too big in the back, shape it to your body by taking small dart tucks in the tissue where it is too large.

Before on Body   **After on Body**

Back yoke is too big at waist.   *Tuck to the shape of body. Lightly tape the dart tucks to hold.*

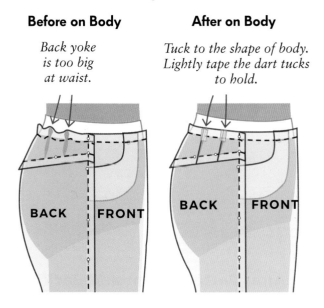

BACK   FRONT   BACK   FRONT

The darts can be anywhere that the yoke is too big in the waist. Usually there are 2-3 very tiny tucks, no more than 1/8" deep at the top. To anchor, place a very small piece of tape over the top of the tuck to hold until you take the pattern off.

Alter the Yoke Pattern

Before opening the tucks, mark the depth of the top of the tuck on the tissue. Then carefully remove the tape and open the tucks. Draw the V-shaped tucks on the tissue.

Draw V-shaped lines.

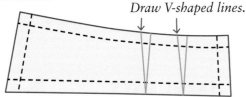

Neatly fold, matching tuck lines and crease tissue. Use two small pieces of tape over the tucks. The top of your yoke will appear more curved and that's okay. It's **your** shape.

Bring lines together and tape.

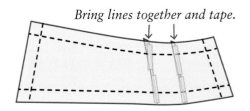

CROCH SMILES

Smiles or **diagonal** wrinkles at the crotch inseam can be in the **front or back.**

Before on Body	After on Body

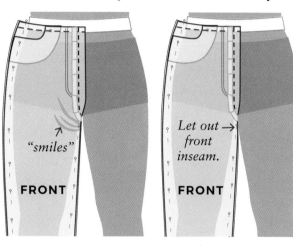

Alter the Inseam

Where you see wrinkles, let that inseam out until you don't see them. Taper to nothing about 5"-7" from the top. You may need to add tissue. If your inner thighs are full all the way to the knee, you may need to let the pattern out to below the knee.

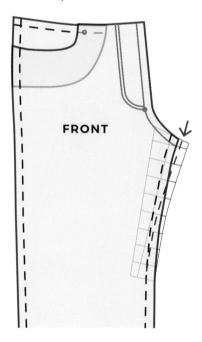

TIP: You may not need the extra crotch length in fabric. You can always sew it away!

Horizontal Wrinkles

Straight horizontal lines across the front, under the seat, and at the knees can be desirable, and unavoidable in snug jeans. Some manufacturers of RTW chemically or mechanically create these "whiskers."

If you prefer looser jeans, let the side and/or inseams out until the wrinkles disappear.

43

CROTCHETY FROWNS

Crotch fullness can be in the front but it's usually in the back with jeans. If you have too much fullness in the thigh area, front or back, take the inseam in where you see it. I often wait to make this determination in fabric. See page 52.

Before on Body

vertical fullness

After on Body

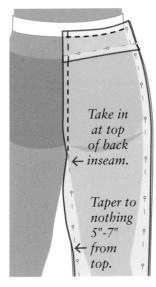

Take in at top of back ← inseam.

Taper to nothing 5"-7" ← from top.

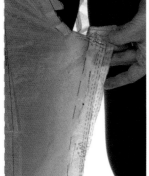

HAZEL SAYS...

I like to just drop the tissue down and pin the back inseam deeper, then pull it up to see if it needs to be even deeper.

"I WANT THE JEANS BUTT FIT"

If the back crotch fits your body snugly but it still seems full in the back thigh and you'd like it more fitted, you can curve in the upper thigh area of the back inseam. This can also be done later in fabric.

Before on Body

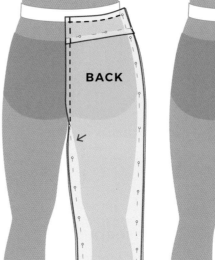

BACK

After on Body

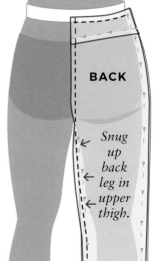

BACK

Snug up back leg in upper thigh.

The Alteration

Start at the back inseam/crotch seam intersection and curve the stitching line in on back only, as shown. Pin the back curved inseam to the front straight inseam.

Alter the Inseam

On a flat surface draw the new stitching line and, after trying on to check fit, trim seam allowance to an even width.

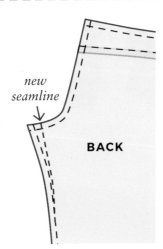

new seamline

BACK

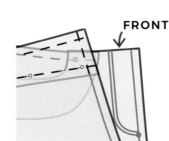

FRONT

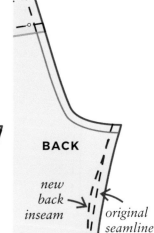

BACK

Deeper back inseam.

BACK

new back inseam

original seamline

SHAPING THE SIDES TO *YOUR* SHAPE

You can now pin the tissue to the shape of your body at the side seams. Move the pins in or out to reflect your shape.

If you have negative ease and added a "chunk" of tissue, you will now have your shape marked even though you might take a deeper seam in fabric to make the jeans tighter.

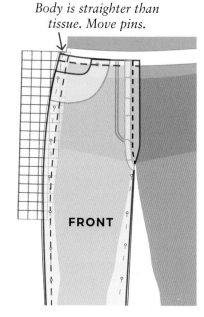

Body is straighter than tissue. Move pins.

FRONT

MARK SEAMLINE CHANGES

Mark Waistline

While you have the tissue on, mark changes at the bottom of the elastic with fine-tip waterproof marker.

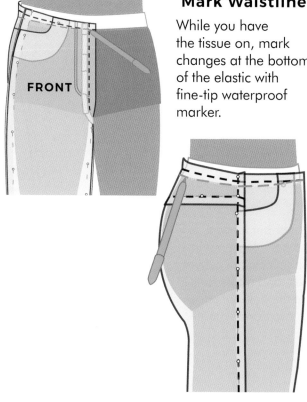

FRONT

Mark Side and Inseams

Take off the tissue. Mark the inseams first, then unpin inseams **only** so the tissue will lie flat. Then mark the side seams.

Lay the tissue flat and record changes by marking on the pins with contrasting color. Let the ink bleed through both layers. Now when you separate the front from back, you have a record of where your pins were.

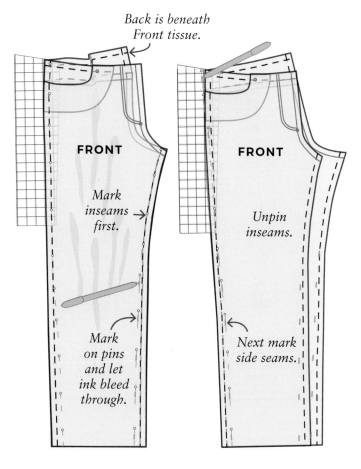

Back is beneath Front tissue.

FRONT

Mark inseams first.

Mark on pins and let ink bleed through.

FRONT

Unpin inseams.

Next mark side seams.

Make Seam Allowances Even

Make all of your seam allowances an even width from your new stitching lines. They should be no narrower than 5/8". Or you can wait until after you've decided whether you want to change the leg shape. If you want 1" in-case seam allowances for fitting, refer to page 111 for how to make 1" seam allowances at sides, inseams, and waist.

REDESIGNING THE LEGS— LENGTH AND SHAPE

Leg Length

If the leg is straight, you can change the length at the bottom. If it is tapered or flared, alter in the knee area.

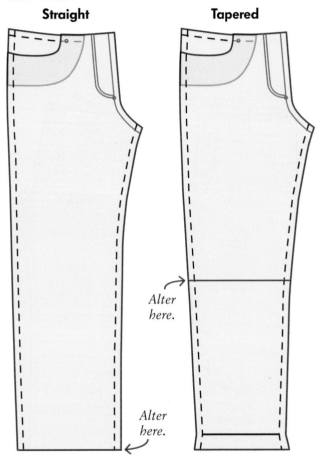

Straight   **Tapered**

Alter here.

Alter here.

When you shorten or lengthen a tapered leg, be sure to **true the lines**. As a general rule, mark the midpoint between the two lines. Then draw from one stitching line to the next through the midpoint. Do this for the cutting line as well.

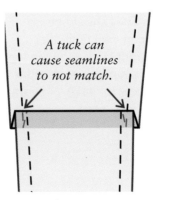

A tuck can cause seamlines to not match.

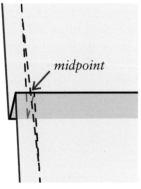

midpoint

Leg Shape

Do you want the legs wider or narrower? Re-pin as shown until you like the width.

Narrower—At the hem, pin in the same amount on inseam and side seam. Taper to original seamlines at the knee, or higher if you have thin legs.

Wider—To widen the legs to a flare, try on the tissue and pin-mark on the side seam and inseam where you want the flare to begin. This can be from the hip or knee.

BACK

FRONT

Taper at knee area.

Tape Perfect Pattern Paper to front and back legs and draw the new shape desired. If you aren't sure how much to add and you have plenty of fabric, go big! You can always take them in to any width in fabric. Cut an even seam allowance outside your new stitching line.

Remember to stack front and back legs together, line up original cutting lines, and make sure that the new cut edges are even and smooth.

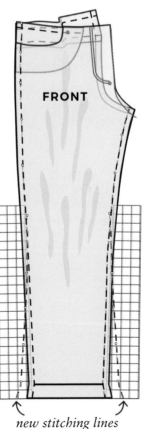

FRONT

new stitching lines

Preserve the Pocket

If you've added to the waist at the side seams, preserve the pocket size and shape this clever way, so you don't have to redesign all of the pocket pieces.

1. With side front and back pinned together, use a ruler to draw a new cut edge from the widest part of the hip to the top of the pattern.

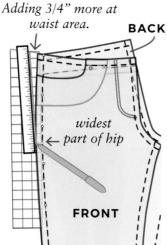

Adding 3/4" more at waist area.

BACK

widest part of hip

FRONT

2. Trim away the excess paper on both front and back at once. Set back piece aside.

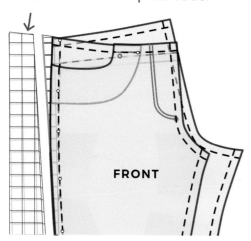

FRONT

3. On front: To retain the shape of the pocket opening curve so the pocket bag piece will still fit, draw a line from the pocket opening to the side cut edge. Trim excess tissue from side front.

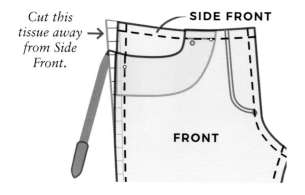

Cut this tissue away from Side Front.

SIDE FRONT

FRONT

4. Separate side front from front and slide it over so the side edges meet.

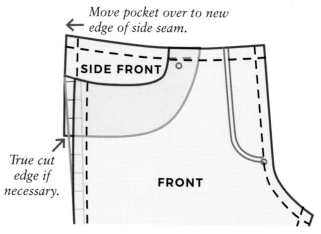

Move pocket over to new edge of side seam.

SIDE FRONT

FRONT

True cut edge if necessary.

5. To keep the pocket opening the same size, draw a box around the curved area of front and cut on the lines.

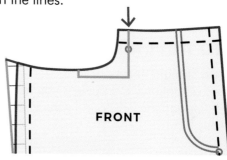

FRONT

6. Slide the box toward the side seam the same amount you added to side seam.

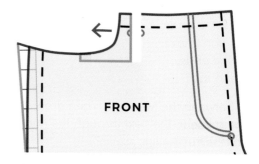

FRONT

7. Anchor to cardboard with pins. Add a piece of tissue to fill the opening and tape to secure. **Trim away excess tissue.**

FRONT

8. Moving over pocket on front means you don't have to add to sides of side front or pocket bag at waist. But If you changed the side seam anywhere above the bottom of the pocket, **make sure the side front, the front leg and the pocket bag pieces all fit together.**

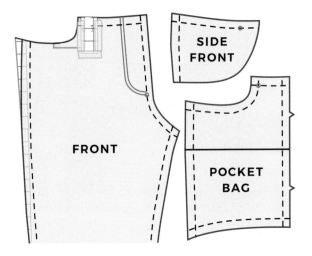

FIT AND ALTER WAISTBAND

If you have a straight, faced, or fold-over waistband there are no alterations to do unless you need to lengthen it. Position the waistband where you had your elastic.

Fold-over waistband —Fold the waistband tissue in half lengthwise and wrap it around your waist. Mark where the ends lap. If you don't have 3" left on the ends, add tissue to the ends.

Two-piece straight waistband—Wrap the waistband around your waist. If the center back is cut on the fold, place the fold at your center back, and mark your center front on the tissue. If you don't have 3" left at the end, add tissue.

Convert a Straight Waistband to Contour

Place the 1½" elastic where you want your waistband to sit on your body. Align bottom seamline of waistband to lower edge of elastic and pin in place.

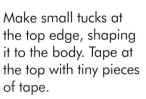

Make small tucks at the top edge, shaping it to the body. Tape at the top with tiny pieces of tape.

Take the waistband off and lay it flat. Tape the dart tucks into place.

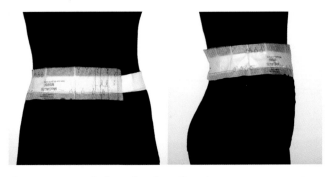

A contour waistband—A pattern's curve may not match yours. If you are curvy, your band will need to be curvy. If you are straighter, your band will be straighter.

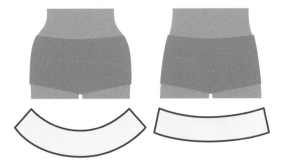

48

Some contour band pattern pieces are for half the body. If your sides are different in size and shape, trace the tissue to make a whole piece. Tape them together at center back.

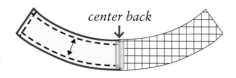
center back

Fitting a contour waistband

Fit this the same way as converting a straight waistband to contour. You may need to take only one or two tucks, or you may have to straighten it by taking a tuck at the bottom edge to fit your body.

You've tried on the waistband and pinned or taped tucks to shape it to your body. Now lay the waistband flat and tape the dart tucks into place.

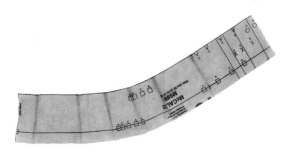

FULL DERRIERE

Wrinkles point to the derriere. Jeans won't come up to waist in back.

Generally, you add only to the back inseam. Rarely do we add at the top as shown.

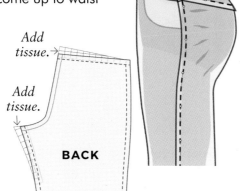
Add tissue.
Add tissue.
BACK

A way of adding even more length for a full derriere without letting out the inseam even more is to sew a more acute crotch curve. This new stitching line measures longer than the old one.

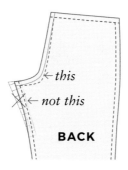
← this
← not this
BACK

BACK CROTCH SHAPE

Each of the patterns below has a different back crotch angle. Ready-to-wear jeans often have a back crotch that is so angled it is on the bias. In theory, the bias crotch may stretch to fit more people, especially if the jeans are very fitted.

Does this work for everyone? Or is it the reason you can't find a pair of jeans you love off the rack? This is why we sew. If you need more or less angle in the back crotch it will be revealed in tissue and fabric fitting. That is why in this chapter we showed you examples of when to change the back crotch shape. A clue: How slanted is your body from the center back waist to fullest part of bum? And is your bum full and high or is it so low that your pattern needs to be scooped to make more sitting room?

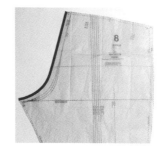

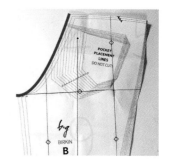

YOUR NEXT PAIR OF JEANS

Wouldn't it be great to be able to cut and sew jeans, never having to try them on? Can you just do the fitting process once and sew up your pattern the next time in any old order? Not really. Unless the fabric is identical, you are always 100% accurate in your cutting and sewing, and your body size and shape haven't changed, you will always need to fit as you sew. It's worth the effort if you want great fit.

In Chapter 5, Real People Fitting Jeans, read how we fit each person in both tissue and fabric. In the rest of this chapter we walk you through all the things to look for in fabric, followed by each alteration.

YOUR JEANS BODY MAP ALTERATION WORKSHEET

( ) = page reference

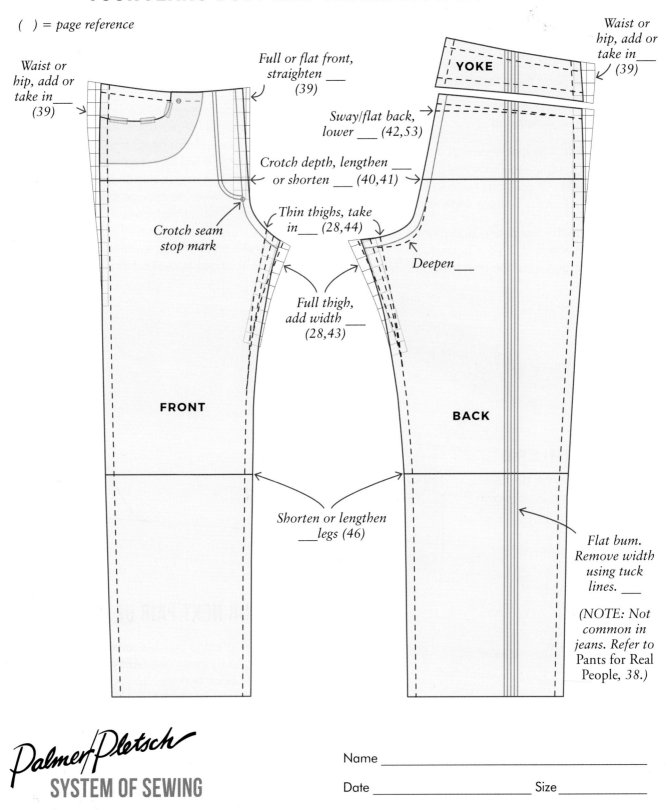

Waist or hip, add or take in___ (39)

Full or flat front, straighten ___ (39)

YOKE

Waist or hip, add or take in___ (39)

Sway/flat back, lower ___ (42,53)

Crotch depth, lengthen ___ or shorten ___ (40,41)

Crotch seam stop mark

Thin thighs, take in___ (28,44)

Deepen___

Full thigh, add width ___ (28,43)

FRONT

BACK

Shorten or lengthen ___legs (46)

Flat bum. Remove width using tuck lines. ___

(NOTE: Not common in jeans. Refer to Pants for Real People, 38.)

Palmer/Pletsch
SYSTEM OF SEWING

Name _____

Date _____ Size _____

NOTE TO TEACHERS: You have our permission to copy this page for students.
During the first tissue-fitting, circle the alterations and add approximate amounts such as +3/4" or -1/4".
© *Fit and Sew Custom Jeans* by Helen Bartley — www.palmerpletsch.com

FABRIC FITTING

WRINKLES POINT TO FIT PROBLEMS

Wrinkles in your garments **can** indicate a fit issue. You may need to look at both ends of the wrinkle for clues as to what they are pointing to. After you have basted your jeans together for a first fitting (page 139), try them on and take a good look in a full-length mirror at your front and back. If you see wrinkles and lines that you don't like, it's likely one of the following issues. For each fit issue we'll show what it looks like and the how-tos to resolve. Use this "wrinkle dictionary" to help you create your best-fitting jeans.

Horizontal wrinkles

—Horizontal lines just beneath the waist indicate a tight waist.

If you don't want to be uncomfortable, let out the side seams at the waist. Jeans you buy can grow when worn, but we recommend interfacing the waistband to prevent that stretch.

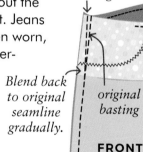

new basting

Blend back to original seamline gradually.

original basting

FRONT

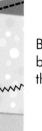

bump

Blend stitching to prevent a bump. Sew farther down on the side if necessary.

Diagonal wrinkles—

When pointing to the inseam, they indicate tightness. They can be seen in the front and/or back thigh area. Let out the inseam where you see these wrinkles. Here, they are in the front.

Remove crotch basting for 2" on each side of the inseam. Let out the front inseam, tapering to the original seamline 6"-8" from the top. The back inseam stitching line remains the same. **This may make your crotch intersection uneven at the top.**

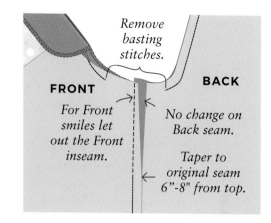

Remove basting stitches.

FRONT

BACK

For Front smiles let out the Front inseam.

No change on Back seam.

Taper to original seam 6"-8" from top.

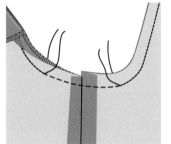

You will need to re-connect the crotch stitching line. This will deepen or narrow one of the seam allowances depending on how you decide to re-connect. Re-baste and try on.

Vertical wrinkles in hip and/or thigh area—

If the jeans are too loose, you will see vertical wrinkles.

Where you see vertical wrinkles, pin sides deeper to fit your body. Place pins horizontally at start and stop points.

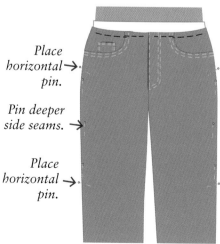

Place horizontal pin.

Pin deeper side seams.

Place horizontal pin.

On the inside, chalk-mark pin position to mark new seamlines. (See photo tutorial on pages 58-59.)

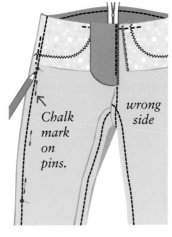

Chalk mark on pins.

wrong side

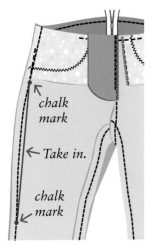

chalk mark

← *Take in.*

chalk mark

Then draw the new stitching lines. You can also take in front, back, or both of the inseams to snug things up.

NOTE: If the **crotch feels too long**, taking in the inseams will shorten it. If it feels a little short, letting out the inseams will lengthen it. You can change front and/or back inseams.

About fullness in the back—If the length of the back crotch seam feels too long and there is vertical fullness below the seat, take in the back inseam starting at the top, tapering to nothing about 6"-8" down. This will shorten the back crotch length and take away some back thigh fullness.

Remove enough of the crotch basting to lay inseams flat.

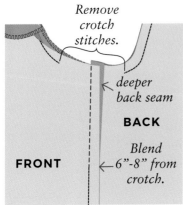

Remove crotch stitches.

← *deeper back seam*

BACK

FRONT

Blend 6"-8" from crotch.

Chalk new stitching line on the back inseam. Pin, matching new back inseam to original front inseam. Re-baste and try on for fit.

Jeans "butt fit"—If there are no back wrinkles and the back crotch length feels good, but you want less fullness under your seat, there is a way to get that look.

Before

After

Draw a curved stitching line on the back leg inseam. Remove inseam basting and re-pin, matching new curved back inseam stitching line to the straight front inseam stitching line. Re-baste and try on for fit. Deepen if necessary.

← *old seamline*

← *new*

BACK

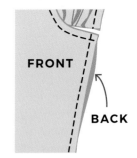

FRONT

BACK

Back puddles—If the front crotch feels good, yet you have a baggy back, you might be "sitting on" the back crotch seam and pushing it down, causing the wrinkles.

If you lower the back crotch seam, making room for your bum, you can then pull up the center back and the wrinkles will go away. Sometimes the amount you lower the back crotch seam is the same amount that you pull up in back.

puddle

Mark how much lower you want the crotch and draw new seamline. Stitch, then trim seam to 3/8".

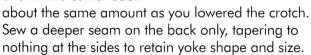

BACK

Mark amount to lower.

FRONT

To hold the back up, you will need to unstitch the yoke seam and lift the center back about the same amount as you lowered the crotch. Sew a deeper seam on the back only, tapering to nothing at the sides to retain yoke shape and size.

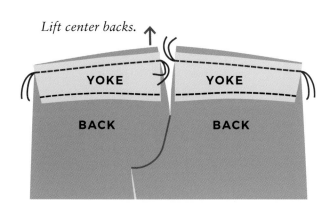

Lift center backs.

YOKE   **YOKE**

BACK   **BACK**

Back crotch cleavage—This has been called "hungry butt" by the image it creates. Usually, straightening the center back seam the amount needed at the spot where the fabric has pulled into the cleavage solves the problem.

Seam goes into cleavage.

If you can't pinch the amount out, estimate the amount.

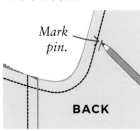

Mark pin.

BACK

On the wrong side chalk the pin position (or transfer your chalk mark to the wrong side if you couldn't pin) and straighten the CB seam to the pin mark. Go a little lower than the crotch curve, then blend in.

Sway back—If you have puddling at your center back, lower the yoke on the back until the puddling disappears. On the back only (not the yoke), take a deeper seam at the center back, tapering to nothing at the sides.

Straighten back crotch.

Blend.

BACK

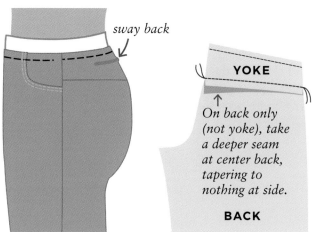

sway back

YOKE

On back only (not yoke), take a deeper seam at center back, tapering to nothing at side.

BACK

Crotch oddities—Changing the shape of any seam is tricky. This wrinkle can be in the front or back. Try pinning out a tuck in the middle of the bubble. That is the amount you need to sew the crotch curve deeper to get rid of the fullness.

When the wrinkle is in the front, you need to sew a more acute angle where the crotch curves.

When the wrinkle is in the back it usually means you need less width where you pinned out the excess. Straightening the back crotch takes away width.

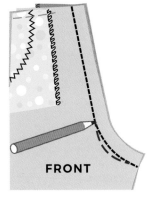

FRONT

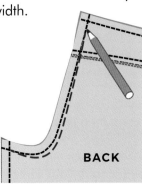

BACK

NOTE: The shape of the front crotch curve is rarely changed, but for a prominent pelvic bone you may need a deeper or more acute front curve. If your bone is more slanted, it will feel like you have too much fabric there. Raise the crotch seam at the curve making it less acute and closer to the body. You might have to try both to see which works.

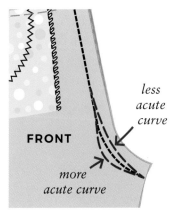

FRONT

less acute curve

more acute curve

Inseam shape—Some people have full inner thighs. Sometimes they are full to the knees. Straighten the slanted inseam as low as needed and gradually taper back to inseam toward hem. Mark the final stitching line on your tissue and the new cutting line for the next time you sew jeans.

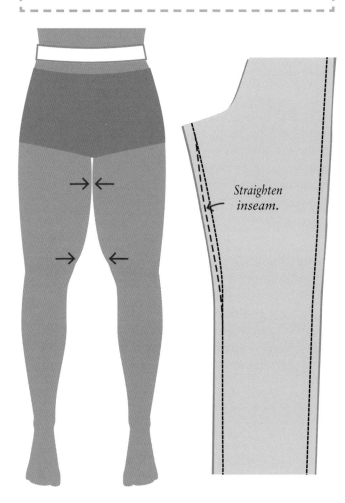

HAZEL SAYS...

It would be better to do this in tissue-fitting. Hopefully you took the suggestion to use 1" seam allowances. Be sure to look for this the next time you tissue-fit.

Straighten inseam.

54

Pillow, puff, and fluff—These wrinkles look similar to the ones on the preceding page but also include smiles pointing to the inner thigh about 2"-3" from the crotch. That usually means you need to let out the front thighs.

Also, you may see light through the legs at the top of the inseam above where the thighs touch.

Crotch depth feels fine. Thighs touch about 1/2"-1" below crotch, causing this wrinkle.

Note that this body has an inner thigh "pillow." It doesn't work to let out the inseam at the top because the thighs don't come together there. Width is needed lower.

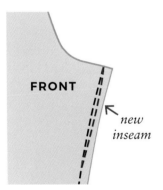

new inseam

Curve out the front thigh inseam only in the area of the pillow. Mark, then pin the curve to the back inseam on its original seamline.

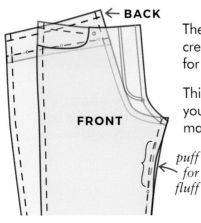

The little "puff" you create makes room for the "fluff."

This is an alteration you may want to mark on your tissue.

puff for fluff

Curvy sides—
The side seams often need careful shaping.

You may have a hollow area that is emphasized when sewn to fit. You can straighten it out just a little so the hollow is less noticeable.

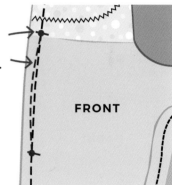

Chalk-mark pin locations at beginning and end points. Gradually let out seam.

FRONT

Uneven hips—
If one side is fuller and higher, pull down on the side seam on the high side or up on the low side, depending on your crotch comfort. You may need to let out the high side below the waist if it is also fuller and/or take in the low side because it may be flatter.

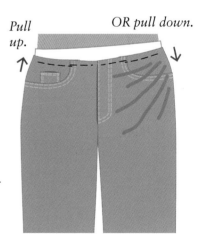

Pull up. *OR pull down.*

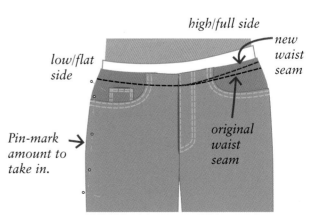

high/full side

new waist seam

low/flat side

original waist seam

Pin-mark amount to take in.

Prominent calves—If you have full calves and jeans with narrow legs, the side seam will pull toward the back and you will see wrinkles pointing to the calves. Let out the seams on the back only from just above the knee to the hem. This is another reason we like 1" seam allowances. Next time you tissue-fit, check for extended calves, especially in narrow-leg jeans. You won't see it in fuller pant legs.

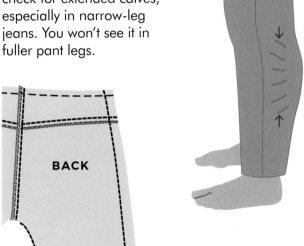

BACK

Start about 3" above knee.

Let out back seams only.

Starting about 3" above the knee use a chalk wheel and a ruler to draw new stitching lines for the BACK inseam and outseam to make the BACK leg wider for the calf. In the future, look for this while tissue-fitting.

Full derriere—If your side seam bows to the back, you may need more back width across the derriere. You may also need more length to fit over the bump.

Let out the side seams in this area of back only. Let out back inseams. Re-mark center back of waist higher. If you still need more center back length, lower the back crotch seam.

Next time, make this alteration in tissue because it may not work in fabric if you didn't cut 1" seam allowances.

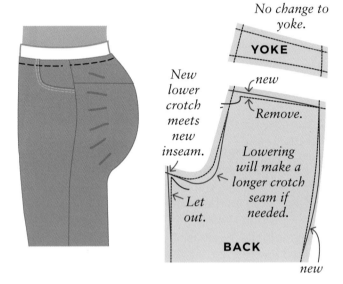

No change to yoke.

YOKE

new

Remove.

New lower crotch meets new inseam.

Lowering will make a longer crotch seam if needed.

Let out.

BACK

new

FITTING THE YOKE

If the yoke gaps just a little in the back you can take a slightly deeper seam at the center back and in the sides if necessary.

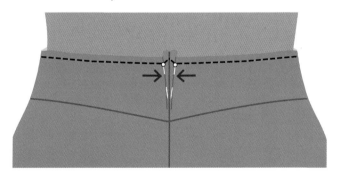

Sometimes, even if you tucked the yoke to fit your body curve in tissue, it may still gap in the back too much to be corrected without making a new yoke.

Cut a New Yoke

Pin small tucks in the fabric from the waist, tapering to nothing at bottom of yoke. Depending on your shape, the tucks might be deeper on one side than the other. Then remove yoke and undo the center back seam. Use the yoke as a pattern to cut a new yoke. If one side of your body is smaller than the other, use both pieces to cut a yoke for each side.

SEAMS FINAL CHECK

Side seams—
Do they need to be taken in or let out? See pages 58-59 for how-tos.

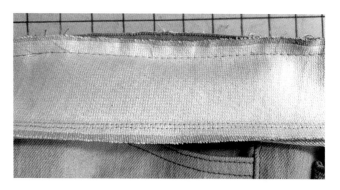

Vertical pins mark how deep to make new seam.

Horizontal pins mark start and stop of change.

TWEAKING THE WAISTBAND SEAM

Fitting the basted waistband—This wrinkle below the waistband means you need to sew the waistband lower on the pant in this area. We see it on both sides, but you may see it only on one side.

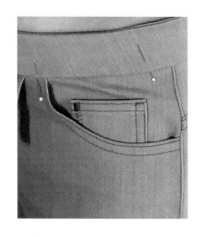

First, push the excess toward the waistband. Pin the amount you need to remove. Place vertical pins at the beginning and end of the change.

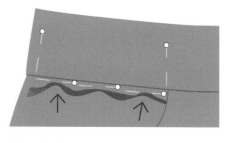

On the wrong side, chalk-mark the new waist stitching line where the pins are. Sew waistband on new seamline, removing excess fabric at the waist.

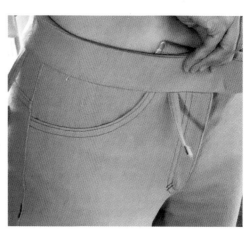

The waistband is sewn on and there are no wrinkles on either side.

LENGTH

Consider how you're going to wear your jeans before cutting off length. You might leave a 2" "in-case" hem when fitting. Tapered legs may look better shorter and wide legs longer, but again, you choose.

MASTER CHALK-MARKING YOUR CHANGES!

Having conducted many workshops, I've learned not to gloss over this step. Now that you've pinned your jeans into the shape you want, how the heck do you record this on your fabric so you can actually sew what you changed? Follow these steps. It's not quick, but it works!

While on your body you can put horizontal pins where you want to start and stop and vertical pins to mark how much you want to take in. If you are letting out, you will decide how much, and still use your horizontal start and stop pins.

2. If you've taken in a seam, chalk where the pins are. Rub hard.

The new seamline is marked at the pins. When you mark pins that are on the right side, you'll get two marks—one on the pants and one on the seam allowance. Follow the row of lines that are the innermost marks. Ignore the second set.

1. Turn jeans wrong side out and on the wrong side, chalk-mark the horizontal pins and then remove them.

Chalk-mark horizontal pins.

3. With a chalk wheel, draw a line where you will baste the new seam.

4. Machine baste on the new seamline.

6. Draw the new cut edge with a chalk wheel, making even seam allowances.

5. Remove the old basting stitches. Try the jeans on to make sure you like the fit.

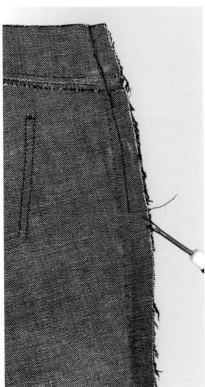

7. Trim on new cutting line.

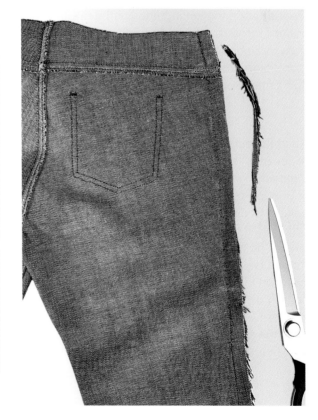

TRACING A PDF PATTERN FOR TISSUE-FITTING

Some patterns are available only in PDF. These patterns must be traced onto tissue in order to tissue-fit them with success. Regular paper is just too stiff. We recommend tracing your pattern onto Perfect Pattern Paper because it works so well for tissue-fitting, as noted on the next page.

Whether you've taped 8.5" x 11" sheets together or are tracing one large sheet, place it on a surface where the entire pattern can lie completely flat.

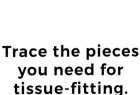

Trace the pieces you need for tissue-fitting.

1. To clearly see the cutting lines of the original pattern through the tissue, darken the cutting lines for your size with a thick marker on the Front, Side Front, Back, and Yoke as shown on PDF pattern upper right in next column.

2. Place Perfect Pattern Paper over the pattern. Match the grainline of one leg of original pattern to a line on the PPP. Hold it in place with pins or pattern weights. Trace. Use a #2 pencil that won't tear the pattern or a waterproof marker to carefully trace the pattern onto your tissue.

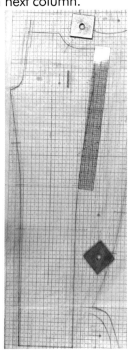

Darken cutting lines for your size.

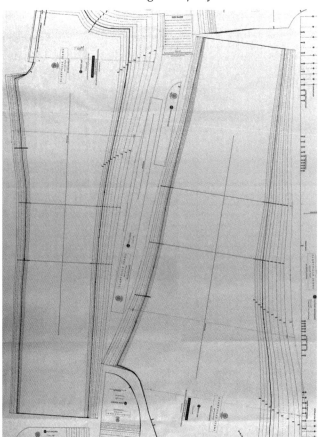

3. Shift PPP over the other leg until the grainline matches a line on the Perfect Pattern Paper. Trace. Continue with the smaller pieces.

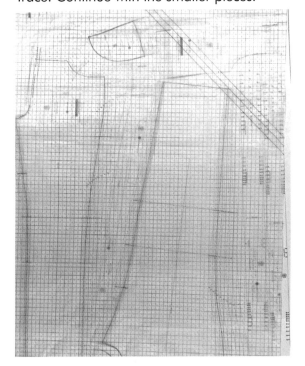

Trace all grainlines, pattern markings, and notches.

4. If your pattern has no ease or negative ease (see page 34) draw 2" x 18" side extensions onto the sheet of tissue on front, back, yoke and side front before you cut out the pieces.

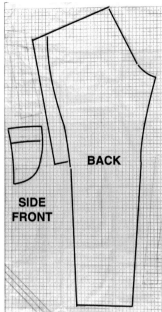

5. Cut pieces out.

6. Mark your seamlines (see page 33). Also mark a horizontal grainline at hip, just above crotch as shown. The vertical and horizontal grainlines will help you fit. They should be perpendicular and parallel to the floor.

7. Reinforce pattern crotch with tape. See page 33.

8. Pin pattern together for tissue-fitting following the instructions on page 34.

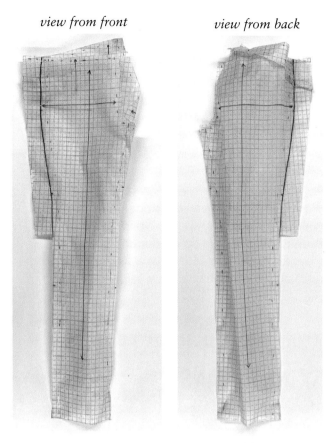

view from front   *view from back*

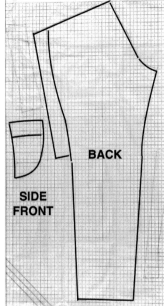

Your pinned pattern is ready for tissue-fitting. You can trim the pieces not needed for fitting later.

NOTE: During the 15 years that I've been studying and teaching tissue-fitting in Palmer/Pletsch workshops, I have seen every kind of pattern tracing paper/nonwoven fabric product imaginable. I love Perfect Pattern Paper for tissue-fitting because it drapes like fabric. It is tougher than it looks and it doesn't get hung up on the other garments you're wearing when fitting. The printed grid makes altering easier.

CHAPTER 5
REAL PEOPLE FITTING JEANS

Regardless of the shape of the pattern pieces, you can fit any jeans pattern to your body. We'll show you how in this "Real People" chapter. We have fitted different body types in a variety of jeans patterns using both rigid and stretch denim.

AVA IN HIGH-WAISTED SKINNY JEANS

First, so you can see the whole process from start to finish and to help you learn to think through jeans fit, we will start with my daughter Ava, who is 5'11" and slim, with a 40" hip. She wants a snugly fitted stretch jean that comes up to her waist. For Ava we chose the Megan Nielsen "Ash" jeans in the skinny version. Ava is very picky about her jeans fit. Follow along.

HAZEL SAYS

Be like a cat and never compromise. YOU know how you want your clothes to fit.

AVA FINDS HER WAIST

Ava has placed her elastic where she wants her waistband, in this case at her natural waist at the bottom of the elastic.

megan nielsen
patterns

The ultimate stretch jean pattern set. Includes four cuts and multiple lengths for tall, regular and cropped. Pattern features a comfortable rise, close fit through the waist and hips, and classic jeans details.

ash

WAIST 24-36" (61-91cm)
MN2211
www.megannielsen.com
SKILL ●●○○

SIZING & YARDAGE

IMPERIAL

		24	25	26	27	28	29	30	31	32	33	34	35	36
BODY MEASUREMENTS (inches)														
waist		24	25	26	27	28	29	30	31	32	33	34	35	36
hip		34	35	36	37	38	39	40	41	42	43	44	45	46
FABRIC REQUIRED (yards)														
v1	60"	1½	1½	1½	1½	1½	1½	1½	1⅝	1⅝	1⅝	1¾	1¾	1¾
	45"	2⅛	2⅛	2⅛	2⅛	2⅛	2⅛	2¼	2¼	2¼	2⅜	2⅜	2⅜	2⅜
v2	60"	1½	1½	1½	1½	1½	1½	1½	1⅝	1⅝	1⅝	1¾	1¾	1¾
	45"	2⅛	2⅛	2⅛	2⅛	2⅛	2⅛	2¼	2¼	2¼	2⅜	2⅜	2⅜	2⅜
v3	60"	2⅛	2⅛	2⅛	2⅛	2⅛	2⅛	2¼	2¼	2¼	2¼	2¼	2¼	2¼
	45"	2½	2½	2½	2½	2½	2½	2½	2½	2½	2½	2½	2½	2½
v4	60"	2⅛	2⅛	2⅛	2⅛	2⅛	2⅛	2¼	2¼	2¼	2¼	2¼	2¼	2¼
	45"	2½	2½	2½	2½	2½	2½	2⅝	2⅝	2⅝	2⅝	2⅝	2⅝	2⅝
FINISHED GARMENT (inches)														
waistband		24⅜	25⅜	26⅜	27⅜	28⅜	29⅜	30⅜	31¼	32¼	33¼	34¼	35¼	36¼
hip		32⅝	33⅝	34⅝	35⅝	36⅝	37⅝	38⅝	39⅝	40½	41½	42½	43½	44½
rise*		9⅜	9½	9⅝	9¾	9⅞	10⅛	10¼	10⅜	10½	10⅝	10⅞	11	11⅛

CHOOSING AVA'S PATTERN SIZE

The size on the envelope of Ava's chosen pattern for a 40" hip is size 30. The finished garment measurement (FGM) for size 30 is 38½". We did the wrap test just to be sure that 38½" would stretch to 40 to account for **negative ease**. This shows us that 38½" of fabric does fit comfortably snug. We will still use 1" just-in-case seam allowances at side seams, inseams, and waist.

THE FRONT BEFORE

The tissue has been prepared for tissue-fitting: the crotch was taped and clipped and extra tissue was added to the upper side front and back because of **negative ease** so Ava can try it on. The excess tissue at the sides will be removed before cutting fabric. Since these are skinny jeans in a stretchy fabric, ignore that the lower legs don't meet at the outside seams. They will stretch to fit.

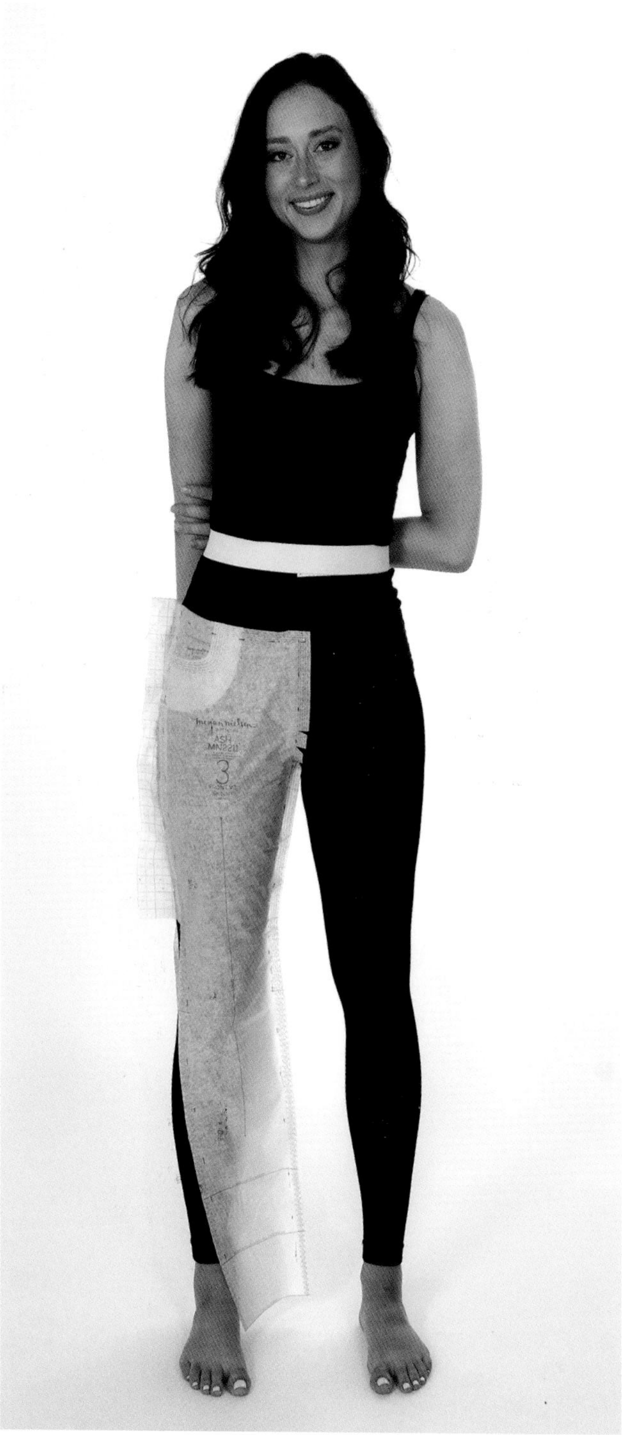

THE SIDE AND BACK BEFORE

Ava needs to add crotch depth. We will add 3" to get the waist seamline on the tissue to the bottom of the elastic. After molding the tissue to her shape, we will reduce the amount we added.

THE FRONT AFTER

The front and back crotch have been lengthened 3". She puts on the tissue and pulls it up until the crotch seamline touches her body and the top touches the waistband elastic.

THE SIDE AND BACK AFTER

The side seam is perpendicular to the floor. The back inseam has a few "whiskers" or horizontal wrinkles below the seat, a typical jeans look, but the top of the yoke is buckling—it is too big.

We will now shape the yoke to fit.

We darted the tissue at the back waist, tapering to nothing at the bottom of the yoke. Now it lies flat.

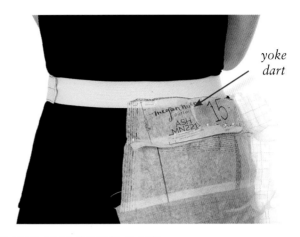

yoke dart

THE WAISTBAND

To fit the waistband, Ava wraps it around her waist to make sure it comes from center back to 2"-3" past center front. That gives her plenty of extra for the underlap and just in case she needs a little more length.

The contour band shapes perfectly to her body.

65

We added crotch depth to get the tissue up to Ava's waist in order to shape the yoke and side seams to her body.

However, we know that denim fabric will grow, so we will remove some of what we added in crotch depth before cutting out the fabric. If you don't, your jeans may come up higher than you like them and if you cut this excess off at the top, you'll lose a portion of your front pockets.

How much to shorten the crotch depth? It depends on the fabric. Below is a guide to help you determine where you want the tissue waist after all tissue-fitting is completed and before you cut your fabric. *We feature this guide more than once in the book because it's unique to jeans fitting and we consider it key to getting proper fit. See page 110.*

CROTCH DEPTH GUIDE

Nonstretch or rigid denim
Pattern waist seamline can be 1/2" to 1" below your waistband seamline (bottom of the elastic). Example: If you added a total of 2" of depth, you can fold out 1/2" to 1" before cutting.

Stretch denim (moderate stretch)
Pattern waist seamline can be 1" to 1½" below your waistband seamline (bottom of the elastic).

4-way stretch denim
Not common. Stretch-test both directions to be sure it really is 4-way. Pattern waist seamline can be 1½" to 2" below your waistband seamline (bottom of the elastic).

We always recommend using 1" waistline seam allowances—just in case.

We added 3" to Ava's crotch depth to reach her preferred waist level in tissue for shaping. Before cutting we removed a portion of that tissue using the Crotch Depth Guide.

Ava's denim is moderately stretchy, so we want the tissue to be 1" to 1½" from the bottom of her elastic. I chose to remove 1½" and work with 1" seam allowances at waist, sides, and inseams. Refer to Chapter 6 page 110 for step-by-step instructions.

FABRIC FIT

I sewed the front pockets and fly front zipper, then basted the rest for a first fabric fitting.

They look good. I turned up the hem to her preferred finished length, but will check length again later before cutting off and leaving a 1" hem allowance. Ava likes to wear booties in the fall and winter and have a little bit of skin show above the shoe, so precise length is important to her.

The crotch depth is perfect! The upper thigh feels just a little loose to her, so we will take the inseams in 3/8" at the top, front and back, tapering back to the 5/8" seam allowance about 8" down the leg.

WAIST AND LEG WIDTH

The back waist gaps a bit, so we will take in the center back seam at the waist, tapering to nothing at the full hip. This adds a little more slant to the crotch seam to fit her slant.

pinched in waist at center back

The pockets are pinned in place and we marked the corners and bottom point with chalk.

67

The jeans look great while standing, but Ava did the "sit test" and decided she needs a little more leg width. These jeans feel tight through the knee and calf. We will let the inseams and side seams out 1/8" starting at the horizontal pins just above the knee.

Letting out these seams an even 1/8" means adding 1/2" in total width. This type of tweaking is what makes your jeans fit perfectly!

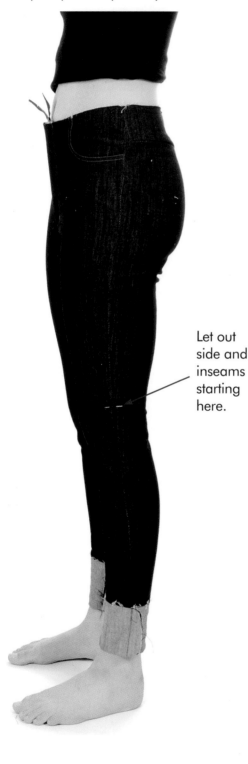

Let out side and inseams starting here.

THE WAISTBAND

The top waistband seam is sewn, trimmed, graded and ready to wrap around her waist to check fit. The contour of the band perfectly fits her contour and comes to her natural waist, which is her preference. Off to finish sewing!

THE FINISHED JEANS

Ava loves her new custom jeans and Mom loved sewing them! They are paired here with the Grainline Studio "Archer Button Up" shirt in a flowy rayon crepe.

69

ALLI IN DARK WASH STRETCH JEANS

Meet Alli, a barre instructor and hair and makeup stylist who says she has a terrible time finding jeans that fit. She is tall and curvy and firm. We've chosen the Ames Jeans pattern by Cashmerette, a company that specializes in patterns for curvy bodies. It features two interchangeable pelvis shapes and leg widths. We started with the "apple" shaped pelvis and the "skinny" leg.

We are using 1½" elastic, the same as her waistband width, and asked her to put it where she wants her jeans waistband. She prefers a higher waist because they will stay in place better.

As you can see from the side view, her waist is higher in the back than the front and that is where her jeans waistband will be. If you tried to make the waistband level, it would just fall down in front.

CHOOSING THE PATTERN SIZE

Stand in front of a full-length mirror when you are measuring to make sure the measuring tape is parallel to the floor. Alli measures her fullest place at the hip so we can decide on the best size pattern to use. She measures 52". The size we picked has a finished hip measurement of 48". We are using a stretch denim and Alli wants a snug fit. Let's find out if 48" of her fabric will stretch to fit her hips.

ALLI DOES THE WRAP TEST

We measured 48" of her stretchy denim fabric folded along the crosswise grain and wrapped it tightly around the fullest part her hips. It easily stretched the 4" needed at the fullest part of her hips. Therefore, we don't need to add to the pattern at the side seams.

FIRST TISSUE-FITTING

The pattern is 4" smaller than Alli, but her denim will stretch that much and she wants her jeans tight. We added width temporarily to the pattern so we can tissue-fit. We will then be able to quickly check the crotch depth, crotch curve shape, inseams, and length. We will trim the extra tissue away from the sides before we cut from fabric. We will do the rest of the fitting in fabric.

For your first tissue-fitting, pull up the tissue evenly in the front and back until the taped and clipped crotch seam touches your body. Don't pull up the front then the back. You won't be able to get the back up. Treat the tissue like an elevator, raising it up as a unit.

Alli needs a higher rise (aka more crotch depth). We want to add the amount she needs to get the tissue to the bottom of the elastic. However, the amount is different in the front, side, and back. Since we don't want to lose the front pocket, we will add only the amount needed to get the front waist seamline to the bottom of the elastic in the front. When she tries the tissue on again we will decide how much to add to the top of the side and back tissue to fit.

NOTE: Because Alli's denim is quite stretchy, after we fit the top front and back yoke parts to her body and before we cut from fabric, we will fold out the amount that will bring the pattern waist seamline to 1½" from the bottom of her elastic for this stretchy denim. See page 66 for your best-bet formula for determining this crotch depth adjustment.

We've added 3¼" crotch depth and tried on the altered pattern, pulling it up evenly as she did in the first fitting.

Ignore the open side seam from the knee down. The denim will stretch AND we will have those 1" just-in-case seam allowances.

We will add some tissue to the top at the side and back to reach her waist.

The wrinkle to the front inseam usually means you need to let out the front inseam, but for a jeans fit in this stretchy denim, we won't. We'll have our 1" seam allowances, so we can adjust at the fabric-fit stage if needed.

The pattern has enough leg length.

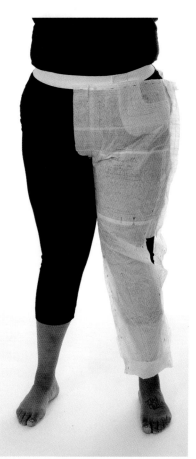

Tissue has been added to fill in the space from the top of the pattern to reach the bottom of the elastic at sides and back.

Alli curves in at the back waist so we darted the tissue to fit her curve. You can do this alone. *Yes, you can!* Stand with your back facing a full-length mirror while using a handheld mirror to look over your shoulder.

Try on to see if what you pinned out is the right amount. Adjust if necessary.

The darts in the tissue taper to nothing from the waist to the bottom of the yoke. The side seam has been pinned deeper, curving in to fit her waist.

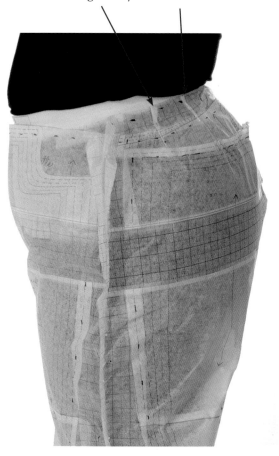

Here's a close-up of the yoke, flat and ready to cut.

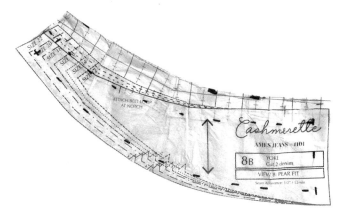

THE WAISTBAND

The waistband is contoured, or curved.

We wrapped half the waistband around Alli's waist, starting at the center back, and marked the center front. We always add 3" beyond the center front to make sure the band is long enough. Just the thickness of the denim can eat up some length.

It curves to her body shape and lies smooth.

The waistband back is tricky. Alli curves in a lot at the waist. It's difficult to mimic fabric here, but the tissue looks as if it needs to have a little more shaping near the center back. We mark with a pencil where two more darts are needed and then fold them in when the waistband is flat.

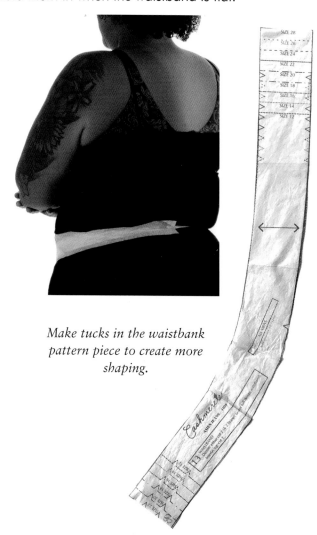

Make tucks in the waistbank pattern piece to create more shaping.

Finalize the Pattern

Remember! Before cutting Alli's denim we will fold out a portion of the crotch depth. We know the denim will stretch and "grow" to bring the crotch depth up to the level she needs. See page 110 for a full explanation and how to do this.

We will cut off the side extension (page 110), because this fabric has lots of stretch to allow for negative ease. However, we will save the extension because it will remind us of the shape of her side from hip to waist.

FABRIC FITTING

Alli's front pockets and zipper have been sewn and the rest is basted together.

The jeans fit well at the waist and through the hips and thighs. Even though Alli has full inner thighs (page 54), the fabric had enough stretch to accomodate the inner leg width.

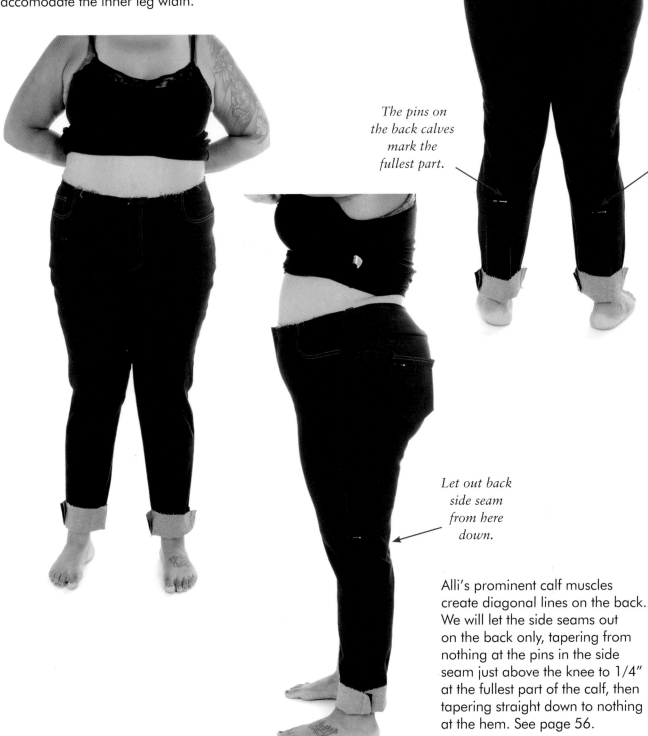

The pins on the back calves mark the fullest part.

Let out back side seam from here down.

Alli's prominent calf muscles create diagonal lines on the back. We will let the side seams out on the back only, tapering from nothing at the pins in the side seam just above the knee to 1/4" at the fullest part of the calf, then tapering straight down to nothing at the hem. See page 56.

THE WAISTBAND

Before we make the changes determined on page 74, we will fit the contour waistband. The facing has been sewn to the top of the waistband and understitched. It is wrapped around Alli's waist and fastened with a clip. The contour waistband fits her very well and is at the height she wants to wear it.

BACK POCKETS

We repositioned the pockets until we loved the way they looked and marked the top corners and bottom point with a chalk pencil.

Now to finish up the sewing!

THE FINISHED JEANS

Alli looks great in her dark wash denim!

FITTING PATI

Pati is smaller just above her hip bones and a trend right now is high-waisted (meaning normal waist). Since this will be a snug-fitting, stretchy denim jean, she thinks the higher waist will be more comfortable. And these will be pull-on jeans.

This pattern was converted to be pull-on jeans.

TRYING ON THE TISSUE

Pati has turned up the bottoms 2½" just so they don't crumple up at her ankles.

Try on the tissue carefully. If you pull the front up to the waist first, you won't be able to get the back up to the waist, and the side seam won't be perpendicular to the floor.

Instead, pretend the tissue is an elevator and pull up the front and back evenly, having the side seam perpendicular to the floor.

Pati levels out the pattern so the side seam is straight and makes sure the crotch seam is touching her body and the centers front and back of the tissue are at her centers.

HAZEL SAYS

The crotch seam MUST touch the body!

Tissue not touching the body

Perfect— tissue touching the body

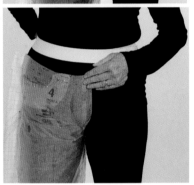

The pattern is 1" below her elastic in front and 2" below the elastic in back. Pati will lower the back crotch curve 1" to bring the back up and level the pattern.

Pati lowers the back crotch curve 1" and the pattern now reaches the same distance from the elastic in both front and back.

Pati stands with her back to her full-length mirror and uses a hand mirror to look at the back first.

The tissue is being pushed down in the back, causing wrinkles below the seat and puddles below the knee. The back crotch needs to be lowered, but how much? See page 53.

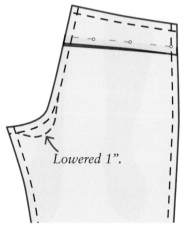

Lowered 1".

For Pati to have her waistband at the level she wants, she needs to lengthen the crotch depth 1" front and back. We still need a 5/8" waist seam, but this stretch denim should stretch enough to accommodate it.

The tissue and elastic are also showing that Pati's right hip is a little higher and rounder than her left hip. Since we are tissue-fitting the fuller, higher side, we will adjust the left side in fabric.

Note that where we turned the hem up looks like a good finished length. Since the jeans have a 1" hem, we can trim the hem allowance to 1" before cutting the denim, or we can wait until the jeans are finished, which would allow for changes in length during fabric fitting.

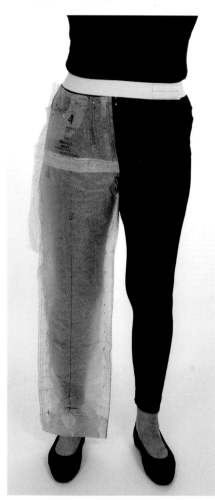

THE BACK CLOSE UP

Pati's back cleavage is where the arrow is pointing. The center back seam needs to be placed there. Pati is a little flatter and straighter in the back than the pattern. Straightening the crotch seam will move the seam over to her center back and take away some width.

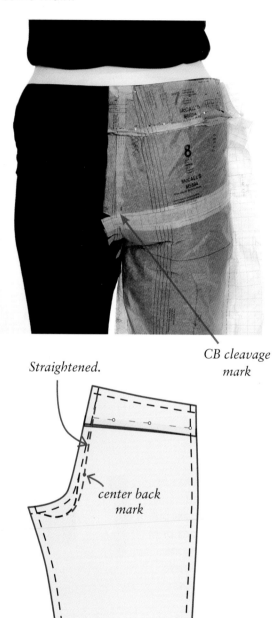

Straightened.

CB cleavage mark

center back mark

Before cutting out fabric, trim the back crotch seam to an even seam allowance.

THE FRONT CLOSE UP

The center front is slanted. The seam should come to Pati's center where the pin is.

We straightened the center front 1/2" at the top, tapering to nothing where the crotch starts to curve.

There is a wrinkle pointing to her thigh.

Pati drops the tissue and unpins the inseam, then lets out the front inseam until the wrinkle is gone. She has 1" in-case seam allowances.

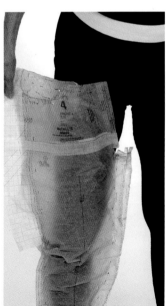

A FINAL LOOK AT THE SIDE AND BACK

Because her fabric has so much stretch, we used a size 12, planning on using that stretch to fit her width. Therefore, the jeans will be more fitted in the back than we are seeing in the tissue. See page 30, where she wraps the fabric around the hip and calculates her size.

Pati is straighter from hip to waist than the pattern, so we will add 3/4" to the waist at the top.

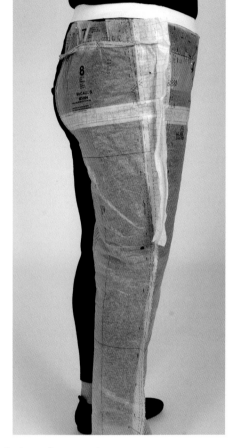

The back yoke is too big in the waist. We taped in some small tucks to shape the yoke to her body.

tucks in yoke at waist, tapering to nothing at bottom of yoke

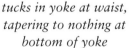

Pati likes a tapered leg (13½" to 14" circumference at the bottom), so we marked on her pattern in red where we will begin tapering and will use a yardstick to draw a seamline, add seam allowances by marking new cutting lines, and trim away the excess tissue.

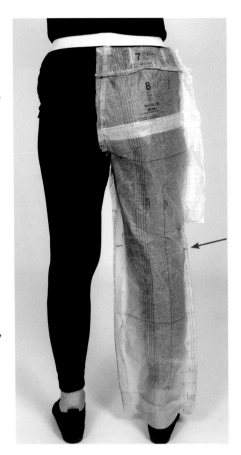

FITTING THE WAISTBAND

Pati's jeans will have a pull-on waistband with elastic. She folded the band in half and wrapped it around her waist to make sure it will fit her. We will leave 1" on each end to fit the top of the jeans. (See page 113.)

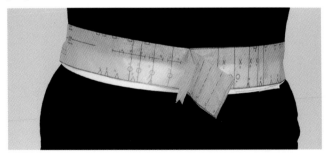

WHAT DID WE LEARN FROM TISSUE-FITTING?

We saw in tissue what may have been difficult to see in fabric, such as needing to lengthen the crotch, straightening the front, lowering the back crotch, and shaping the yoke. Now fabric fitting will be easier. If Pati needs more calf room or front thigh room, or to take in the back inseam, all can

be done in fabric and she will be happy to have 1" seam allowances on inseams and side seams.

If her fabric had little or no stretch, Pati might have started with a size 14 instead of a 12. There are things to consider depending on your fabric and your own fit preferences.

THE PATTERN READY TO CUT FROM FABRIC

The side seam is pinned 3/4" from the cut edge of the pattern at her waist. That will be her stitching line. A wedge of tissue will be needed at the waist.

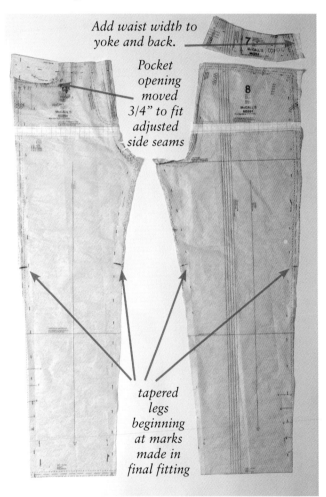

Add waist width to yoke and back.

Pocket opening moved 3/4" to fit adjusted side seams

tapered legs beginning at marks made in final fitting

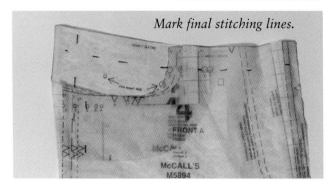

Mark final stitching lines.

FIRST FABRIC FITTING

Pati's front pockets and mock front fly were sewn (page 209), then the jeans were basted together for a fitting. The tissue-fitting worked well, and the fabric wrap test helped us know how much smaller the jeans could be through the hips and waist. We are very happy with how they look. We could finish them now, as is, but we love tweaking because it makes us love them even more.

The back looks good, but we decided to take in the back inseams to get a more snug jeans fit.

The pinned tuck shows how much to slip the back inseam in. It is a 1/2" tuck, meaning we will slip the back inseam in 1". If you can't sit in them after doing this, take out the basting. This is such a stretchy denim, Pati could sit comfortably.

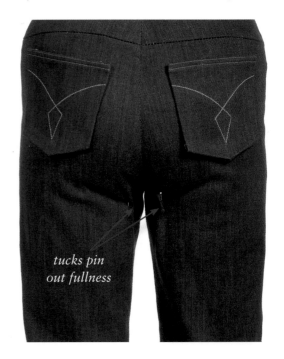

tucks pin out fullness

The back now has whiskers under the seat and Pati likes the way they look.

Pati is higher on her right hip We need to mark the bottom of the elastic on the left side where the waistband seam will be a little deeper.

We turned the hem up to touch the top of her shoes, then cut off all but 1" for the hem.

The last little bit of tweaking we did was to taper the legs a little more on the side seam from above the knee and the inseam starting at the knee. Mark the pins with chalk on the inside of your jeans to record your new stitching lines. See page 58, 59 to learn how to mark your changes on fabric.

Time to finish sewing!

PULL-ON JEANS ADVANTAGE

Pull-on jeans don't need a zipper because the waistline will stretch to go over the hips. There are no gathers caused by the elastic because Pati's waist is just a few inches smaller than her hips. For instructions for the mock fly front see page 209. For the elastic waistband see page 213.

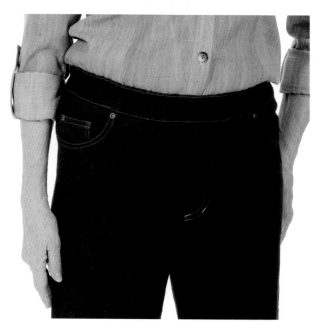

83

PATI'S FINISHED JEANS

Pati loves her new pull-on jeans. They are very comfy. They also stay in place very well. She wears the legs turned up for summer and longer in winter.

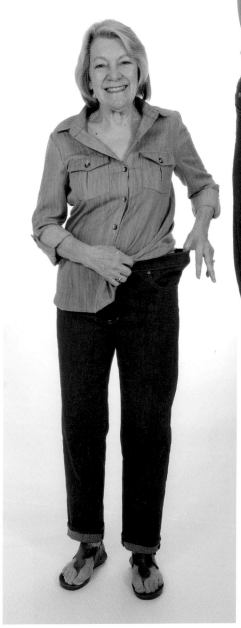

The back fits well with no puddles. It's snug, but not too tight.

MY FLANNEL-UNDERLINED JEANS

I have been dreaming of making flannel-lined jeans for many years. I've seen them in mail order catalogs (pricey!) and always thought the combination of rugged denim and cozy flannel sounded like cold-weather heaven. I wanted them to fit at the waist, be a tad snug at the hip, and roomy enough in the legs to comfortably sit around the campfire on brisk mountain mornings while I enjoy a tasty beverage. I wanted a cute, turned-up cuff to show off just a bit of the flannel and I'd smile every time I looked down and caught a glimpse of bright pink at my ankles. They turned out better than I ever imagined. Here is the story.

FITTING RIGID, STRAIGHT-LEGGED JEANS

These jeans will be for camping and winter walks. This is the first time I am making this type of jean and it is a learning experience. The pattern is Closet Core "Morgan Boyfriend Jeans." They are designed with straight-grain side seams suitable for selvedge denim and have a button fly.

I am using 12 oz. denim and underlining with a thick cotton flannel.

CHOOSING THE PATTERN SIZE

To satisfy my curiosity about the ease needed for the two layers of fabric, I wrap the fabrics around my hips comfortably and mark with pins where the fabrics come together.

Measuring from pin to pin was 38". That is what the pattern needs to allow in the hips for the two layers.

I chose the pattern size with a finished garment measurement closest to 38" at the hip. As we often do, I will use 1" inseam and side seam allowances, "in case" I need more room.

85

A LOOK AT THE FRONT

Since these jeans will fit more like a regular pant versus jeans with negative ease, we can tissue-fit without adding an extra chunk of tissue to the side seams.

The crotch depth is good, front and back. The tissue reaches the elastic with a 5/8" seam allowance. This is important with this style of jeans and weight of denim. I won't assume the denim will stretch to allow for a waist seam allowance.

The front comes to my center front. It needs no alterations but I will cut 1" side seams and inseams in case I want to add hip or thigh width later in fabric.

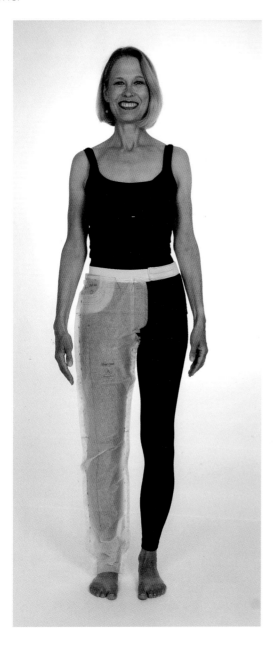

THE BACK

The back comes to my center back, but my seat is pushing the back crotch seam down, causing puddling of the tissue below the seat. I will lower the back crotch curve 3/4".

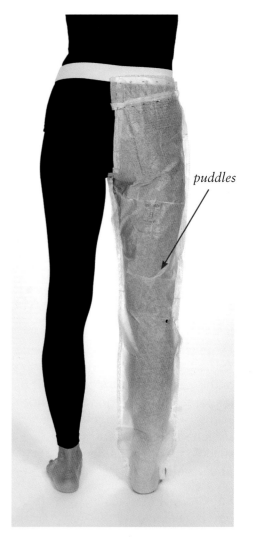

puddles

After lowering the back crotch curve, the tissue is much smoother beneath the seat and the little bit of wrinkle still there will smooth out in denim. The yoke, however, is too big at the waist and it ripples.

We made two tucks in the yoke to shape it to my body.

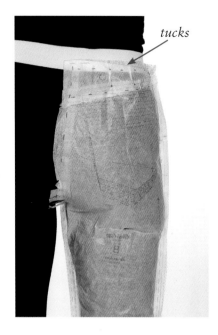

tucks

I cut my flannel underlining so the plaid would match up at the hems for the turned-up cuffs.

FITTING THE WAISTBAND

I love a contour waistband. This pattern just happens to have one. If it didn't, I would shape a straight waistband to fit. This fits well and no alterations are needed.

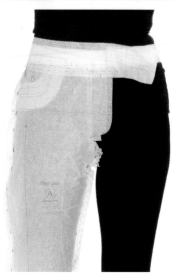

I glue-basted the flannel underlining to the wrong side of my denim in the seam allowances on the legs and yokes.

HAZEL SAYS...

What is the difference between lining and underlining? Lining is attached at the waist and hangs free inside the pants. Lining fabric is generally slippery.

Underlining is attached to the wrong side of each piece of fashion fabric and both layers are included in the seam. If the flannel were used as a lining, it would stick to the denim and possibly even ride up or twist inside the legs.

FIRST FABRIC FITTING

With the flannel underlining glue-basted to the denim, I sewed the front pockets and button fly front. I will wait until the end to install the buttons.

The seams with the flannel underlining and the 12 oz. denim feel very bulky with the 1" side and inseam allowances. Trimming, serging, and pressing the seam allowances will eliminate much of the bulk.

THE FRONT

The fabric clips at the top of the side seams are helping hold up the jeans. I will deepen the upper side seams 5/8" to fit my waist.

I will take in the upper front inseams about 5/8".

However, the lower legs need to be looser so I can still bend my knees and sit comfortably.

This is where the 1" side and inseam allowances come in handy. I will let them out beginning just above the knee, tapering out from nothing to 5/8" at the hem, making each leg 2½" wider at the hem. (5/8" x 4 = 2½")

The crotch curve feels strange. I decided I had made the curve too acute when I lowered the back crotch seam in tissue.

This photo shows how I will raise it for the next fitting, by sewing a shallower seam at the curve.

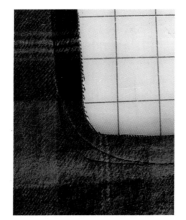

THE BACK

There is still a little puddling under the seat. I pull up the jeans at the center back to relieve this, but the result is "hungry butt." This usually means the back crotch needs to be straightened, which will remove width and pull the seam out of the back cleavage.

We will straighten the back seam, taking it in the amount the back crotch seam is pinched with the clip. See page 53.

I will also take in the back inseams by the amount the clip is pinching, which is 1". See page 44.

The patch pockets are in a good position.

SECOND FABRIC FITTING

THE FRONT

The waist fits well. The legs have been widened for more movement and the back inseams taken in.

I like the length with a 1″ hem. Just enough of the flannel underlining will show with the legs turned up.

THE BACK

The center back crotch seam was straightened and the back looks great. The horizontal "whiskers" below the seat give it a good jeans fit. Yay! Time to finish sewing.

HAZEL'S HINTS FOR SEWING BULKY SEAMS

To reduce bulk at the hem, trim the flannel 1″ shorter than the denim.

After basting for fit and determining the finished length, remove your side and inseam basting and separate the flannel for 1″ at the bottom so you can trim.

After sewing and pressing seams to one side (inseams are pressed toward the front, side seams are pressed toward the back, yokes are pressed down), grade them by cutting the underneath layer to ¼".

Now serge-finish the seam allowances together.

89

For each seam, press again after serging to help reduce bulk and ensure the flattest possible seams: yoke seams down, inseams toward the front, and side seams toward the back.

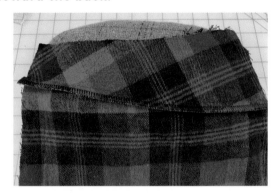

Before sewing the center back/crotch seam, pound the yoke seam at the center back intersection with a hammer to flatten. It will make sewing this bulky seam much easier.

Use a walking foot or a blunt-tipped awl to help feed the four layers through your sewing machine evenly, preventing shifting of the layers.

A walking foot will do the work for you; just sew.

Use the awl on its side in front of the presser foot. Gently flatten and feed the top layer through your machine with short little pushes, so it feeds through at the same rate as the bottom layer against the feed dogs.

the smushed serger stitches after pounding

THE JEANS INSIDE OUT

THE FINISHED JEANS

Here I am in my finished jeans. The fuller legs will allow me to move and bend while camping. They will be warm, too, because of the combination of the 12 oz. denim and the cotton flannel underlining.

I am unreasonably in love with these jeans! I sit here dreaming of camping, the campfire, and hot cocoa. It feels so great to make clothes you can live in.

JULIE IN STRETCH JEANS

Julie made jeans in a Palmer/Pletsch jeans workshop and says they are the only jeans she's ever had that fit. She is very full in the front, swayed at the center back, and slanted from her full seat to her thighs.

CHOOSING JULIE'S PATTERN SIZE

Julie puts the 1½"-wide elastic where she wants her waistband to be—at her waist just above the belly button where the bottom of the elastic sits. But since she doesn't curve in from tummy to waist, we question whether the finished jeans will stay up in the front. They will stay up fine at the sides and back, but she may need to add elastic to the waistband to help the jeans stay in place in the front.

She measures the fullest hip, about 7"-9" from her waist (the bottom of the elastic). She measures 46". We used Butterick 5682. The pattern envelope tells us to sew a size 22 for a 46" hip. The pattern's finished garment measurement at the hip is 49". Since she is using a moderately stretchy denim, this will be too much ease. Size 18 has a FGM of 45" at the hip. We wrapped her denim and found that 45" of her fabric will easily stretch 1" to fit her hip. She wants the jeans snug but not skintight. We cut a size 18.

Julie's pattern

TRY ON THE TISSUE

The tissue was prepared following pages 32-35. Since the pattern has negative ease, we added strips of Perfect Pattern Paper to the sides at front and back and yoke so we could pin the pattern together for tissue-fitting, page 35. Julie tries on the tissue. She is tall and she might need to add to crotch depth normally, but with the rise in this design being low, she will need quite a lot to get the tissue to her preferred waist.

CENTERS

The pattern centers front and back reach her centers front and back, but Julie is rounded below the waist and we need to shape the pattern to her.

THE FRONT, SIDE, AND BACK

We added 3" to the crotch depth to bring the tissue up to the elastic. Remember, some of this depth will be removed before cutting fabric using the measurements in the Crotch Depth Guide chart on page 66.

Julie tries the pattern on again. From this we see that we may need to let out the front inseam because we see smiles. It will probably be less in

First Tissue Try-On

Second Tissue Try-On

fabric. We will be using 1" inseam allowances, so we won't worry about this in tissue.

We need to add tissue at the top on the back where you see the gap. There is fullness below her seat, so we will take in the back inseam in tissue by 3/4". If more is needed, we can do it in fabric since we can pull fabric tighter than tissue.

93

From the knee past the calf, Julie's legs splay slightly to the outside. We will take in the back inseams and let out the back side seams in that area. We notice that the elastic has fallen in the front a little, probably more where it wants to sit.

STRAIGHTENING THE CENTER BACK

Julie is more slanted at the center back than the pattern. We will slant the center back seam, making it 5/8" deeper at the waist and tapering to nothing where the crotch starts to curve.

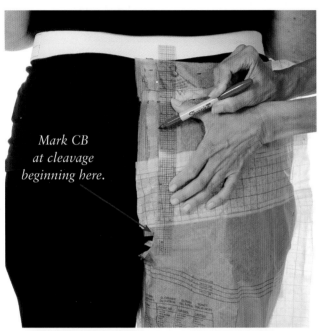

Mark CB at cleavage beginning here.

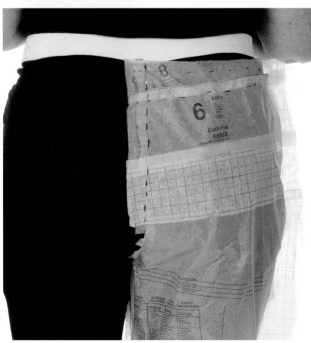

THE YOKE

We've filled in the space at the top of the back and added a small dart in the yoke at the waist, tapering to nothing at the bottom of the yoke, to shape the yoke to her body.

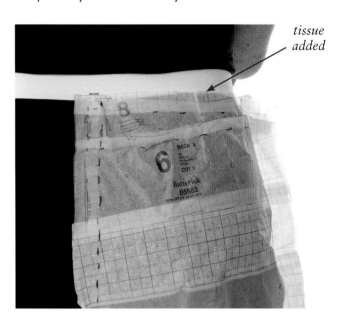

tissue added

THE WAISTBAND

Lastly, we fit the waistband, starting at the center back. We mark the center front on the front piece.

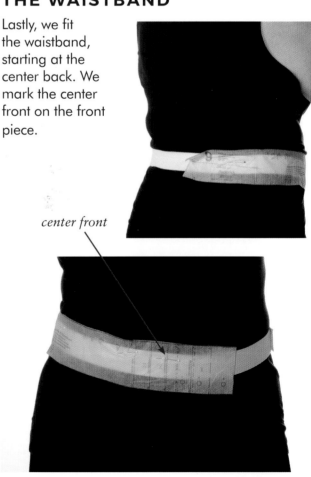

center front

BEFORE CUTTING, RECONSIDER CROTCH DEPTH

We decided to take out 1" of the 3" (on both front and back) of crotch depth previously added to the pattern. See page 66 for how to estimate denim stretch in crotch depth. This pattern alteration is shown in detail on page 110. Because Julie's denim is just moderately stretchy, we wanted the final waist seamline of the tissue 1½" below her elastic. We also will make the waist, side, and inseam allowances 1".

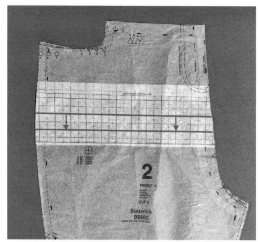

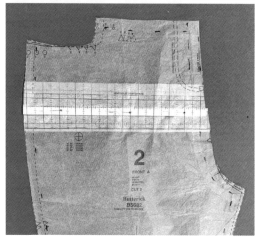

FABRIC FITTING

For Julie, we basted the side fronts to the fronts and basted the center front instead of finishing the pockets and zipper. We took this precaution because Julie's waistband naturally drops in the front and she was not positive where its position in fabric would end up. The tissue also told us we may need to let her inseams out. This could result in too much crotch depth in fabric because crotch length and depth are interrelated, page 28. If we had

the pockets and zipper sewn, we might have had to cut off too much of them at the top. Basting it all takes longer, but allows more opportunity to achieve great fit. We are glad we waited to sew the details!

THE FRONT

The jeans are looking good. We pulled them up in the front and will lower the waistband that amount.

There are some pulls coming from the front inseam. We will let the upper inseam out 1/4".

Julie also wanted the legs more tapered, so we pinned the side seams in deeper. Just before Julie took the jeans off we asked her to do the sit test to make sure she was comfortable. Glad we did! She could hardly bend her legs enough to sit. We ended up just tapering a bit at the ankle.

lower waistband

THE SIDE AND BACK

We removed the pins from the side seams.

Julie's seat is sitting on the crotch and pushing wrinkles down the leg, so we will lower the back crotch 5/8".

We can now remove the basting and sew the pockets, zipper and yoke. The next fitting will be with just the back crotch, side, and inseams basted.

THE FRONT IN A SECOND FABRIC FITTING

Here, the front pockets and zipper have been sewn, the back crotch curve lowered, and the front inseam let out.

The front crotch looks fine, but Julie has to hold the jeans up in this photo, so we will lower the center front 1/2" to nothing at the side seams. We will use elastic in the waistband to help hold them up in front.

A LOOK AT THE WAISTBAND AND POCKETS

With waistband pinned in place and lowered a bit in the front, the jeans are ready to finish. The back crotch was lowered a bit more and we will evaluate the pocket placement.

We can now finish sewing the jeans!

JULIE IN HER FINISHED JEANS

FITTING MEN IN JEANS

Does fitting men differ from fitting women? There are the obvious differences, but when you get right down to it, our basic body shapes are not that different. Because we tissue-fit, we can make any jeans pattern fit any body.

We fit the three men in this chapter in the Palmer/Pletsch straight-leg, mid-rise jeans pattern. It was originally designed and marketed as a women's jean. For the last model, Taylor, we ended up using the Workroom Social Claryville Jeans. Generally, these are the differences we discovered while fitting men. Most apply to any body.

- Most people, men included, need a straighter (less slanted) center front crotch seam than some patterns have.

- Men may need a lower front crotch curve for more body parts room.

- The type of underwear worn, with more or less support and/or bulk, may affect fit choices, as do bra types when fitting women's upper bodies.

- A longer zipper opening is advisable, especially in more fitted styles.

- Larger hands need larger pocket openings.

- Men's belt loops are usually bigger to accommodate a wider belt. It's best to attach them with bartacks top and bottom after the waistband is complete instead of sewing them into the waistband.

- If the jeans are loose-fitting, a longer crotch depth may add comfort. As with any fit choice, it is a personal preference.

FITTING JEFF

CHOOSING JEFF'S PATTERN SIZE

Jeff measures himself at the hip, above the crotch. He measures 40½". He says he does not want tight jeans. With this in mind we chose size 16 in the Palmer/Pletsch jean. The FGM at the hip is 43½".

THE FRONT AND SIDE IN TISSUE BEFORE

Jeff tries on the tissue. I unpinned the tissue at the side to get the center front to Jeff's center front. That created a wrinkle pointing both to the front inseam and toward the center front near the waist. I will straighten the center front and possibly let out the front inseam. The side seam hangs straight.

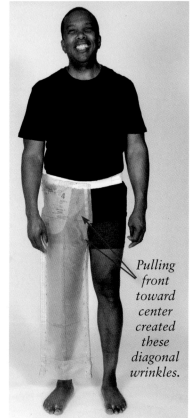

Pulling front toward center created these diagonal wrinkles.

THE BACK BEFORE

The crotch is too long. You can see more clearly from the back that the crotch seam is not touching his body. We will shorten the crotch depth by 1".

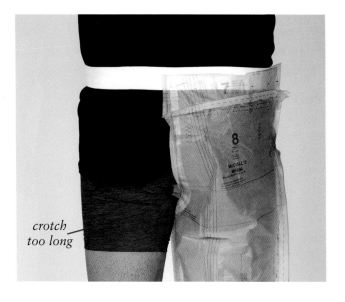

crotch too long

THE FRONT AND BACK WITH TUCK

We pinned a tuck across the front and back. Now the crotch seam touches his body. It will grow a bit in fabric. We will tape the horizontal tuck in place.

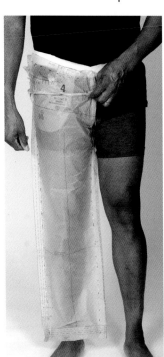
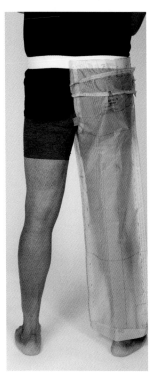

THE SIDE AND BACK

I added tissue at the sides for more waist room. Some may be removed before cutting because the denim will stretch enough to fit snugly. Plus we have 1" in-case seam allowances.

There are puddles beneath the seat.

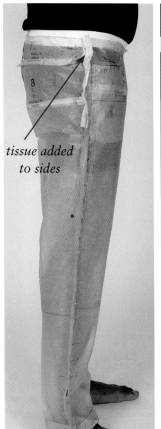
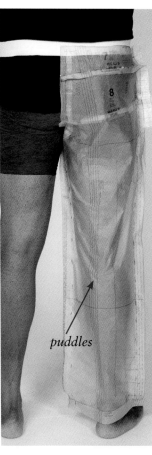

tissue added to sides

puddles

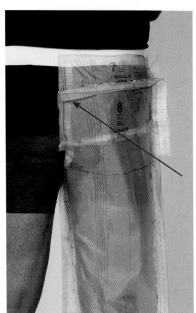

We pulled the tissue up and took a deeper seam at center back, tapering to nothing at the side in the back piece only. The yoke stays the same size. The puddles are gone.

The center front has been straightened. The front crotch is snug, so we will lower the front crotch curve. We didn't need to let out the front inseam because the lower crotch curve added length as well.

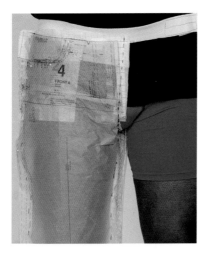

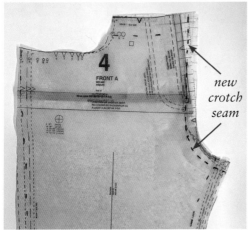

new crotch seam

FIRST FABRIC FIT BEFORE SEWING

The quickest fit check in a looser fitting jean can be done before sewing pockets and zipper. Baste the pieces together and pin the side seams on the outside for easy adjusting. We will taper the leg 1/2" deeper at the hem on inseams and side seams.

We need to widen the front pockets to a 5¾" finished opening to fit his hands. Time to sew!

JEFF IN HIS FINISHED JEANS

Jeff's wife, Toni, was at each of the photo sessions. When she saw Jeff in the final shots, she covered her face in awe.

She told us that he had lost nearly 50 pounds and she hadn't seen him in clothes that fit for a couple of years. They were waiting to buy new clothes until he met his goal.

Oh, but would those jeans look this good?

FITTING GREG

Meet Greg, also known as the Sergin' General. He sews and knows how he wants his jeans to fit. He likes a higher rise and slimmer leg than what he is able to find in RTW and would like a waistband that fits well enough to make wearing a belt optional. Let's go.

Greg measures his hip at 37½". We are using a rigid denim and he doesn't want a super-tight fit. The pattern size 14 has a finished garment measurement at the hip of 41½". We decided to start here with 4" of hip ease and see where it takes us.

Since I have sewn up all the sizes in this Palmer/Pletsch pattern for our workshop attendees, we decided to try the unaltered jeans on the guys just for fun. Greg tells us the waist is too tight and the legs too long. I see hungry butt, back puddles, and the need for a bit more front inseam room. Now, let's see what the tissue tells us.

FRONT BEFORE

The center front doesn't come to Greg's center. Also, the front crotch needs a bit more length. I will straighten the center front and lower the front crotch curve which makes the crotch seam longer.

The leg length is too long.

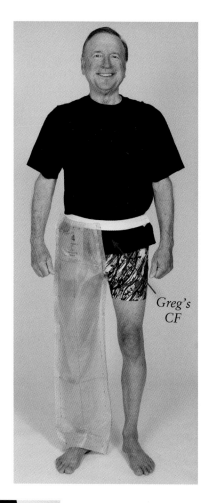

Greg's CF

SIDE BEFORE

Greg's side hangs straight. We will add tissue to the upper side seam to straighten it, giving Greg more waist room.

The hem has been deepened to get the extra length out of the way.

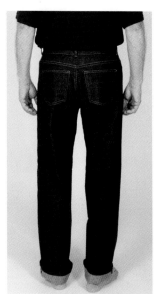

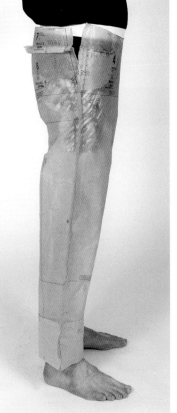

BACK BEFORE

Greg needs more sitting room. We will lower the back crotch 1/2". Then we will be able to pull up the center back so it will hang more smoothly.

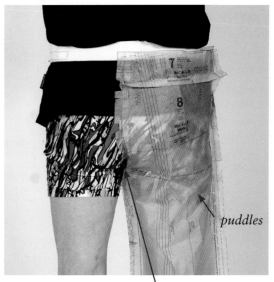

Greg is "sitting" on the crotch seam. Lowering will allow center back to be lifted and these droopy lines or "puddles" will disappear.

BACK AFTER

The back crotch has been lowered about 1/2". See page 42. This allows the back to be pulled up at the center to nothing at the side. The puddles are gone. The size of the yoke remains the same.

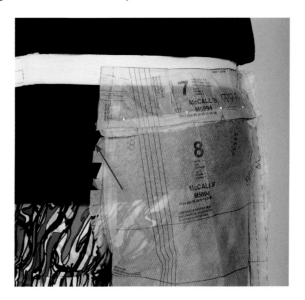

FRONT AFTER

Tissue was added to straighten the front. The front crotch has been lowered.

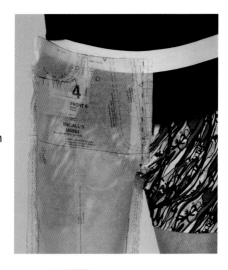

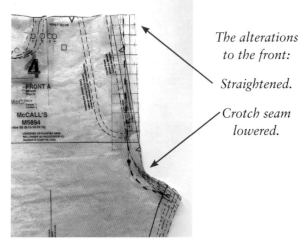

The alterations to the front:

Straightened.

Crotch seam lowered.

If you don't straighten the center front, you will see this wrinkle from the thigh to the center front. It disappeared after straightening as shown above. Remember, wrinkles point to the problem.

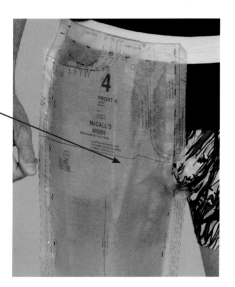

SIDE SEAM AFTER

Tissue was added to straighten the sides so the tissue would meet at the waist.

The back hangs straight with no puddles.

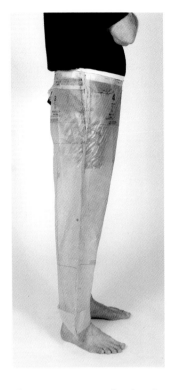

THE YOKE

A close-up of Greg's yoke shows a gap at the back waist. It needs shaping.

gap

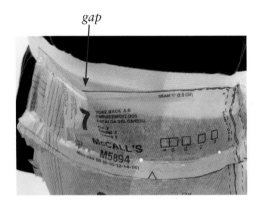

We made two 1/8" tucks and taped the tops with tiny pieces so we could tidy them up on a flat surface. These adjustments made the waist an even 1" seam allowance as well.

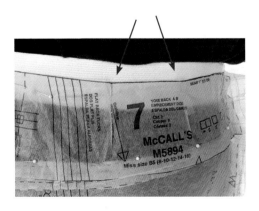

THE WAISTBAND

Greg wraps the tissue around his waist to make sure it's about 3" past center front on both sides. It will be a little long, but we will fine-tune this in fabric.

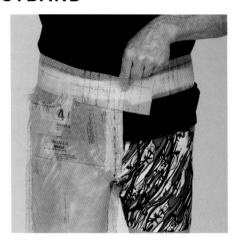

FABRIC FITTING

The front and side:

The front fits well. Greg says they feel comfortable. No front wrinkles point to the waist.

The side seam hangs straight. Jeans fit well in the waist.

THE BACK

There is a little too much fullness across the back, although Greg says they feel fine. We pinned out 1/2" of fullness at the center back and will take the back inseams in 1/2".

GREG'S FINISHED JEANS

Greg loves his jeans. They fit well, look great, and he says they are comfortable. Mission accomplished!

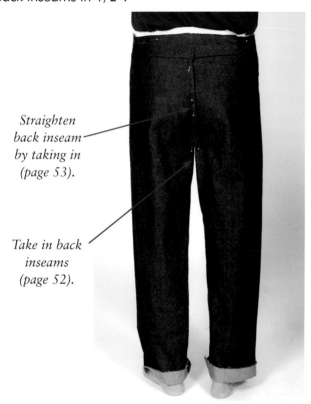

Straighten back inseam by taking in (page 53).

Take in back inseams (page 52).

THE WAISTBAND

Greg puts the prepared waistband snugly around his waist.

The CF is chalk-marked on each end of the band.

TAYLOR'S JEANS

Taylor wants a slim fit and referred us to a favorite pair of his jeans. They are tapered but have a lower rise than he says he wants and they are too big in the waist, causing them to constantly slide down. He said from the outset that he wanted tight jeans. I didn't listen and really understand *how* tight he wanted to wear them. Because I made "tryon" jeans for teaching, Taylor tried on the straight leg Palmer/Pletsch jeans in size 14, the size with the FGM closest to his hip measurement. They looked pretty good, but we noted some changes and decided to tissue-fit this style.

The jeans fit well in both tissue and fabric, but it just wasn't the fit he wanted, even after narrowing the legs. Back to the drawing board.

Taylor in one of my "tryon" jeans

The fit in tissue.

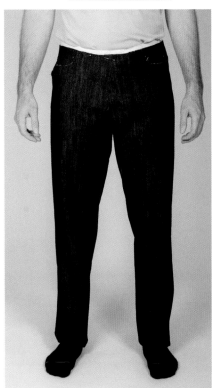

The fit in fabric.

Taylor was tissue- and fabric-fitted in the Palmer/ Pletsch jeans pattern.

105

Next Taylor tried on his RTW jeans for us and then I understood—he wants *tight* jeans!

THE PATTERN WE PICKED

The Claryville jean by Workroom Social is a pretty slim fit. Since I sewed them in all sizes as workshop try-on jeans, Taylor tried on the size 12. He said, "Perfect." Okay, they aren't quite perfect, but they "felt" the way he wants his jeans to feel through the hips and legs.

They are too tight in the waist, so we will add width. He also needs more leg length.

Taylor in the Claryville jeans size 12.

Yes, this is a women's jeans patterns, but we are sewing to fit and it really doesn't matter what pattern we use or what changes we make—as long as we ultimately get them to fit. The the Palmer/ Pletsch jeans we used for Greg and Jeff is also a pattern designed and marketed for women.

Because of the "end-of-book time crunch" we decided to go straight to fabric fitting based on what we saw from the try-on jeans.

TAYLOR'S JEANS IN FABRIC
First Fabric Fitting

I sewed the pockets and zipper and basted the rest for fitting. I pinned Taylor's jeans 3/8" deeper at the waist for a more snug fit. The leg width is good. The front looks good. The back has some bagginess under the seat at his inner thigh.

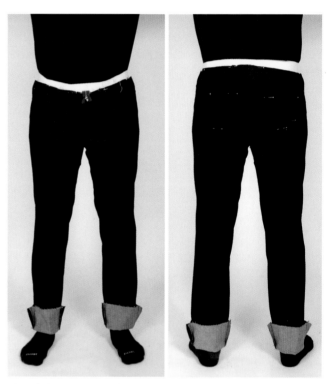

This fabric is stretchier than the try-on jeans, which is why there is more fullness in the back. I pinned 3/8" tucks at the upper thigh. I will take in the back inseam 3/4" and baste the side seam deeper at the waist at the same time.

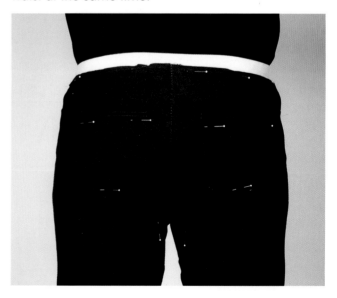

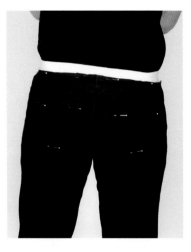

The back looks good now with a little horizontal whiskering under the seat as expected in snug jeans.

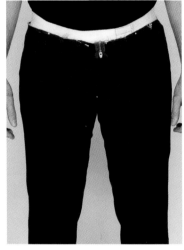

Taking in the back inseam has made the front a bit too tight. Cause and effect! I will let out the front inseams 1/2". Taylor is also a little fuller on his left side. I will let the left side seam out 1/8".

Waistband

Taylor wraps the waistband around his waist and I marked the center front with chalk. Off to finish sewing.

TAYLOR'S FINISHED JEANS

It took a little work to get here, but it paid off in the end. Taylor has jeans that fit and feel the way he likes to wear them. We all love the results.

WE KEEP LEARNING FROM THE "REAL PEOPLE"

Sewing for someone else? Your subject may not know how they want their jeans to fit or how to describe it. You may choose to baste the jeans together before sewing any details and have the person try them on to see how they feel. Then ask them how they would like to change the fit if at all. Basting jeans together gives you a starting point.

Even after a zillion pant and jeans workshops, Pati and I continue to learn about fitting. Learning to fit and sew any type of garment is an ongoing process. All our "real people" students, while attending class to learn, teach us so very much. Thank you! I hope you'll jump in, make mistakes, find answers, and ultimately enjoy sewing jeans.

CHAPTER 6

BEFORE YOU SEW

PREPARING TO SEW

Yes, I know, everything in this book so far has been "before you sew," but this chapter explains the actions to take with your pattern, fabric, and sewing space that bring about the best sewing magic.

GOOD SEWING HYGIENE

"Good sewing hygiene" refers to best habits for setting up and maintaining your sewing area and order of your projects. It's a silly phrase, but quite descriptive. I'm a naturally messy and disorganized sewing person. It's taken years of teaching to make me break my bad habits and stay tidy and in control of my space. Whether my sewing space was in a corner of the bedroom under a few storage shelves, or was taking up the largest portion of my home (my living and dining room are my studio space at the time of this writing), I have learned that being *tidy all the time* really helps.

I won't go as far as the old *Singer Sewing Book* that advises us to dress up and do our hair before sewing, but getting your space set up to sew without clutter can make the experience more Zen. Aren't we sewing because we love it?

Make your space the best it can be whether you have a dedicated room or you're nested in a closet. Put away everything you're not using for your project. I mean it. If you've got a T-shirt up next in your rotation, put those supplies together and tuck them away. I find having another project stacked in my peripheral vision distracting.

Canberra, Australia, sewist Amanda Adams, aka @bimbleandpimple of Instagram sewing fame, has a wire mesh basket where she gathers her projects together and ritualizes the planning stage of sewing. What's up next in Amanda's basket? I tune in to see. So cute! Staging your next project makes it more likely to happen too.

Amanda says: "Jeans making is something that intimidated me at first, but after experimenting with lots of different patterns it's become one of my favorite sewing projects. I love all the details,

experimenting with pocket designs, and ending up with an awesome pair of jeans that feel great on."

We couldn't agree more!

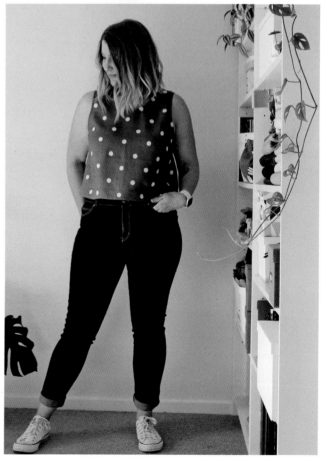

Amanda Adams, Canberra sewist

WASTE NOT, WANT NOT

After cutting out your project, deal with all of your scraps immediately. Toss those too small for stitch testing or anything else. If you're saving them for stuffing, Closet Core Patterns has a groovy, free "pouf" ottoman pattern by which you can reuse all those bits and scraps. If this isn't your bag, move them out of your life and space. Even better, find a place in your locale that wants scraps. Here in Portland, we have SCRAP Creative Reuse, which takes and sells or reuses in classes many of your crafty things you don't need. See Resources, page 235.

Clear the space around your sewing machine to include only snips or small scissors and a place for pins if you're a pinner. I have a plastic bin close by with recycled glass jars to hold my essentials.

Okay, enough of me being a bossypants. You get it. Make your routine *yours*. Honor your art by keeping the chaos within your brilliant designs and out of your workspace.

HAZEL SAYS...

- **Hold your threads each and every time you start a line of stitching.**

- **Clip all thread ends immediately, at your machine, unless you need to pull them through and tie... more about this later.**

For more practical tips to make sewing easier, check out the Palmer/Pletsch book *Painless Sewing*, available at palmerpletsch.com. It's a delight.

FABRIC PREPARATION

Wash and dry your denim three times using warm water and a medium dryer setting. Your goal is to preshrink your fabric before cutting out your jeans. If you can grab your denim right after the dryer stops to prevent wrinkling, do it. This also helps limit creasing and fading on those crease lines. Denim will start to fade right away.

With stretch denim, after this initial washing and after the jeans are constructed, always wash in cold water and hang them to dry. The elastic fiber will deteriorate pretty quickly when using a dryer. The result is a puckering in the stress areas of the pant and loss of stretch retention in the knees and seat. The higher the elastic content, the more the damage potential from a hot dryer.

If you want to retain the indigo color longer, you can add two cups of white vinegar to your first washing. You can also use a product called Retayne to help set the dye. Remember that the dyeing process of denim generally does not penetrate the entire warp yarn, and the weft yarn is generally not dyed at all, so fading is a natural and expected process. You might be surprised how much color is released in these first washings.

109

PREPARE THE ALTERED PATTERN FOR CUTTING

1. Unpin the pattern. If wrinkled, press the tissue from the wrong side (the side without tape).

2. Trim away the side width extensions if added for negative ease allowing you to tissue-fit without tearing the tissue.

NOTE: If you end up adding width to the waist, see page 47 for adjusting side seams and pocket area.

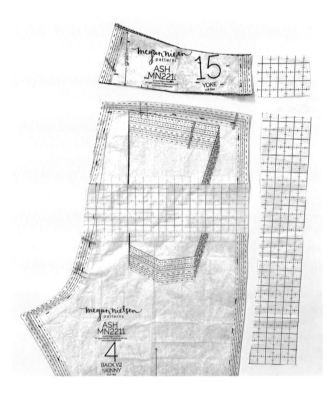

3. Decide on your best finished crotch depth.

Base this on your fabric after all of your alterations and shaping to your curves are done. You needed the extra depth so you could shape the yoke and sides to fit your body.

The crotch in denim will grow, so you will need to remove some of the crotch depth. If you don't, your jeans waistline may come up higher than you like it. If you cut this excess off at the top in fabric, you may lose a portion of your front pockets. How much do you shorten?

CROTCH DEPTH GUIDE

Nonstretch or rigid denim
Pattern waist seamline can be 1/2" to 1" below your waistband seamline (bottom of the elastic). Example: If you added a total of 2" of depth, you can fold out 1/2" to 1" before cutting.

Stretch denim (moderate stretch)
Pattern waist seamline can be 1" to 1½" below your waistband seamline (bottom of the elastic).

4-way stretch denim
Not common. Stretch-test both directions to be sure it really is 4-way. Pattern waist seamline can be 1½" to 2" below your waistband seamline (bottom of the elastic).

We always recommend using 1" waistline seam allowances— just in case.

USE OUR CROTCH DEPTH GUIDE TO ADJUST YOUR PATTERN

1. Shorten the amount required by drawing two lines through the width of your crotch depth addition.

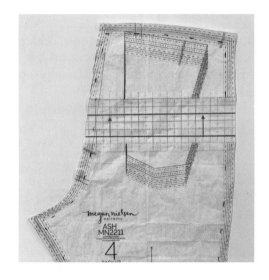

2. Bring one line to meet the other, and gently fold and pin or tape to secure. Be sure to shorten both front *and* back, equally.

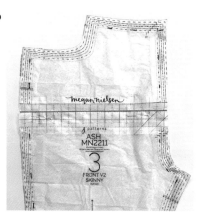

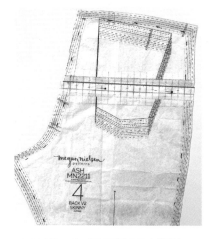

3. If necessary, straighten the center back seamline and true side and crotch edges (page 46).

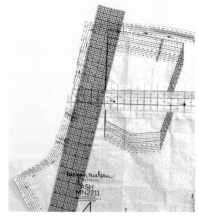

4. If you make changes to crotch depth, adjust the fly facing and fly protector.

5. If you lowered or changed your crotch curve, trim seam allowance to an even amount before cutting.

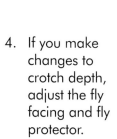
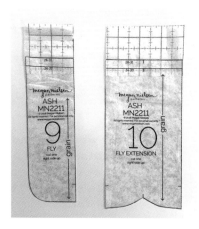

ADDING 1" SEAM ALLOWANCES

Now is the chance to make your seam allowances 1". Add the amount needed in these locations.

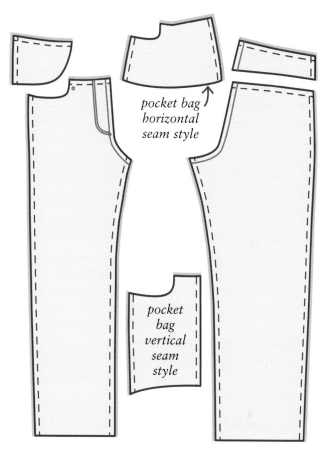

pocket bag horizontal seam style

pocket bag vertical seam style

I like to draw my in-case seam allowances directly on the fabric with a chalk wheel.

If you'd rather, add tissue to these areas in the amount that makes your seam allowances a full 1".

LAYOUT AND CUTTING

If your fabric is larger than your cutting surface, fold the excess back to rest on the table to prevent distortion of the fabric.

There is a theory that cutting each leg out single layer and in opposite directions, reversing the diagonal of the twill weave on each side of the leg, will eliminate twisting. This could be a practice in manufacturing to conserve fabric. We've sewn dozens of pairs of jeans cutting double and had no problem with twisting. Use quality denim, cut on grain, and this should not be a thing. But hey, it's not *wrong* to cut single layer and in opposing directions; it's just more work! Do it your way.

1. Fold fabric in half lengthwise right or wrong sides together, whichever you prefer. Lay it out on the cutting surface with selvedges stacked on top of each other and the edges even. If the selvedges are straight and the fold isn't twisted (diagonal lines), it means you are ready to cut. Don't worry if the ends are not even. In other fabrics you would straighten the grain to make them even, but don't do it in denim. After washing, the grain will just bounce back to where it was before.

2. Arrange your pattern pieces on the fabric using the layout diagram suggested in your pattern, or fit the pieces as your fabric limitations dictate. For rigid denim, cut the waistband on the lengthwise grain, especially if you are interfacing only the ends.

3. Measure pattern from grainlines to selvedges or the fold to ensure pattern is placed on grain.

4. Secure all pattern pieces to the fabric with pins or use weights if you prefer to cut with a rotary cutter. I love these metal concrete anchors for pattern weights. They are available at most building supply centers.

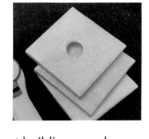

5. Cut around pattern pieces using your preferred method. Leave all pattern pieces in place until after you complete the marking in the next section.

wide denim layout   narrow denim layout

HAZEL SAYS...

1. Place pattern grainline parallel to the selvedge.

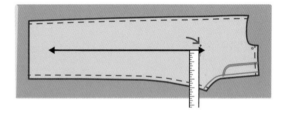

2. Anchor one end of the pattern grainline using a "pivot pin," pinning with just a pick of fabric. Or if using a cardboard cutting board, anchor by pushing a pin into the board.

3. Measure distance from grainline to selvedge. Note measurement.

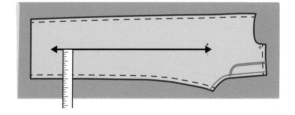

4. Measure at other end of grainline marking, rotating the pattern as necessary at the pivot pin until both ends are the same distance from the selvedge or fold.

6. Cut belt loops easily using a ruler and rotary cutter. Cut a lengthwise strip 1¼" by 25", longer than you need, but you may want an extra loop in back. This will also give you extra length to practice bartacks later.

BELT LOOP LENGTH AND PLACEMENT

Your belt determines the length you cut your belt loops and the method by which they are attached.

For belts up to 1¼" wide: Cut them 3¾" long, sew on with waistband. Bring to top and turn under 1/2". Bartack at top and bottom.

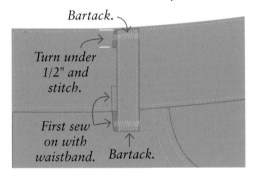

Bartack.

Turn under 1/2" and stitch.

First sew on with waistband.

Bartack.

For belts more than 1¼" wide: Cut belt loops the width of the belt plus 2", which allows for 1/2" turned under at each end, space for bartacking, and room for the belt to pass through.

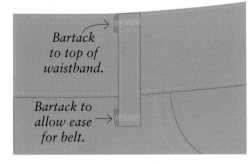

Bartack to top of waistband.

Bartack to allow ease for belt.

More on belt loops:

TRANSFER PATTERN MARKINGS

Before you remove any pattern pieces from your fabric, transfer the pattern markings as follows:

Snip-mark with 1/4" clips into fabric edge:

- center front

- notches on side seams, inseams, and yoke

- foldline on pocket bag lining

- facing foldline on top edges of coin pocket and back pockets

It's not necessary to snip-mark the fly facing, fly/zipper protector, or crotch. Too many markings become confusing and these areas are easy to line up unmarked.

Mark with a chalk pencil:

- Coin pocket placement on right side front (Xs). Don't worry if your pattern doesn't have these marks. Some patterns use snips along the bottom edge of side front for this.

- Mark where faced pocket edge on front laps on side front. It's important for accuracy.

- Back pocket placement marks will be for reference only. You will fine-tune during fabric fitting. (Chapter 7, page 142.)

- Mark on the wrong side of fabric the crotch seam stop mark on fronts and fly facing.

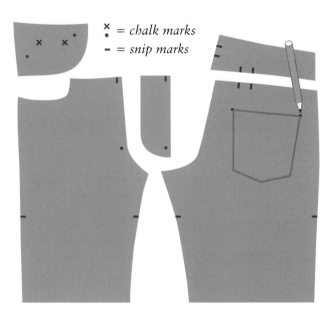

× = *chalk marks*
– = *snip marks*

HAZEL SAYS...

An easy way to mark accurately is to pin into the markings, lift pattern and mark with chalk where pin is going in.

CUTTING POCKET FACING/ BAGS

It's fun to see the right side of a cotton print on the inside of your jeans. Well, it's fun for me, anyway. Maybe a cat print will make you smile too. Pocket bags can also be sewn from a light to medium weight cotton broadcloth in a solid color.

Upside Right!

If your pocket bag pattern has a horizontal fold forming the bottom edge and you want to see your print top side up, place the pattern **top** edge opposite the direction of the print. For example, I want this kitty print to be cat heads up. Here's how I lay the pattern on the fabric.

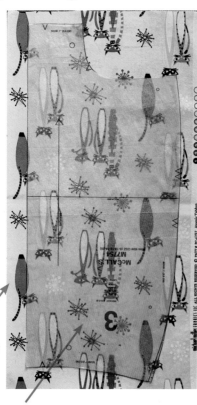

Place one-way print upside down. The print will be right side up inside the finished jeans.

Pattern piece pocket opening is at top.

SEAMS, TOPSTITCHING, BARTACKS AND BUTTONHOLES

Test all your stitches, seams and seam finishes on your project fabric. Practicing on larger pieces of fabric will allow you to see clearly if your stitches are sound. A few pieces of 4" x 8" scraps work well.

SEAMS

Use regular polyester thread for both top and bobbin. Start your testing with a 2.5mm stitch length. Sew a seam, pull it open and examine your stitches.

Seams in jeans are under more stress than those of the average garment, especially if they are snug. Adjust stitch length and tension until you love them. You may not need to adjust anything but length, but test to be sure.

On stretch denim you may want to start with a 3mm or longer stitch length just as you would with a heavier knit. The stretch of the fabric as it goes through the machine can shrink up stitches when it recovers. Complete your test by pressing as you would while sewing.

PRESSING FOR THE FLATTEST, PRETTIEST SEAMS

1. Set your stitches by pressing on the closed seams to meld thread and fabric fibers together, helping to reduce bulk.

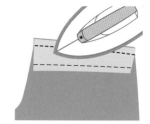

2. Press the seam open.

A seam stick or roll is helpful when pressing leg seams.

3. Press the seam allowances to one side.

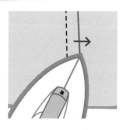

SEAM FINISHES

Serge seam allowances together, trimming to 1/2". If you don't have a serger, trim seams to 1/2" and zigzag together.

For the serger, use the widest stitch width possible when using the right-hand needle position and a stitch length of 2.5-3mm. For zigzag, use a 3.5mm width and 3mm length.

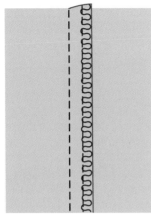

TOPSTITCHED SEAMS

Seams can be edgestitched, edgestitched and topstitched, or just topstitched.

The inseam is often edgestitched next to the seam and sometimes flat-felled with two rows of stitching showing. The front and back pockets and yoke are edgestitched and topstitched. The crotch seam is flat-felled.

Mock Flat-Felled Seam

This is easier than a flat-felled seam. After finishing the seam allowances, edgestitch next to the seam, then topstitch.

wrong side

right side

Flat-Felled Seam

Try this traditional option if you want a durable seam finish or if you don't have a serger. Sew seams **wrong** sides together with **topstitching** thread in the needle. **Sew with the seam allowance that will be folded over on top.**

Trim the under seam allowance to 1/4". Press top seam allowance over the trimmed one. Fold the edge of top seam allowance under 1/4" to encase the trimmed one. Press.

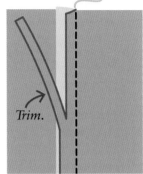

Trim.

Edgestitch next to the fold with topstitching thread.

If you have a felling foot for your machine, make a test sample to check that your topstitching thread will end up on the right side of the fabric.

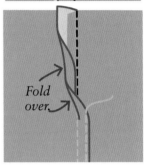

Fold over.

Topstitching

Experiment with different kinds of topstitching threads. See page 22 for more information. My favorite combo is Tex 40 topstitching thread in the needle and a Tex 30 regular thread in the bobbin.

Start your testing with 3-4mm stitch lengths. Stitch a few lines to see what looks best. You may need to increase your upper thread tension. Record the settings for next time.

Play around with different spacing and numbers of rows. They don't always need to be parallel. RTW does all kinds of variations. You are the designer!

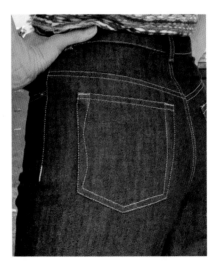

Topstitching tips for test samples

- Try different kinds of threads.

- Try a size 100 topstitching needle.

- Use a point on your presser foot as a guide.

- Try the triple stretch stitch for a bolder look.

- Sew with double thread. Use two spools of regular thread through the same thread path and needle. Test!

- Chain stitch on your cover-stitch machine. RTW uses a chain stitch for most topstitching on jeans.

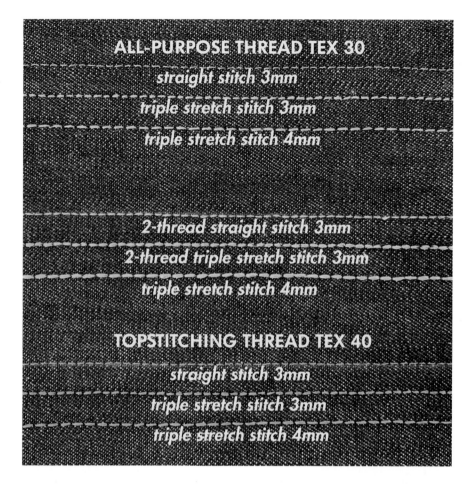

ALL-PURPOSE THREAD TEX 30
straight stitch 3mm
triple stretch stitch 3mm
triple stretch stitch 4mm

2-thread straight stitch 3mm
2-thread triple stretch stitch 3mm
triple stretch stitch 4mm

TOPSTITCHING THREAD TEX 40
straight stitch 3mm
triple stretch stitch 3mm
triple stretch stitch 4mm

A topstitched seam

1. Find a visual point on your presser foot to use as a guide for easier and more accurate edgestitching (shown here) and topstitching.

2. For the flattest seams, gently pull apart the seam as you stitch.

3. Your topstitching can be any distance from the edgestitching. I line up the edge of my presser foot with either the edge-stitching or the seam.

Topstitch perfection paralysis? Get over it!

If you can't see a topstitch blemish from four feet away, *it isn't there!* If you feel you need to fix something, try these options:

- **Bartack over errant zipper topstitching.** In the words of Heather Lou, Closet Core Patterns, *"Put a bartack on it!"* Cover up detours in your topstitching with a bartack. It will look like a design feature.

- **Unsew + re-sew.** Carefully remove enough stitches to pull your thread to the wrong side and be able to tie a knot with the thread you are joining it with. Re-sew your stitches, leaving a long tail of thread at the beginning and end.

  Turn to wrong side and pull on bobbin thread until you see a loop of the needle thread, then pull the needle thread to the wrong side. Tie a square knot close to fabric. A square knot will not work itself loose. Bury your threads.

HAZEL SAYS...

Tying a Square Knot

1.

2.

3.

4.

BARTACKS

Bartacks are short lengths of closely spaced zigzag stitches that are functional as well as decorative. They provide a measure of durability to the stress areas on your jeans such as the side seams at pocket bottoms, belt loops, back pocket tops, and base of fly topstitching—important because it anchors the fly protector to the front.

Tips for bartacking

- Pound extra-thick seam intersections with a metal hammer to flatten and soften fibers.

- Use a brand-new denim needle in Size 100.

- Use pins to mark placement and length of bartacks. If they are on the side seams, compare sides to make sure they match perfectly.

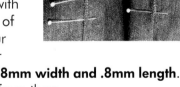

- Sew test samples on actual seams and belt loops with the same layers of thickness as your jeans. Start your testing with a **1.8mm width and .8mm length**. Test and adjust from there.

- Try your sewing machine's automatic bartack if it has one.

- Make sure there is nothing underneath your bartack that you really don't want tacked down!

- Hold thread ends as you start to prevent a nest from forming on the underside.

- Don't be too hard on yourself as to the quality. Rip only if you must. Slide a seam ripper between the belt loop and jeans and pull them apart a bit so you can cut the stitches. It's really not that hard!

- Use thread tweezers like like these to help grab threads.

Bartack on your Belt Loops

Belt loops are bartacked to the top of the waistband and again below the waistband. Placement below the waistband depends on the length of the loop. You may have already sewn them into the waistband seam or you may be attaching both top and bottom now. A dot of fabric basting glue can hold the loops in place while bartacking. (See page 22 for glue tip.)

Lower the needle into the belt loop with the presser foot up. Slip the leveler under the back of the foot. Lower presser foot and sew bartack.

Alternative to Bartacking

Sometimes the combination of thread, fabric, and machine just won't cooperate to sew pretty bartacks. You can substitute multiple rows of straight stitching for any bartack. Play around.

BUTTONHOLES

Sewing buttonholes on jeans can be frustrating, but they are doable with practice. Remember, RTW uses an industrial machine designed solely for buttonholes. Most importantly, practice, practice, *practice*. And do that practice on samples of the real terrain. It's worth the time and effort to make a couple of mini waistband ends to use for this purpose. Ripping out buttonholes is not fun, but can be done just like errant bartacks to the left.

A few tips:

- Trim seam allowances aggressively but carefully on the overlap (left) end of your waistband during the finishing steps.

- Press the buttonhole area and steam well. Use a clapper to flatten. Allow fabric to cool with clapper in place. Flatten with a hammer if necessary.

- Use a thread color that matches your denim to minimize imperfections until you've mastered your favorite method. Traditionally, topstitching thread is used.

Length and Placement

Make your buttonhole 1/4" longer than the diameter of your button. For a 17mm jeans tack button, make it 7/8" long (about 22mm).

1. Find the center of your waistband quickly by folding lengthwise and marking with a pin.

2. Draw placement line with chalk starting 3/8" from the end of waistband. Farther in will cause the end of the waistband to curl up and away at the center front.

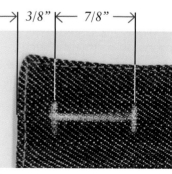

3. Be sure that you have the waistband very smooth and flat behind the needle before you begin.

4. Sew your buttonhole by machine or by hand (page 120). For a standard machine buttonhole, it's usually best to stitch from the fabric edge inward.

Four Machine Buttonholes

Fully Automatic Buttonhole

Today's computerized machines allow for many buttonhole sizes and shapes.

Follow the instructions in your sewing machine manual. If you are using topstitching thread, you may need to adjust stitch length because the automatic buttonhole tension is set for regular thread.

Here's a classic keyhole machine buttonhole made with a vintage Singer template style buttonholer.

Try using a piece of plastic on top of the waistband to help slide the fabric under the buttonholer into position. Remove the plastic before sewing.

Manual Machine Buttonhole

If the automatic buttonhole on your sewing machine won't perform because of bulk and inconsistent fabric levels, try using the manual buttonhole mode. This sometimes requires a special-order presser foot but it's well worth the investment. It will take some practice, but this is a reliable way to make jeans buttonholes. Start with a 5mm width and .5mm length.

The buttonhole has four parts: side one, bartack at end, side two, bartack at other end. Refer to your sewing machine manual for specifics. Some machines have a "manual" setting that actually sews the buttonhole automatically except for your input on where to start and stop. Your manual will guide you. The simplest setup will work like this:

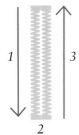

Step 1: Straight ahead with zigzag stitches.

Step 2: Bartack across one end.

Step 3: Straight back with zigzag stitches.

Step 4: Bartack on opposite end.

A Freehand Machine Buttonhole

Make a freehand keyhole-style buttonhole using a narrow zig-zag stitch. This takes practice, too, but it's the closest thing to RTW. The wider looped end accommodates the shank on the tack button and reduces distortion of the area.

1. Mark a 7/8"-long buttonhole with chalk.

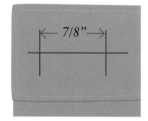

2. Draw the "keyhole" to make it easier to follow the shape while stitching.

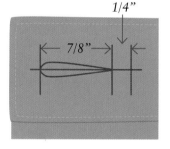

3. Practice following your line using a zigzag stitch **1.8mm wide x .8mm** long, similar to your bartack stitch. Sew in the direction of the arrows. The stitches at the beginning and end overlap for 1/4".

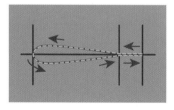

4. Open the buttonhole with small, sharp scissors or a button-hole cutter.

Hand-Sewn Keyhole Buttonhole Designed for Jeans

Three reasons to hand-sew a jeans buttonhole: your sewing machine just won't cooperate with multiple layers of heavy denim; you want to completely enclose the buttonhole edges to reduce fraying; you love a little hand-sewing Zen after so much time behind the machine.

You can sew your buttonhole by hand with topstitch or buttonhole thread using the buttonhole stitch.

Consider making your life easier by matching your thread color to your denim. As you become the buttonhole master you may want contrasting thread for a little pop.

Prepare Buttonhole Opening

1. Before finishing your waistband, press a 1" x 2" piece of fusible web into the overlap end of the waistband to secure all the layers together and reduce fraying. Now finish the waistband and edgestitch.

2. If you are using a standard 17mm jeans tack button, draw your buttonhole with chalk 7/8" (about 22 mm) long. Your buttonhole should be 1/4" longer than the diameter of your button.

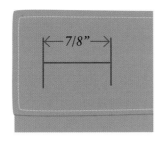

3. Using a handheld or tabletop hole punch, make a 4mm hole (less than 1/8") at the end closest to edge. Make the hole inside the chalk line. This hole will accommodate the shank on your tack button.

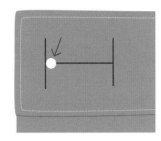

4. Carefully cut buttonhole open from hole to chalk line at end with a buttonhole cutter or small, sharp scissors.

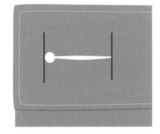

Sew Buttonhole

Work the stitches in this direction.

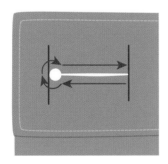

NOTE: The following illustrations will show the jeans positioned away from you as you sew.

1. Sew around a piece of filler cord or gimp to strengthen the buttonhole and help it keep its shape. In tailoring, this gimp is usually silk and a very specific size. For jeans I use a 10" length of my topstitch or buttonhole thread. The illustration shows where the gimp will be stitched over as you go. It won't stay in this position. You'll have to guide it into place so you can sew over it.

Secure it to the waistband with a figure 8 twist around a pin near the buttonhole as shown.

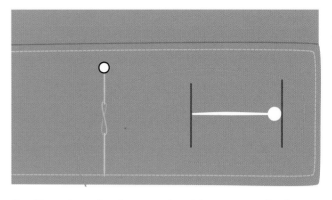

2. To reduce fraying use the thinnest needle that you can still thread. Working with about a 20" length of single thread, make a tiny backstitch on wrong side opposite the hole-punched end of buttonhole. Leave a 2" tail of thread to tie off at the end.

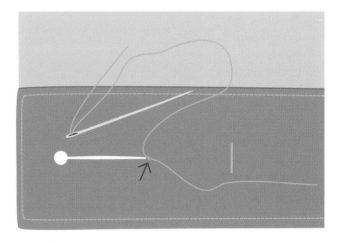

3. Bring needle and thread up from wrong side through slit. Now you're ready to start working the stitch.

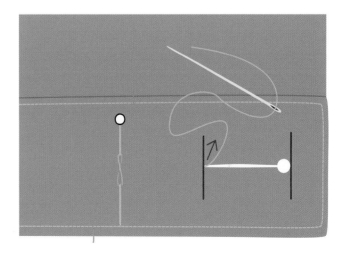

Working the Buttonhole Stitch

1. Insert needle under edge of buttonhole through to the right side about 1/16"-1/8" from the cut edge. Don't pull the thread through yet.

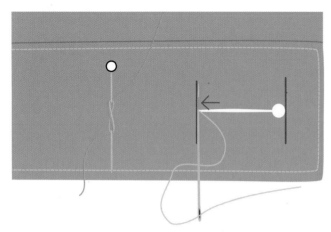

2. Pick up double thread near needle's eye, bring toward you and under point of needle, clockwise. Pull needle through and then pull the thread down toward the raw edge to form a purl. Repeat.

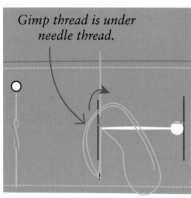

Gimp thread is under needle thread.

3. The first purl stitch looks like this.

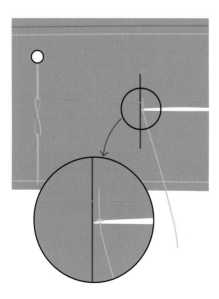

4. Continue working the stitch around the cut edges until you reach the beginning. Move the gimp so that it is always under your stitches.

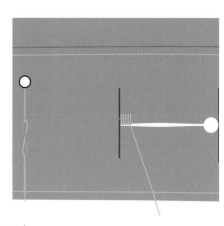

It takes some practice to get your stitches the same size and tension. Turn your work so the needle continues to go up under the fabric in the same direction.

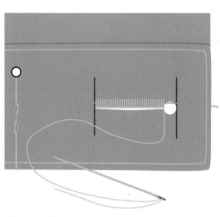

Finish Buttonhole End

1. When you reach the end, leave your needle threaded and unpin your gimp thread. Gently pull on both ends of the thread to smooth out the edges of your buttonhole.

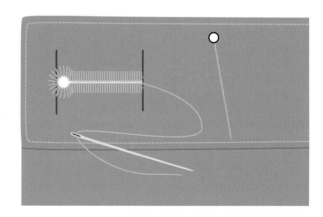

2. Tie the thread ends in a square knot, being sure not to pull too tightly causing the buttonhole to pucker. Bring the thread ends to the back and leave them for the last step.

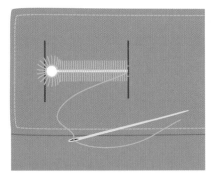

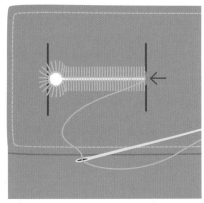

REALITY CHECK

If you make a mistake on your buttonhole (machine-sewn *or* hand-sewn), don't sweat it! Just use it and know that your button will mostly cover it up! Try for a better one next time. People will be so blown away that you sewed your own jeans and no one will notice the buttonhole. Trust!

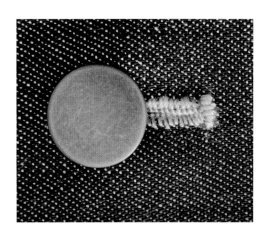

3. Cover the inside end of the button-hole with three bartacks across the end.

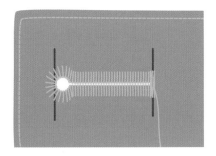

4. Stitch over your bartacks with a row of 1/16" satin stitches or buttonhole stitches if you prefer. On last stitch, bring thread through to the back. Tie a square knot with beginning and ending threads and bury under stitches.

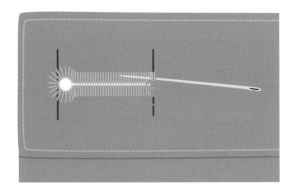

CONSTRUCTING JEANS

It's time to sew! Let's have a show of hands. How many of you turned straight to this page without reading the preceding chapters? No shame. I'm just so happy you are here! I do recommend that you read (or at least skim) this entire chapter before you start sewing, even if you don't fully comprehend it all until you are at each step, fabric in hand (me!). There are hints and suggestions throughout, so reading first gives you a heads-up as to what's coming.

FIT WHILE YOU SEW

This sewing order is for a classic jean with fly front zipper. See Chapter 8 for many modifications. When a mod requires that you sew the jeans in a different order, a Snap-View Order is included with its directions. At right is your Snap-View jeans construction order. You save time by marking, interfacing, and serging right after cutting. But if that is confusing, wait and do it when you see it in the construction steps. I'll give you little reminders throughout the process. Marking tips are found on page 113.

A note about fabric fitting: You will do your first fabric fitting after you have finished the front pockets and fly zipper. However, sometimes it is worth basting all of the pieces together before doing any sewing if there is a chance you might need less crotch depth. See Julie page 95. Otherwise, your first fitting will be after the front pockets and zipper have been sewn. What's going to work best for you?

QUICK STITCH GUIDE

Needle size:
16/100

Stitch length:
2.5mm

Topstitch length:
3.5mm

Bartack:
width 1.8mm
length .8mm

Buttonhole for
17mm tack button,
length 7/8" (22mm)

Always TEST first!

Snap-VIEW CONSTRUCTION ORDER

- ☐ Cut out jeans, page 112.
- ☐ Transfer pattern markings, page 113.
- ☐ Fuse interfacing, page 125.
- ☐ Prepare pockets, fly pieces, belt loops, page 125.
- ☐ Sew front pockets, page 128.
- ☐ Sew fly front zipper, page 133.
- ☐ Baste & fabric fit, page 139.
- ☐ Sew yokes, page 143.
- ☐ Sew back pockets, page 144.
- ☐ Sew inseams, page 146.
- ☐ Sew crotch seam, page 146.
- ☐ Sew side seams, page 147.
- ☐ Baste belt loops to waist, page 148.
- ☐ Baste & fit waistband, page 148.
- ☐ Sew waistband, page 149.
- ☐ Finish belt loops (sew or bartack), page 118.
- ☐ Sew bartacks, page 117.
- ☐ Sew buttonhole, page 119.
- ☐ Sew hem, page 154.
- ☐ Install hardware, page 155.

INTERFACING

Fusible interfacing prevents stretching and provides body and stability.

Stretch denim: Interface the following pieces with lengthwise stable strips of PerfectFuse Sheer interfacing:

- Back pockets – Fuse tops with 1" strips covering foldline 1/8".

- Coin pocket – Fuse top with 1" strip covering foldline 1/8".

- Fly facing – Fuse entire piece.

- Right front fly – Fuse a 5/8" strip lined up even with the edge of right front. Make it long enough to overlap the crotch seam stop mark.

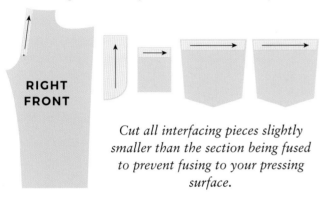

Cut all interfacing pieces slightly smaller than the section being fused to prevent fusing to your pressing surface.

- Waistband and waistband facing – Use your pattern pieces and fuse to both waistband and facing. Use PerfectFuse Medium because it is stable in both directions. If the band is contoured, place the lengthwise stable grain as shown by the arrows. You can always lap interfacing when you need more length than you have.

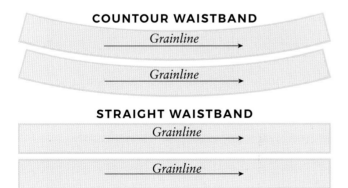

Rigid denim: If you are using rigid or nonstretch denim and a straight waistband, interface the fly facing and right front fly area only. See page 150 for how to interface waistband ends to stabilize for button and buttonhole. Even rigid denim on the lengthwise grain can stretch a little depending on the fabric. If this is a concern, interface the entire waistband.

EFFICIENCY SERGING

Set your serger for a **3-thread stitch**, needle in the right position, stitch width of 4-5mm, and stitch length of 2.5-3mm. Serge with the fabric right side up for the best-looking stitches. Test on a scrap to see what you like.

Serge the following, barely skimming the edges: the curved edge of the fly facing, the curved bottom edge of the left side front (**the right front will be serged after the coin pocket is sewn on**), the long sides of the back pockets and the coin pocket, along the crotch curve of the right front, and one long edge of the belt loop strip.

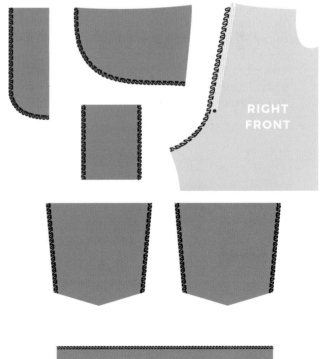

BELT LOOPS CLOSE UP

NOTE: Your finished belt loops will be 1/2" wide.

1. Even if you have a pattern piece for loops, cut a strip of fabric 1¼" x 25". Use a rotary cutter and ruler to make it easier and more accurate. See page 113.

2. Serge finish one lengthwise edge with a 3-thread narrow stitch.

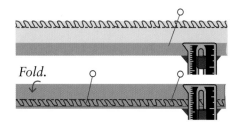

3. Fold the strip in thirds. Press. The first fold will be about 1/4". Fold again with serging on top.

Fold.

HAZEL SAYS...

To avoid burning your paws while working with a hot iron and steam, "pin and press." Pin one side at a time into your pressboard. Angle the pins away from you, press between pins, remove pins and press again. Turn the piece and repeat on the other side.

---

4. Press so serged edge is no more than 1/16" from the edge. With **topstitching** thread sew two lines of edge-stitching 1/8" from each long edge, or use a cover-stitch machine.

BACK & COIN POCKETS

Prep for both coin and back pockets:

1. Fold top toward wrong side at snips.

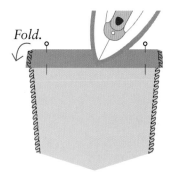

Fold.

2. Fold under raw edge 1/4" or refer to pattern measurements. Press.

3. With **topstitching** thread, stitch 1/16" from top edge and again 1/4" from the first line.

Do these steps for all three pockets.

4. For back pockets, press all raw edges under according to pattern measurements. Here we are using 5/8".

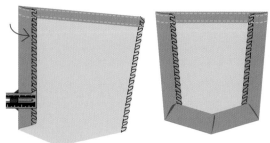

5. Fold pocket in half to check that both sides match.

6. Use the same trick with pocket #2. Then place it over the first pocket to make sure they are the same size.

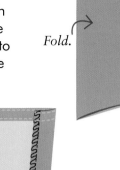

Fold.

Compare the two pockets.

7. Plain or embellished pockets? See page 180 for pocket design inspiration. Now is the time to decorate your pockets if you desire.

Plan a design to sew with a regular sewing machine. Open up creased edges. Sketch or trace a design onto one pocket using a chalk wheel. Draw a thick line using lots of chalk.

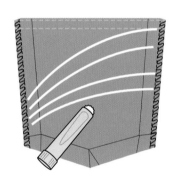

Stitching lines should begin and end past the folds in order to be secured when the pockets are topstitched to the jeans.

8. Place the first pocket on the second pocket right sides together and carefully rub the surface to transfer the design.

9. Lift a corner of the pocket and make sure the chalk transferred. Separate the pockets. You may need to chalk over the lines a bit on the second pocket to clearly see your design for stitching.

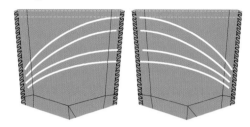

10. Sew your stitched, appliqued, hand- or machine-embroidered design. Try different techniques using your machine's triple and satin stitches or decorative

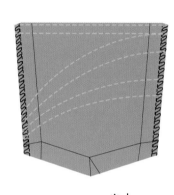

stitches. You can also use your cover stitch machine with a single-needle chain stitch with the chain on the right side. Go bananas!

11. Re-press your pockets to set the crease. Use a clapper or ham to help crease stubborn fabric.

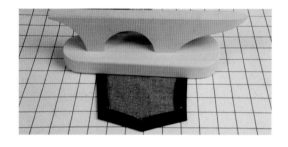

FRONT POCKETS

COIN POCKET

Set your back pockets aside and complete your coin pocket. The coin pocket will be stitched to the **right side front**.

Coin pockets can be sewn in a variety of ways. See page 177. Or follow the directions in your pattern. It may have a unique shape and construction order. For a two-sided method for a coin pocket, sew as follows.

If you followed the prep steps for the coin pockets (page 126), start with step 4.

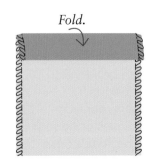

Fold.

1. Fold top toward wrong side and press.

Fold under.

2. Fold under raw edge 1/4", or refer to your pattern directions. Press.

3. With **topstitching** thread, stitch 1/16" from top edge and again 1/4" from the first line.

4. Turn under 5/8" along sides or refer to pattern measurements. Press.

Turn under.

5. Match top of pocket to the placement markings you made on your side front or follow your pattern instructions.

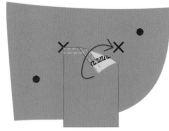

6. With **topstitching** thread, edge-stitch pocket to side front, starting at bottom and stitching in a "U." Topstitch 1/4" from edge on each side. Serge lower edge of side front, trimming away excess coin pocket at lower edge.

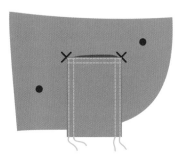

If you haven't already, serge finish the curved edge of the left side front.

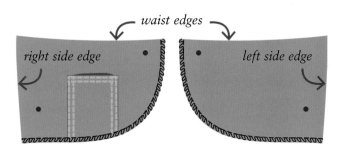

waist edges

right side edge   *left side edge*

7. Press to set stitches.

HAZEL SAYS...

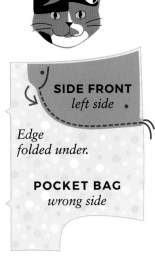

Keys and coins can get caught on the serged stitches used to finish the side front lower edge. To add strength, finish the edge by turning under the edge 1/4" and stitching to pocket bag with a straight stitch.

SIDE FRONT *left side*

Edge folded under.

POCKET BAG *wrong side*

Sew for your needs! If you really use your front pockets a lot, consider lengthening the pocket bag. (See page 171).

A WORD TO THE WISE OR THE ULTRA-CAUTIOUS:

I usually sew the front pockets and the zipper before basting seams and trying the jeans on. However, if I have fitting concerns, I will baste the side fronts to the fronts, center front, inseams and side seams for a quick try-on. See Julie on page 95.

FRONT POCKET BAGS

The following instructions are for a pocket with the seam at the inner side of the pocket. I prefer that because a fold across the bottom is less bulky than a seam along the thigh in a snug jean.

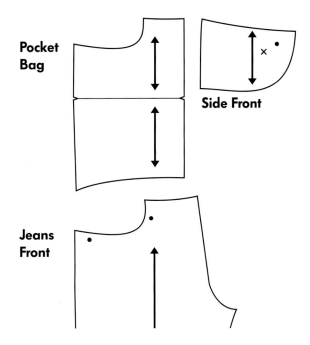

Pocket Bag

Side Front

Jeans Front

The quick view below shows how the pieces go together. Step-by-step instructions follow.

Pocket from the right side.

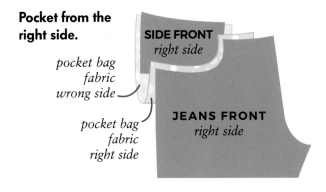

pocket bag fabric wrong side

SIDE FRONT *right side*

pocket bag fabric right side

JEANS FRONT *right side*

Pocket from the wrong side.

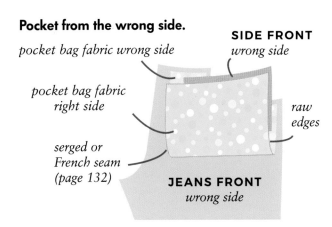

pocket bag fabric wrong side

SIDE FRONT *wrong side*

pocket bag fabric right side

raw edges

serged or French seam (page 132)

JEANS FRONT *wrong side*

FRONT POCKETS

1. Zigzag the lower edge of the side fronts to the lower part of the wrong side of pocket linings. Zigzag on top of the serged stitches and slightly over the edge of your jeans fabric. Set your zigzag stitch at 4mm wide and 3mm long. Test first!

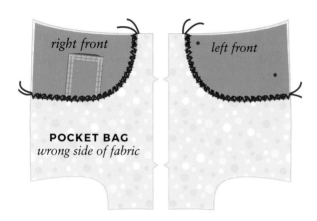

2. Baste the raw edges of side fronts to lining along top and side.

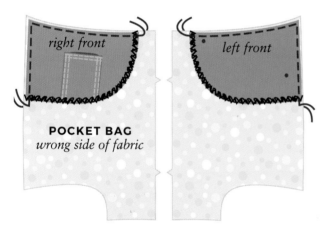

HAZEL SAYS...

Try spraying temporary adhesive on the back of the side front pieces to prevent slippage while sewing to pocket bags. Spray inside a spray box.

3. Sew wrong side of pocket bag to right side of front following pattern-specified seam allowances.

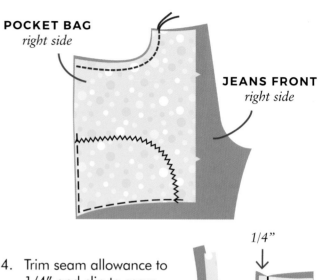

4. Trim seam allowance to 1/4" and clip to seam on curves.

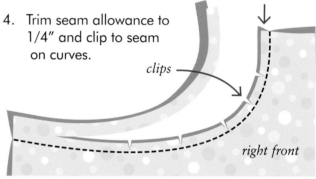

5. With jeans right side up, flip pocket bag up over seam allowance tightly against the stitching and press.

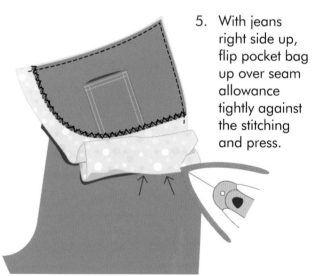

6. Turn pocket bag to inside. Press 1/16" to the inside so bag will not roll forward and show from the front.

7. Carefully pin along pocket front to prevent shifting during topstitching.

8. With **topstitching** thread, stitch 1/16" from the pocket opening and again 1/4" from first line of stitching.

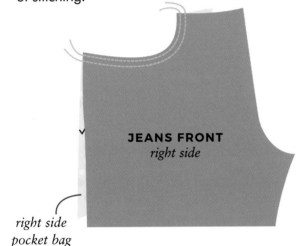

right side pocket bag

JEANS FRONT
right side

9. **From the wrong side** flip the bottom of the pocket bag up to the top edge of the front.

right side
POCKET BAG

JEANS FRONT
wrong side

10. Smooth the pocket and pin the raw edges together. Then pin top edges together.

Repeat this process to complete the left side front pocket (with no coin pocket).

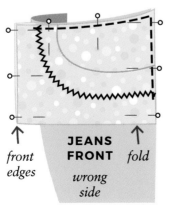

front edges

JEANS FRONT
wrong side

fold

11. Then flip over and make sure both the pockets are the same distance from the top.

12. Serge pocket bag edges together, or sew a French seam as shown on next page.

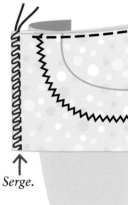

Serge.

13. Bury serger tail in the serged seam on the underside so it won't show.

14. Press the serged seam to set stitches, then press the entire pocket flat from the wrong side.

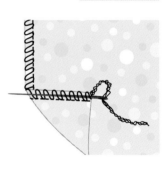

15. Baste pocket at waist and sides to hold the layers in place.

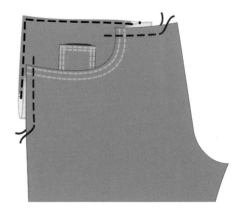

Now you're ready to move on to the fly front zipper!

131

FANCY FRENCH SEAM POCKET

1. To make an enclosed French seam on your pocket bag, bring the lower edge of pocket to the waist, right sides together, by folding on the foldline (at snips) and matching notches.

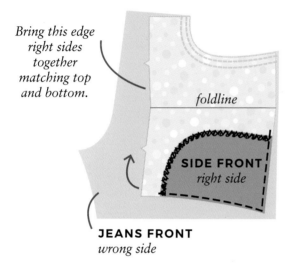

Bring this edge right sides together matching top and bottom.

foldline

SIDE FRONT
right side

JEANS FRONT
wrong side

2. Fold pants front out of the way.

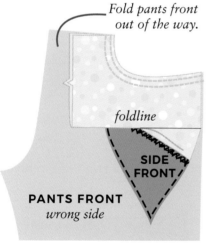

Fold pants front out of the way.

foldline

SIDE FRONT

PANTS FRONT
wrong side

3. Sew a 1/4" seam.

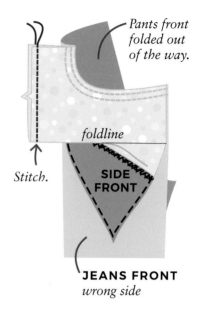

Pants front folded out of the way.

foldline

SIDE FRONT

Stitch.

JEANS FRONT
wrong side

4. Turn seam to inside, wrong sides together, and press. Stitch 3/8" from the edge enclosing the raw edges.

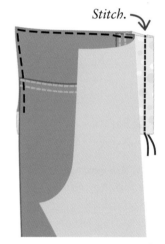

Stitch.

French seam

FLY FRONT ZIPPER

After sewing dozens of pairs of jeans and making many samples of different methods for a fly front zipper, I determined that this method is my favorite. It's sturdy, can be done with most household sewing machines, and finishes off the inside, covering the fly area nicely.

See Chapter 8 for button fly and other front closure options.

Most ready-to-wear jeans have the fly lapping the left side over the right. Decide how you prefer your fly to open and make it that way. The following instructions are sewn like RTW, left over right.

We covered pattern preparation, cutting, and marking on pages 112-113 and interfacing on page 125. Because they are important, some instructions will be repeated in these construction steps.

INTERFACING REVIEW

Right front

If you haven't already, fuse a 5/8"-wide lengthwise stable strip of PerfectFuse Sheer lined up even with the front edge. Make it long enough to overlap the crotch seam stop mark.

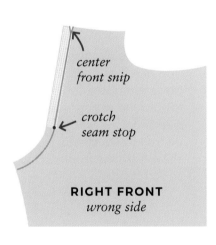

center front snip

crotch seam stop

RIGHT FRONT
wrong side

Fly facing

Fuse interfacing to the wrong side of the fly facing.

Mark crotch seam stop using the marking on your pattern.

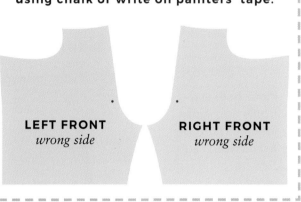
SERGE FINISH REMINDER

Serge finish side and bottom of curved edge of fly facing. Serge with right side up so upper looper thread shows on top—it's prettier. If your pattern has a cut-on fly facing, follow its instructions.

FLY PROTECTOR

Fold fly protector in half right sides together. Sew bottom edge with a 1/4" seam allowance. Trim curved edges with pinking shears because they also notch. Turn right side out, press and finish long side of raw edge.

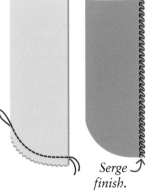

Serge finish.

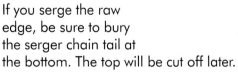

If you serge the raw edge, be sure to bury the serger chain tail at the bottom. The top will be cut off later.

PREPARE FLY OPENING

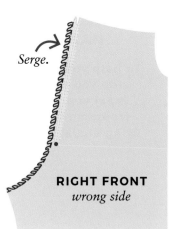

Serge.

RIGHT FRONT
wrong side

1. Serge finish right front crotch from top to inseam.

2. Place both fronts right sides together and sew front crotch seam. Sew from the crotch seam stop mark to 1½" from inseam. Backstitch at both ends. This 1½" opening allows you to adjust inseams later during fabric fitting.

RIGHT FRONT

wrong side

1½"

3. Pin fly facing to the **left** front, right sides together, pinning from the **wrong** side since you will more accurately sew to the crotch stop circle from that side.

   Sew your seam, backstitching at both ends.

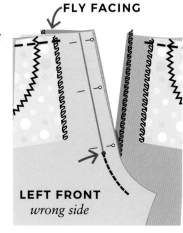

FLY FACING

LEFT FRONT
wrong side

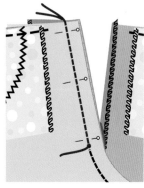

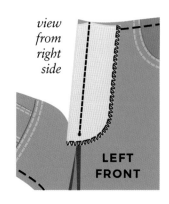

view from right side

LEFT FRONT

4. Grade seam. Trim facing seam allowance to 1/4". Trim front seam allowance to 1/2", top to bottom.

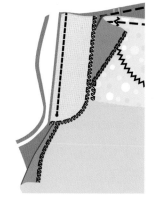

5. Press fly facing seam open.

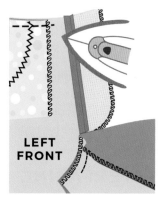

LEFT FRONT

Turn to the wrong side of left front and press seam slightly toward the wrong side so facing will not roll forward and show from the front.

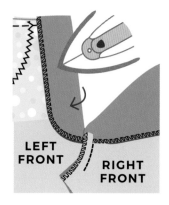

LEFT FRONT

RIGHT FRONT

6. Edgestitch the overlap edge with **topstitching** thread, stopping at the crotch seam, leaving long thread tail at the bottom.

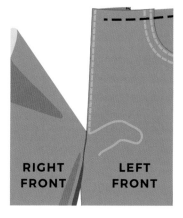

RIGHT FRONT

LEFT FRONT

7. Turn to wrong side and tie off threads. Tie a square knot close to fabric. (See page 117.)

A square knot will not work itself loose. Clip threads close to knot. This whole area is covered up. No need to bury threads.

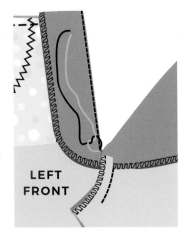

LEFT FRONT

INSTALL ZIPPER

HAZEL SAYS...

Both metal and synthetic coil zippers work great and can be longer than your opening. We'll show you how to manage excess length later in the construction.

1. With zipper facing up, apply 1/8" basting tape very close to the left edge of zipper tape. It is not intended to be sewn through. You could also use a wash-away 1/4" tape that can be sewn through. We find that the 1/8" basting tape adheres better and eliminates the need for pins. Peel away the protective paper.

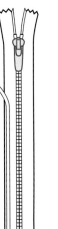

2. Stick zipper face down onto right front, lining up edge of zipper tape with serged edge. The zipper stop should be about 1/2" above where the crotch seam stitching stops.

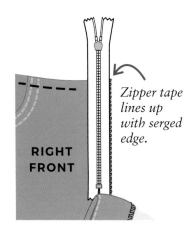

RIGHT FRONT

Zipper tape lines up with serged edge.

3. Using a **zipper foot** and **regular** thread, sew zipper in place down the center of zipper tape so you don't sew through the basting tape. Continue stitching to bottom of zipper tape to hold it in place.

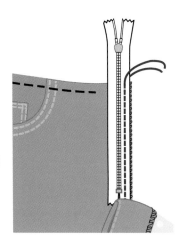

4. Fold zipper under tightly against the line of stitching. Use a few pins near the edge of the fold to prevent slipping.

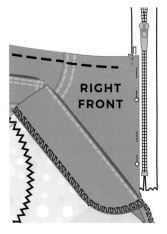

RIGHT FRONT

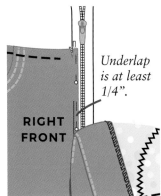

RIGHT FRONT

Underlap is at least 1/4".

Check your underlap before stitching.

You should have an underlap of 1/4"-3/8" here. Adjust the fold so that you have at least 1/4".

5. Using a **zipper foot** and **topstitching** thread, sew close to folded edge to the bottom of the zipper tape.

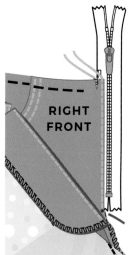

6. Clip **right** front crotch seam allowance just below zipper stitching to allow a flat crotch seam allowance when pressed toward the **left** front.

   This step helps neaten up the inside of your fly area so all layers lie flat in the crotch seam when you join the front to the back.

1/4" snip

7. Gently press crotch seam toward **left** side so all layers lie flat.

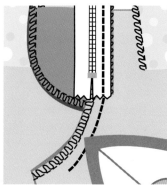

8. Place 1/8" basting tape on the inside edge of the fly facing.

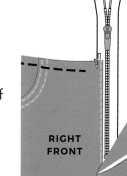

1/8" basting tape

9. Remove the paper backing and stick the left fly extension over the right front. Keep your overlap amount even, bottom to top. It should lap over the front at least 1/4".

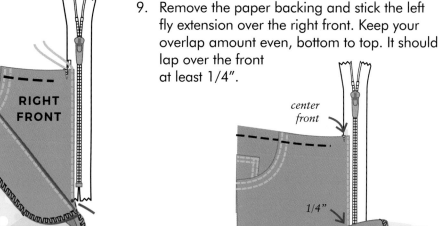

center front

1/4"

RIGHT FRONT

10. Turn over so fronts are stacked, with the **right** front on top and fly facing folded out. Pin zipper to fly facing.

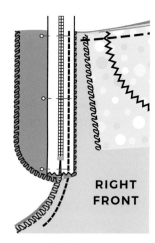

RIGHT FRONT

11. Using a **zipper foot** and **regular** thread, sew zipper tape to fly facing only. Sew two rows of stitching, one close to zipper tape edge and the other 3/16" in from the first, no closer than 1/8" from zipper teeth. Sew from the bottom up to keep the rest of the jean to the left of your machine. It's okay to use topstitching thread if you want.

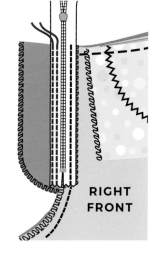

RIGHT FRONT

TOPSTITCHING

1. On the right side, place two strips of 1/2" Scotch Magic tape as topstitching guide on the left front, flush with the center front opening.

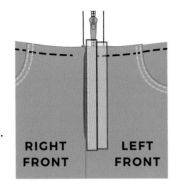

2. For accurate marking, from wrong side, put a pin through all layers right below center of the zipper stop.

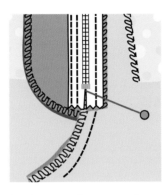

3. Mark zipper end from the front with a pencil and draw your curve on the tape.

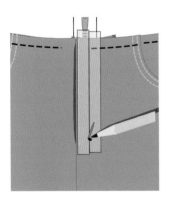 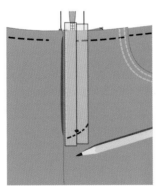

4. Before topstitching, smooth all of the layers around the zipper so that they are all flat. Pin to keep the top layer from scooting as you sew.

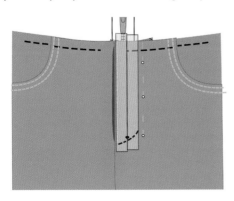

5. Using **topstitching** thread and a **regular foot**, topstitch zipper to front with two rows 1/4" apart. Start at the top along the edge of the tape and stitch to the center front. With needle down, pivot and stitch for 1/4", then pivot again and stitch up to top.

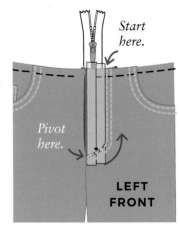

Start here.

Pivot here.

LEFT FRONT

6. Don't worry if these lines don't all meet. You can join them in a later step when you topstitch the crotch seam.

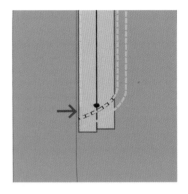

7. Remove tape.

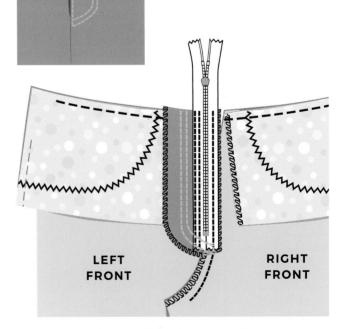

LEFT FRONT   **RIGHT FRONT**

The view from the wrong side—everything is nice and flat.

ATTACH FLY PROTECTOR

1. Bring bottom of fly protector to just below zipper tape, covering left facing at bottom. If zipper tape is unusually long below the stop, cut it shorter. The folded edge of the protector should just cover the serged edge of the left front facing. If it doesn't, don't fret, make it wider the next time. The bottom is the most important part here for a neat-looking inside.

   Pin parallel to the edge from the wrong side. Turn over and pin again on right side through all layers with pins pointing to the top. Remove the pins from the underside. Remove basting tape from fly opening.

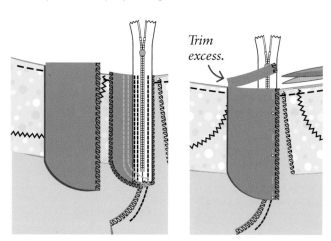

Trim excess.

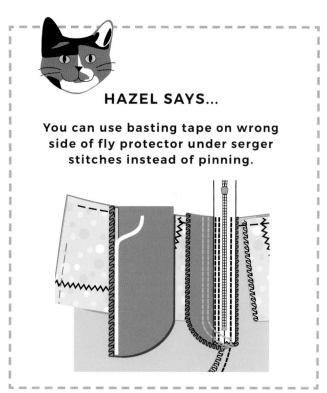

HAZEL SAYS...

You can use basting tape on wrong side of fly protector under serger stitches instead of pinning.

2. Using a **zipper foot** and **regular thread**, edgestitch right next to previous stitching through all layers.

   Stitch as far down as your zipper foot allows. Backstitch to secure.

Here's what it looks like from the wrong side. The stitching won't come all the way to the bottom of the protector.

The fly protector will be secured by the crotch seam topstitching in a later step and with bartacks along the topstitching lines.

You choose bartack placement and whether you do them now or later. I prefer to do all my bartacks later at the same time I secure the belt loops to the waistband.

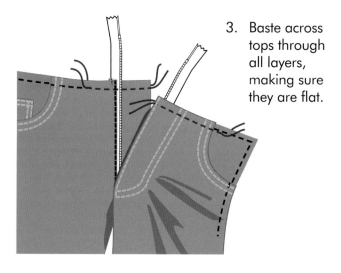

3. Baste across tops through all layers, making sure they are flat.

Whew! You did it!

FIT AS YOU SEW

Here's where the fit-as-you-sew technique really pays off. By basting, trying on, adjusting and marking changes now, you end up with a much better fitting jean than crossing your fingers and hoping for the best! So that I don't interrupt your sewing flow any more than necessary, I will cue you throughout the jeans construction for what to look for at each fabric-fitting stage. You can find detailed instructions on how to do your fit fixes as you sew in Chapter 4. Let's go!

BASTE FOR FIRST FABRIC FITTING

You will be basting your jeans together using a long sewing machine stitch. Use a 5mm or 6mm stitch length or the longest your machine will allow. Using a long stitch will make it easier to remove later. Some machines have a built-in loose-tension basting stitch. To keep seams together while you are fitting, backstitch at both ends.

NOTE: We don't pin-fit jeans like we do pants because of the negative ease. It just plain hurts to be stabbed with pins! Basting will also give you a better reveal of the final fit.

1. Staystitch top of yokes 1/2" from edge to keep them from stretching when you try the pants on.

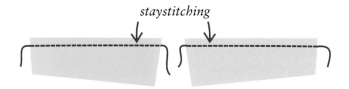

staystitching

HAZEL SAYS...

Staystitching the tops of yokes will not only keep them from stretching out, but it will also remind you that these are the top edges when pinning the yokes to the jeans.

2. Baste yokes to backs, right sides together.

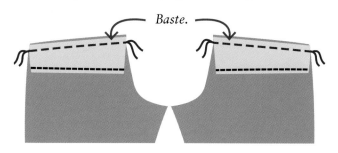

Baste.

3. Pin on a flat surface then baste inseams, right sides together. Pinning first, matching hem edges, ensures accuracy. Don't stretch.

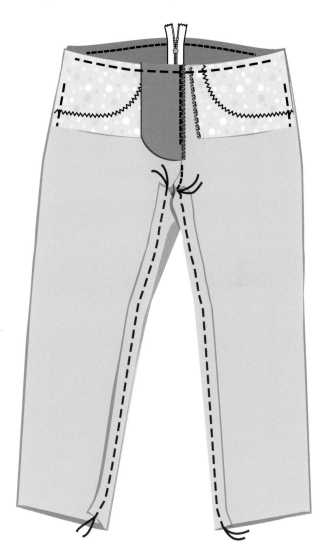

4. Baste crotch seam from back waist to meet stitching line in the front.

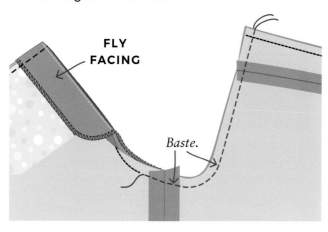

FLY FACING

Baste.

5. Baste side seams, right sides together.

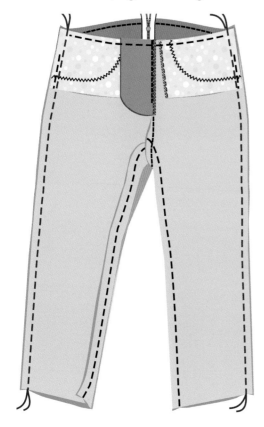

HAZEL SAYS...

Sew Velcro to each end to make a permanent "fitting" elastic.

TRY ON YOUR JEANS

Place 1½" elastic comfortably snug around your waist where you want your waistband to be. Try on the jeans. Bring the waist seamline to the bottom of the elastic. Be sure to pull jeans up at the back first, then the front until the crotch is comfortable. (See Taylor page 105.)

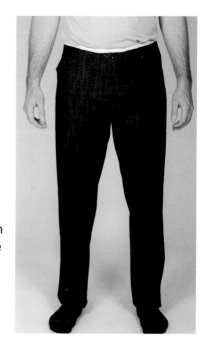

Sometimes you want a super-quick fit check. Baste everything together. These jeans don't have negative ease, so we pinned just the side seams wrong sides together. With side seams sticking out, we could easily adjust to Jeff's shape. (See page 100.)

You can see by the grainline that Taylor's center front (above) was cut based on the pattern which has a slight slant. For Jeff (to the right, the center front was straightened for a better front crotch fit for his shape.

FABRIC-FITTING ORDER

Look at your jeans in the following order. Refer to Chapter 4 for in-depth explanations. **You may have no changes. Lucky you!** Otherwise, address these issues now. I can hear Pati whispering in my ear, "Wrinkles point to the problem." You may have to look at both ends of the wrinkle and you may have to try more than one adjustment before you get it right. The more you play, the better you'll become at fitting.

Snap-VIEW FABRIC-FITTING ORDER

1. Width at Waist

Look for this first. It's a common first tweak. If too big, pin-mark your jeans at the waist and hip so they stay up properly and allow you to look at the rest of the fit.

2. Horizontal Wrinkles

Friend or foe? Page 43 will help you decide.

3. Smiles and Other Crotchety Things

Solutions for smiles and frowns begin on page 51.

4. Excess Fullness in Back

See page 52.

5. Jeans "Butt Fit"

Want a snugger fit through the seat? See page 52, a continuation of excess fullness in back.

6. Back-of-the-Leg Puddles

A relatively simple alteration will relieve these symptoms. See page 53.

7. Hungry Butt

A close relative of puddles and not comfortable! Read more on page 53.

8. Sway Back

See page 53.

9. More Crotch Oddities and Pillows, Fluff & Puff

Changing the shape of seams can be tricky and the results of these changes can change your fitting life for the better! See pages 54-55 for inseam shape and curvy sides too.

10. Prominent Calves

A subtle change can increase comfort and remove drag lines at the lower leg. Page 56 is your go-to for calves.

11. Full Derriere

Usually addressed in tissue, but valid in fabric. Your save is found on page 56.

12. Yoke

If you missed a great yoke shape in tissue, you can still master your yoke and cut a new one. See page 56.

13. Leg Width

Address this now if you know the shape is not what you expected. See page 46 for more.

14. Back Pocket Placement

See tips for placement on page 142.

15. Length

If your jeans are longer than you need, you can shorten now. Leave them 2" longer than you think you want them. See page 57 and 154 for more.

MARK CHANGES AS YOU FIT

Use pins to mark how much and where you want to take seams in or out. Use **horizontal** pins to mark where seam changes start and end. If you are letting the seams out, use the horizontal pins only and estimate how much extra room you need. Remember that each measurement quadruples itself. For example: When you sew a seam 1/4" in or out on both sides of the body, you are changing the circumference of the garment by 1". You are basting these changes, so nothing is permanent at this point. See page 58-59 for details on marking changes.

Seam changes start.

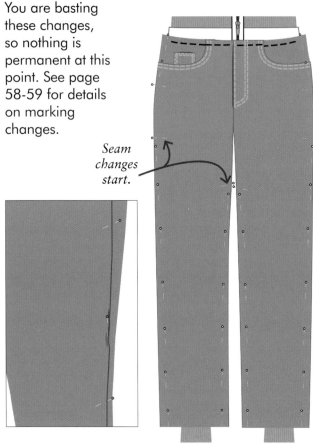

CONTINUE FITTING...

Re-baste your changes and try on again.

REPEAT UNTIL YOU HAVE THE FIT YOU WANT AND ARE READY TO SEW YOUR FINAL SEAMS.

As you work through this process you will need to remove previous lines of basting to see the true fit, especially if you are letting seams out. If you are taking the seams in, it's okay to leave your previous basting in until you are sure you like your changes, then remove it for a tidy inside.

POCKET PLACEMENT

Do this during fabric fitting, before sewing up your jeans. Try a temporary spray adhesive on the wrong side of your back pockets so you can adjust the placement.

While trying on jeans, find your preferred pocket placement and mark the top of the pocket corners with a chalk pencil.

AFTER YOU LOVE YOUR CHANGES, FINALIZE

Mark your inseam and side seam stitching lines with chalk, if the seam allowances have changed during fitting. Trim to an even seam allowance of the widest width possible and at least 3/8". Make a note of your final seam width so it's quick to re-sew later. See page 58-59 for details on recording all your pinned changes.

CONTINUE SEWING YOUR JEANS

By this stage you've done all your fitting adjustments with the exception of the final side seams and the waistband. You can sew like crazy for a bit!

Remove basting from side seams and inseams. *You've marked your changes with chalk, right?*

HAZEL SAYS...
Do I have to remove the basting? It's good sewing hygiene to remove basting stitches so that your seam will press as flat as possible.

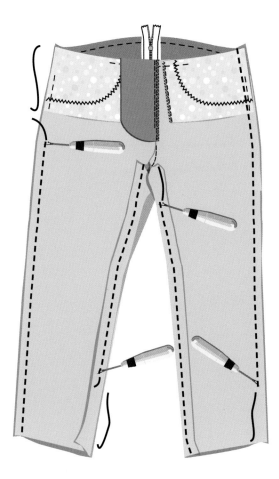

The following sections use a mock flat-felled seam for most areas. You may substitute true flat-felled seams for yokes, crotch and inseams for beautiful, traditional jeans. See page 115 for all the seam types.

YOKES

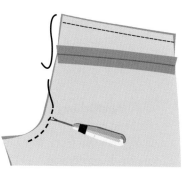

1. Mark any changes in the back crotch seam with chalk. Remove crotch basting stitches. Remove yoke basting stitches.

2. With regular thread, sew yokes to backs.

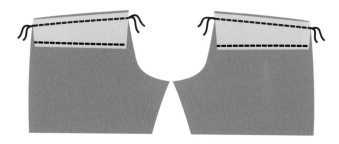

3. Set stitches.

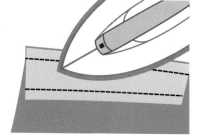

4. Press seams open.

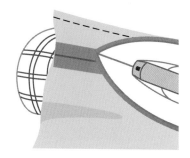

5. Press seams toward backs.

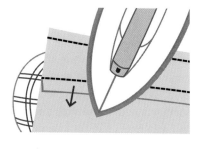

6. Serge finish seam allowances together. See page 115 for seam finishes. Press.

7. With **topstitching** thread sew two lines of stitching below the seam, one 1/16" away and another 1/4" from the first. See page 115 for tips on topstitching.

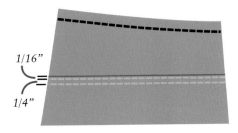

The front and back of your jeans should now look like this.

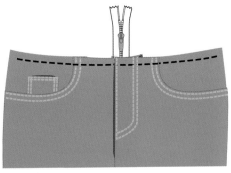

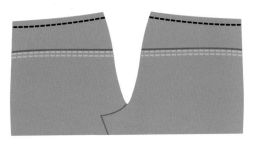

SEW BACK POCKETS TO JEANS

You can sew your back pockets on your jeans at the markings made in the fit stage. Since the crotch seam will be pressed toward the left back and topstitched 1/4" away, place left pocket 1/4" farther toward the side seam. The topstitching tricks the eye as to the real center back.

With **topstitching** thread, sew pockets to backs with two lines of stitching. Start at top corner and edgestitch around pocket, making a U-turn at the opposite top corner and topstitch back to first corner. Remember, you don't have to match the topstitching on the pockets to topstitching elsewhere on the jeans. Go ahead. Break the rules. See page 115 for pocket topstitching ideas. Pull thread tails to the wrong side and tie and bury threads.

INSEAMS

1. With **regular** thread, sew inseams.

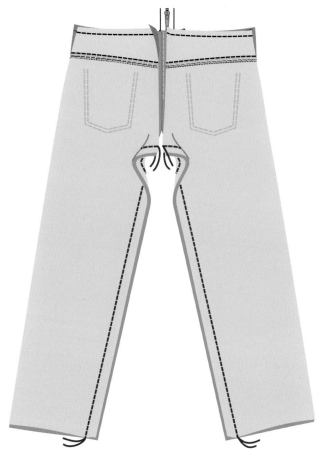

2. Set stitches.

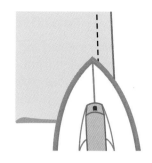

3. Press seams open over a seam roll or seam stick.

4. Press seams toward **fronts**.

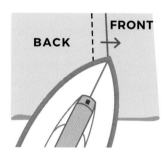

5. Serge finish seam allowances together, leaving a scant 1/2" seam allowance.

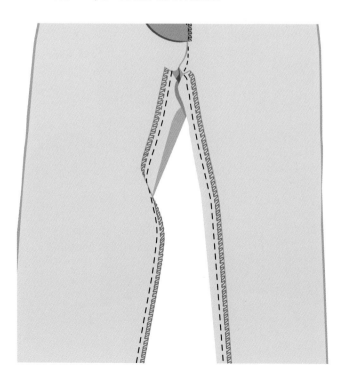

6. With **topstitching** thread, edgestitch 1/8" from the seam, securing seam allowance that is pressed toward front.

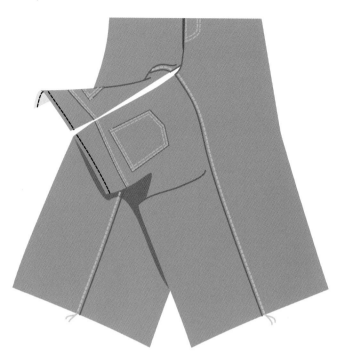

HAZEL SAYS...

In addition to having seam allowances pressed toward the fronts, open up the seam by pulling on the fabric from both sides of the seam while stitching.

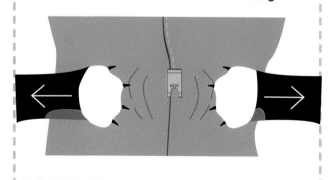

CROTCH SEAM

Sew and Finish Crotch Seam

1. Pin the crotch seam, matching inseams and yoke seams. With **regular** thread, start sewing where front crotch stitching ended, overlapping stitches by about 1/2". Continue to top of center back.

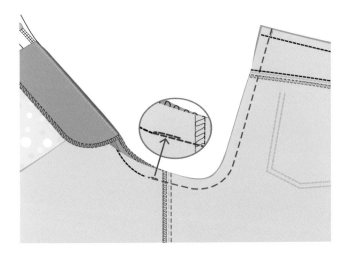

2. To finish crotch seam, carefully serge, starting at the back and joining your previous serger stitching on the front in the fly construction. Lift presser foot, turn work away, lower presser foot and chain off to the side.

Right front crotch serged previously at beginning of fly section.

3. Bury the chain tail through stitches on the underside of the front crotch serging. (See page 31.)

underside of jeans

Topstitch Crotch Seam

To make topstitching easier, press seam allowances toward the left front. The bulkiest areas of the crotch seam are at the yoke and inseam intersections. Press, or pound with a hammer, to flatten.

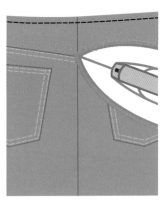

With **topstitching** thread, starting at the center back waist, edgestitch to the bottom of the zipper, pivot, sew for 1/4", pivot again, and sew 1/4" from edgestitching to the back waist. See page 202, step 3, for a variation on this topstitching.

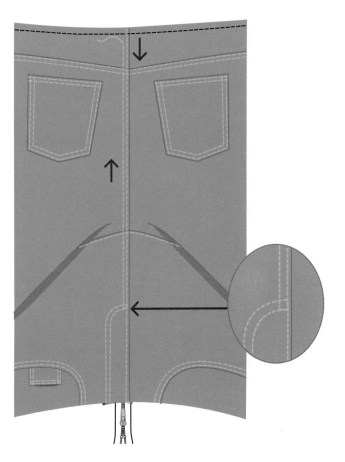

SIDE SEAMS

Now it's time to sew and finish your side seams. We like to baste side seams together for one last fit check before the final sewing. **If you're confident of the side seam fit now, go ahead and skip to step 4 and sew side seams.**

1. Baste side seams, right sides together.

2. Try on jeans with 1½" elastic. See page 36 for tips on using elastic for fitting help.

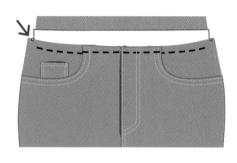

Check that your jeans fit the way you want. Do you need to take in or let out any seams?

3. Take off jeans. Mark any side seam changes you made with chalk on the wrong side. You can now trim so seam allowances are an even width all the way down, or sew on your new chalk marks. See page 58.

4. With **regular** thread, sew side seams.

5. Set stitches by pressing on top of stitching.

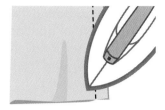

6. Press seams open.

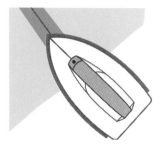

7. Press seams toward the **back**. Pressing over a sleeve board, seam roll, or seam stick makes this easier.

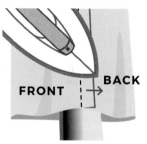

FRONT → BACK

If the hip is curved, press over a pressing ham.

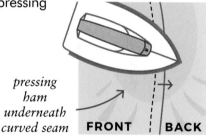

pressing ham underneath curved seam FRONT → BACK

8. Serge finish seam allowances together leaving 1/2" seam allowance.

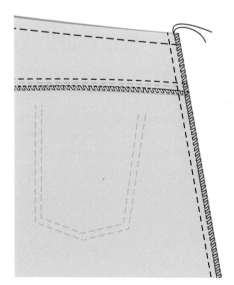

9. With **topstitching** thread, edgestitch from waist to bottom of front pocket bag on side seams. This will secure all the layers of fabric and pockets toward the back and away from the pocket opening.

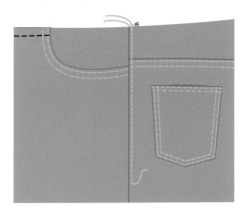

10. With **topstitching** thread add a bartack to the bottom 1/2" for extra strength at the pocket bottom. If you are using a contrast thread (different from your topstitch color) for bartacks, it's easier to wait and make all of the bartacks at the end. See page 117 for bartack how-tos.

← bartack

BELT LOOPS

You've already sewn your belt loop strip, which is ready to cut into individual lengths.

For a deep dive into belt loop length calculation, see page 113, or just cut them 4" long. This works for any 1½"-wide waistband that will hold up to a 1¼" belt.

CLASSIC BELT LOOP PLACEMENT

Traditionally jeans have five belt loops:

Two placed 1/4" to 1" from the front edge of each front pocket.

One at center back.

One placed 3/4" to 1½" away from each side seam.These side loops should not be visible from the front.

You can break all the rules and make your loops bigger, wider, crisscrossed at the center back, or whatever you choose.

ATTACH BELT LOOPS NOW OR LATER

If you want belt loops, you can sew them into the waistband seam now. Or you can sew them on after the waistband is completed.

1. Cut belt loops to length and turn one end to the wrong side 3/8" to 1/2" and press well. I use a little fabric glue to keep the end turned under, then set them under a clapper to dry.

148

2. Attach belt loops to jeans right sides together with a fabric glue stick. Baste over them to secure them so they don't move while sewing on the waistband.

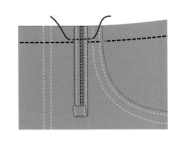

NOTE: After the waistband is attached and finished, this belt loop will come just to the top, and be bartacked in place.

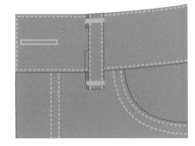

WAISTBAND

If you used a 1" waist seam allowance, trim it to an even 5/8" before you sew on the waistband. Most RTW jeans use a two-piece, straight waistband with a seam at the top. It is usually cut on the crosswise grain and topstitched with a chain stitch, which allows for stretch, in order to fit more bodies. One reason to sew custom jeans is to create a firm waistband that doesn't stretch out or roll. After all, they are designed to fit only your body.

These instructions are for a two-piece (or faced) waistband. It can be either straight or curved. They are sewn the same way. See page 153 for a one-piece fold-over style.

If you're just joining us for the waistband you'll want to make sure your waistband is at least 2" longer on each end of center front than the waist of the jeans. See page 125 for interfacing.

Prepare waistband

1. Stitch waistband to facing along top edge, right sides together. On a curved contour waistband this is the inward curve.

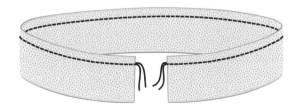

2. Turn up bottom edge of facing to wrong side 1/8" more than your seam allowance and press. Trim to 3/8".

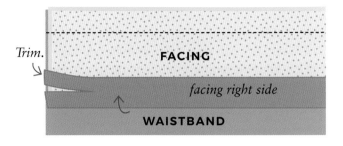

Trim.

FACING

facing right side

WAISTBAND

3. Grade seam allowances to 3/8" on waistband side and 1/4" on facing side. Press facing up over seam allowances.

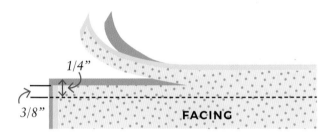

1/4"

3/8"

FACING

4. Flip facing up over seam allowances and understitch to seam allowances close to the seam.

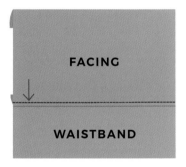

FACING

WAISTBAND

5. Zip up jeans and lay flat, right side up. Mark the waist seamline on both sides of the center front with chalk or pins, so the waistband seam matches on both sides. Again, it will be easier if the waist seam allowance is the same as the 5/8" band seam allowance, so if you used 1" seam allowances, trim to 5/8". **Be sure to unzip the zipper before attaching waistband!**

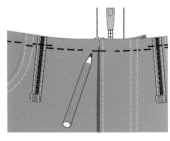

6. Starting at the **center back**, pin unfolded edge of waistband to jeans, right sides together and one to one.

NOTE: You will not be using the pattern markings for the waistband. The two sides of your body may be different, and usually are. We cut the waistband longer than needed and fit the jeans to your waist so the sewing the waistband to your jeans can be one to one, no easing. Be sure you have at least 3/4" extra at each end to finish the ends. Belt loops will be sandwiched between jeans and waistband unless you prefer to sew them on after waistband is complete.

HAZEL SAYS...

Is the waistband lining up at the zipper? If not, before finishing the wrong side of the band, close the zipper and put a pin where the bands should come together. Restitch until even.

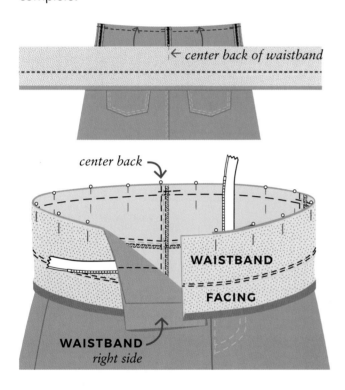

← *center back of waistband*

center back

WAISTBAND

FACING

WAISTBAND
right side

7. Baste waistband to jeans. Or pin in the stitching line parallel to the cut edge and try on. Basting is a little smoother, which makes fitting easier, but it's your choice.

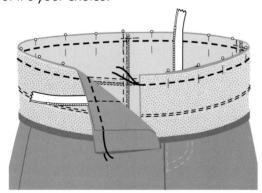

8. Make sure waist seam matches at center front.

TRY ON JEANS

Now is the for-real-last-chance for adjusting in this area. Make sure you love it before you stitch it up.

- Check that **waistband fits snugly** but not too tight. If too loose, remove basting and ease waistband to jeans just a little to make tighter. Or take in side seams.

- It's common to see **little wrinkles below the waistband** in the pocket area. See page 57 for this fix.

SEW WAISTBAND

If you are using nonstretch denim, interface both ends of the waistband with PerfectFuse Sheer or Medium as shown, giving stability to button and buttonhole. Yes, you can cover the seam.

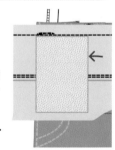

1. Stitch waistband to jeans top. Backstitch twice over area with zipper teeth to strengthen seam so zipper tab doesn't pull off after zipper is cut. If you're using a metal zipper, do this with extreme care. You may need to help the machine skip over the teeth by lifting your presser foot, moving needle over teeth, lowering foot and continuing to stitch.

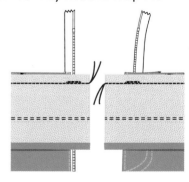

If you used a metal zipper use pliers to pull the teeth off the tape above the seamline. Then you can safely sew over the zipper tape. Trim away tape above waistband leaving 1/4".

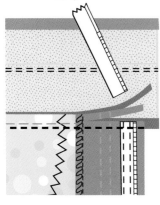

2. Grade seam allowance to 1/4" on jeans side and 3/8" on waistband side.

3. Now you can trim away excess zipper tape above the waist seam, leaving 1/2" of tape.

4. Lay the jeans over a pressing ham and press waistband up over seam allowance.

Waistband Ends

1. For both ends: Fold band in half, right sides together, with seam turned up and bottom edge of waistband unfolded. Trim ends to 3/4".

2. Draw a chalk line on the waistband 1/16" away from the jeans edge, to prevent a pucker.

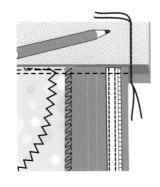

3. Stitch the ends along chalk lines, using short stitch length (1.5-2mm), back-stitching at beginning and end of seam.

4. Trim seam allowance to a scant 1/4" and cut top corner diagonally.

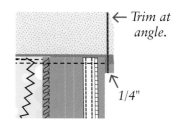

← Trim at angle.

1/4"

HAZEL SAYS...

On the side that gets a buttonhole (left side per these instructions), you can do some EXTREME trimming of this seam allowance to reduce as much bulk as possible to make the buttonhole easier to sew.

---

5. Press both end seams open over the pointed end of a point turner/ clapper.

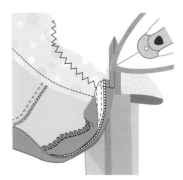

6. Fold seam allowances at end of waistband toward facing and under the facing seam allowance. This will make the right side of the waistband smoother. Press.

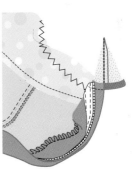

7. Turn ends right side out. Use a point turner to get a nice 90° angle at corners.

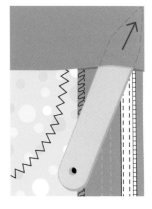

8. The end of your waistband will look like this. The folded edge should cover the waistband stitches. Press this corner well. Use a clapper or hammer to flatten.

WRONG SIDE VIEW   **RIGHT SIDE VIEW**

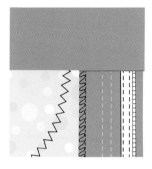 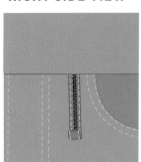

9. To make super-tidy ends and help with topstitching accuracy, from the wrong side, pin the folded edge to cover the waist stitching line. Long, fine quilting "flower pins" work great for this.

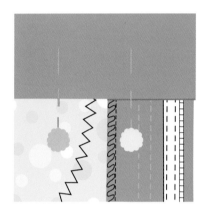

10. Edgestitch from the right side 1½" from ends using matching thread. Stitch off the end and trim threads. You can also do this by hand, but the machine stitching is stronger and faster.

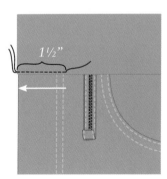

1½"

Finish the Waistband

1. Place folded edge of the rest of the waistband facing just over the waist stitching line. Press well.

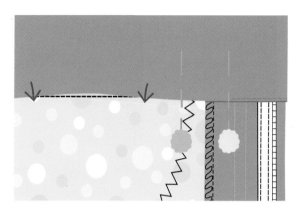

2. From the right side pin 1/16" from the seam using long, thin pins. Pin with heads facing away from center front so you can easily pull them out as you sew.

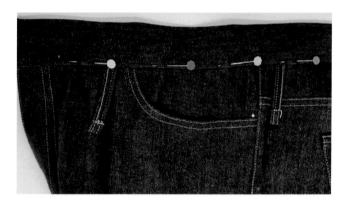

While pinning, check to be sure the pins catch the folded edge on the wrong side.

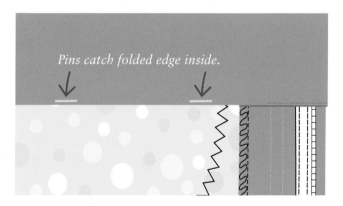

Pins catch folded edge inside.

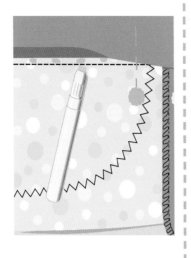

HAZEL SAYS...

A few dots of basting glue in addition to some pins can help hold the waistband in place while topstitching from the right side. Or, like my human, if you'd rather slipstitch the facing to the inside instead of pinning, do it. Then your edgestitching will be perfect.

To get around thick corners evenly, use a "multipurpose tool" or leveling tool under the presser foot. Sew to the corner. With the needle down, raise the presser foot and pivot. Slip the leveling tool under the back of the presser foot. Lower presser foot and continue sewing. Repeat for next corner. Many sewing machines come with this handy gadget. Dritz even makes a notion called the Jean-A-Ma-Jig for this purpose.

3. With **topstitching** thread, edgestitch in one continuous line on right side (public side) of waistband on all edges. Begin at the top of the left front side of jean just above the belt loop. Your stitching ends will be covered with the belt loop. If you don't want belt loops, begin stitching on the top of the band about 4" from the center back. Sew the entire band and join stitches. Leave threads long, bring to the back, tie off, and bury threads under fabric.

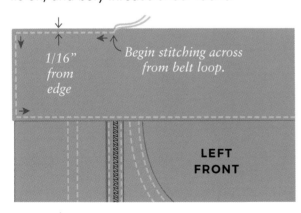

1/16" from edge

Begin stitching across from belt loop.

LEFT FRONT

NOTE: When topstitching and approaching a thick edge, you can get a jamming of thread or a change of stitch length because of the change of thickness. You can level the presser foot with the fabric height using one of the special tools like the one shown in the photo at the top of the next column.

FOLD-OVER WAISTBAND OPTION

Prepare waistband by pressing one edge of waistband under 5/8". Continue with waistband application beginning on page 149, step 5.

Press under 5/8".

FINISHING

Yahoo! Ready for the final touches! You're in the home stretch. Great work! Finish your jeans now with your favorite final touches.

Each technique below has a tutorial in Chapter 6 if you really want to break it down. As always, practice on samples to get the best results with your specific materials.

BELT LOOPS

You'll find detailed instructions for belt loops starting on page 113. Secure your belt loops at the top of the waistband and at the bottom fold with bartacks or multiple lines of straight stitching.

If you didn't sew the belt loops into the waistband seam, turn under each end of your loops 1/2" and bartack them in place at the top edge of the waistband and at the bottom fold of the loop.

BARTACKS

Sew them now. Bartacks are functional as well as decorative. They provide a measure of durability to the stress-bearing areas on your jeans, like the side seams at pocket bottoms, the base of the fly topstitching, and the back pocket tops. They can also be substitutes for rivets if you prefer thread to metal. Refer to chapter 6 page 118 for more about bartack placement and sewing success.

BUTTONHOLE

Sew your waistband buttonhole. Pages 118-123 show several buttonhole options and how-tos.

HEMS

Denim can continue shrinking in length after multiple washings if you dry in the dryer, so it's good to make your finished length a tad longer than you think you want. The days of length rules are gone. Anything goes! See page 215 for more bottom line inspiration.

1. Once you've determined the desired length, trim away excess length leaving 1" to turn under and press. If you don't have that much, use what you have and make the narrowest hem you can.

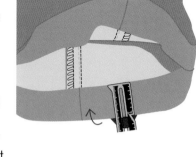

2. With jeans right side out, press legs up 1" all around. Try pressing in quarters, one section at a time: front, back, side seam, inseam. This avoids having to work in a circle and is easier, especially if your leg opening is skinny.

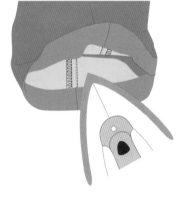

3. Trim away seam allowance at an angle from fold to raw edge to reduce bulk.

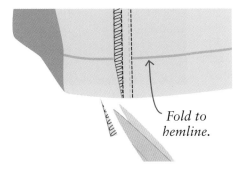

Fold to hemline.

4. Fold under 1/2" of the raw edge and place under machine, beginning just before the inseam on the wrong side of jean. Using matching thread allows you to sew from the wrong side without worry about how straight the stitching is from the right side. Sew 1/16" from the fold in a continuous line, turning under raw edge as you go and backstitching at the meeting of the circle. End with your machine's fix stitch, which stitches in place to lock threads, or pull threads through from front to back and tie off if desired.

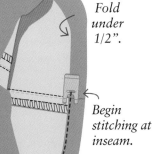

Fold under 1/2".

Begin stitching at inseam.

SETTING HARDWARE

Chapter 2 covers hardware tools, and Chapter 3 describes types of hardware.

Installing Rivets

This section shows simple installation using an awl, tiny anvil, and hammer. **Practice on a sample.** Place your anvil on a piece of wood or a magazine to protect your work surface. No anvil? You can use your garage floor, but it could leave a mark.

1. Mark your rivet locations with a chalk pencil. Your marks should be 1/2" from seams. Rivets are most commonly placed at top and side of front pocket openings and on the top corner(s) of the coin pocket. You choose the locations!

2. Make a hole with an awl or with a 2mm hole piercing punch.

3. Push the stud half of rivet through the hole from the wrong side. Make sure it's all the way in so the back is flush with the fabric.

4. Using your wire cutters, trim the post down to about 1/16" from your fabric. You can experiment with not trimming, but your rivet may not compress tightly to your fabric. If you have a hollow post and it smooshes, reshape it gently with your pliers.

5. Place the rivet top on the stud. It won't "click." You have to line it up and hold it here.

6. Carefully holding all the pieces together, flip the fabric so the rivet top is face down on the anvil. Tap the rivet back with your hammer and then check to make sure the pieces connected.

7. Strike the rivet bottom with hammer a couple of good whacks and look to make sure the rivet is secure.

Practice on scraps a few times until you're comfortable.

Voila! A rivet!—front and back view. Did your rivet get a little smooshed from the hammer? If there are no sharp edges to irritate your skin, move on!

 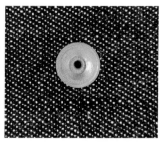

156

Installing Tack Buttons

Tack buttons can be manually installed in the same manner as rivets, but never trim the end of the post. You want the full length and sharp point of the post intact.

The post of most tack buttons has little ridges that grab the center of the button shank. Often the inside of the shank is lined with plastic to help tighten the grip.

Place your button on the underlap side of your waistband so that the shank lines up with the outside edge of your button-hole. Usually this will be right above the zipper teeth.

1. Lay your front flat and mark through your buttonhole to the underlap with a pin.

2. Mark button position on underlap.

3. Make a hole with an awl or use a 2mm hole-piercing punch. See opposite page.

4. Push the stud half of the button through the hole from the wrong side. Make sure it is all the way in so the back is flush with the fabric.

5. Just as you did for the rivet, put the public side of the button on the anvil, and with the waistband folded in half, line up the post over the hole.

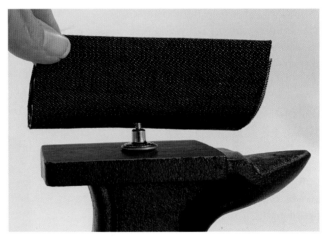

6. Once they are joined, hammer the flat side of the post until the parts are attached.

You are done! Now, go amaze your friends and complete strangers alike with your handmade jeans. When someone compliments you on them say this—loud and proud:

"Thanks! I made them myself!"

CHAPTER 8
DESIGN MODS

MODIFY TO YOUR HEART'S CONTENT

In this chapter I'll take you step-by-step through some great design changes you can use to get the most out of the patterns you've already altered. Different leg widths and lengths, pockets, front closures, hems, and waistbands give you a nice à la carte menu of jeans features to choose from when creating your own designs. Most of these techniques can be used on any jeans you choose to make.

During the first Palmer/Pletsch workshop I attended, Pati Palmer told us, "The pattern is your manuscript, you are the editor." There! The master of the Pattern Design Universe just gave you permission to break the rules. It's *okay* to change your pattern.

TWO BASIC JEANS PATTERNS

Once you've made jeans that fit well, you can easily make your pattern into different styles. I love having two basic jeans patterns that I can change up:

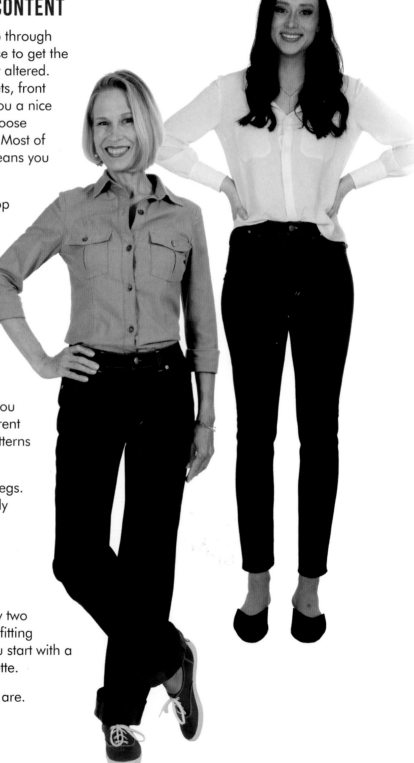

- A slim to skinny style with tapered legs. From this basic style you can literally make any jean.

- A straight-leg style that is looser through the seat and upper thigh.

You can also use just one pattern and achieve many looks. I recommend only two different types because it makes tissue-fitting and modifying easier if, in general, you start with a pattern that has your desired fit silhouette.

What jeans are in style today? They all are. You decide your style, period.

LEG MODIFICATIONS

Widening, tapering, lengthening, and shortening are simple changes that can have big impact. These things are covered in Chapter 4 with fitting. See page 46.

Lengthen the leg and add darts or pleats at front inseam and side seam at the knee. This will allow the leg to bend easily.

This pant has a separate section of fabric for the knee area. I'll call it the knee inset. It can be a functional design feature made from self-fabric or something different. Making the inset a double layer adds durability.

CREATE THE KNEE INSET ON YOUR PATTERN

This hiking pant started with a straight-leg jeans pattern.

1. During tissue-fitting, mark on your pattern the center of your knee with a pin. Bending over to pin can move the tissue, so if you are doing this yourself, stand back up straight and make sure that you've marked accurately. Remove the pattern and mark pin with pencil.

2. Place the front pattern piece flat on your work surface. Draw a line through your center-of-the-knee mark, perpendicular to the grainline.

3. Mark length of the knee inset. It should be a finished length of at least 10" for an adult. Draw two lines—one 5"-7" above and one 5"-7" below the center.

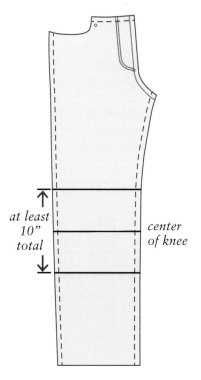

at least 10" total

center of knee

ARTICULATED KNEE

Work jeans and hiking pants become more functional with an articulated knee. I love hiking and do a lot of scrambling over logs and rocks. I designed these shaped knees to allow plenty of movement.

A darted cargo pocket for seat and legs is a great companion detail for these hikers. See page 189 of this chapter for a full tutorial.

WAYS TO SHAPE THE KNEE

Create a rounded or articulating knee shape on the front leg, with or without a separate knee section.

159

4. Cut on top and bottom inset lines.

5. Add 1/2" seam allowances to the top and bottom front pieces with Perfect Pattern Paper.

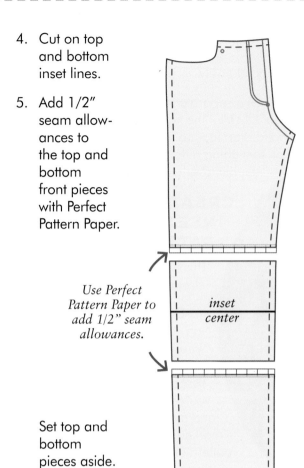

Use Perfect Pattern Paper to add 1/2" seam allowances.

Set top and bottom pieces aside.

2. Draw eight tuck lines. Starting 2" above the new center line, draw four lines 1/2" apart. Repeat, starting 2" below the center line.

3. Label your lines A,B,C,D as shown.

4. Draw 1/2" seam allowance lines at the top and bottom of inset.

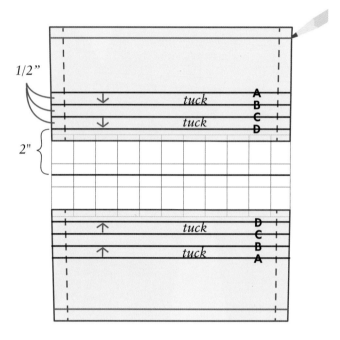

LENGTHEN INSET AND MARK TUCKS

For a finished inset of 10", add 3" to the length of the inset: 2" for four 1/2" tucks and 1" for top and bottom 1/2" seam allowances.

1. Cut inset along center line. Add 3" of Perfect Pattern Paper, tape. Draw a new center line in your addition. The inset is now 13" long.

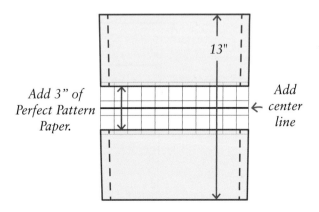

Add 3" of Perfect Pattern Paper.

Add center line →

CUT INSET FROM FABRIC

After you cut out your pants and transfer all your pattern markings, trace your tuck lines A, B, C, and D onto your knee inset pieces.

TIP: A sharp, fine pencil lightly drawn on fabric will be accurate.

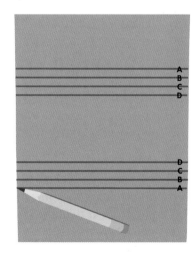

SEW TUCKS ON INSETS

1. Bring lines A to lines B and lines C to lines D. Notice that the tucks point to the center of the inset. Press.

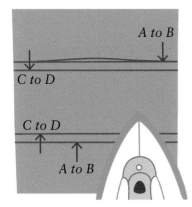

2. Draw stitching lines 2" long and 1/8" from the fold on each tuck.

   Make two perpendicular marks 3/8" apart at the inside end of the stitching line. This is where you will bartack.

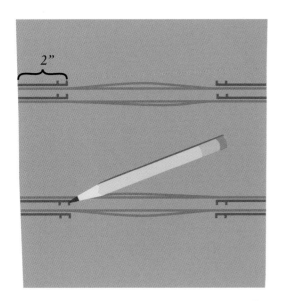

3. Using **topstitching** thread, edgestitch your tucks on your lines, starting at the raw edge. Stitch to the end mark and then backstitch to the second mark.

   Raise your needle and set your machine to zigzag (2mm wide by .8mm long). Sew bartacks, stopping at the end mark (3/8" long). Leave threads long, pull to the back, tie a square knot and bury the threads.

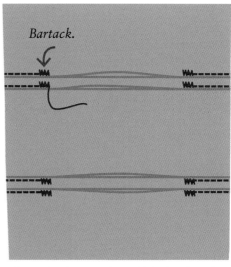

This is how the four tucks will look when finished.

4. Using **regular** thread, sew the tucked inset to the top and bottom front pieces with 1/2" seam allowances. Press seams open and then away from the inset.

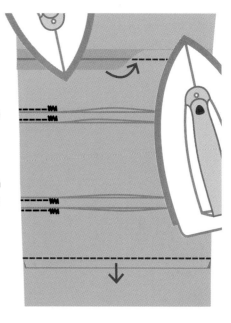

5. Serge finish both seam allowances, leaving them 1/2" wide.

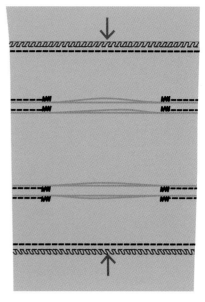

161

6. From the right side, using **topstitching** thread, sew two lines of stitching, one 1/16" from the seam and another 1/4" from the first.

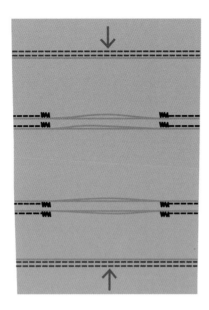

Finish sewing articulated knee pants following the construction order in Chapter 7. If you want to add the darted cargo pocket, follow the instructions on page 189.

VARIATIONS

There are other ways to shape the knee area. Try making 1/2" deep by 2½" long darts instead of tucks. You could make the inset wider instead of longer and do vertical darts at the top and bottom. It's up to you. Experiment and decide which provides you the most comfort and movement.

EASY DESIGN CHANGES TO LEGS

It's as easy as drawing a line on the front or back pattern, cutting on that line, adding seam allowances, and sewing together.

SADDLE SEAM JEANS

Add a seam to the front, curving it below the pocket and continuing it to the center back below the yoke.

Using a striped denim gives you creative cutting opportunities.

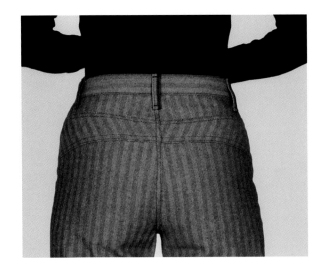

Snap-VIEW CONSTRUCTION ORDER FOR SADDLE SEAM JEANS

☐ **ALTER PATTERN following steps 1-3, below.**

☐ **Cut out jeans, page 112.**

☐ **Pattern markings, page 113**

☐ **Front pockets, page 128**

☐ **Fly front zipper, page 133**

☐ **Baste and fabric fit, page 139. BASTE IN THIS ORDER: front saddle piece to front, back saddle piece to back, yoke to back saddle piece, inseams, side seams.**

☐ **ASSEMBLE FRONTS AND BACKS IN THE SAME ORDER YOU BASTED. PRESS SADDLE SEAMS UP.**

☐ **Sew inseams, page 144**

☐ **Sew, finish, topstitch crotch, page 146**

☐ **SEW SIDE SEAMS-TAKING CARE TO MATCH UP THE "SADDLE SEAM" AT THE SIDES.**

☐ **Complete jeans from belt loops, page 148 to the end.**

1. Sketch your idea. In my first sketches I deleted the side seam but then while tissue-fitting my altered pattern I decided that I wanted to be able to adjust the fit at the side, just in case.

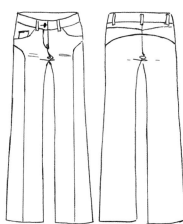

2. Pin pattern pieces together and draw design lines. Overlap the side seam at the seam allowance at the widest point of the hip. Draw a line from center back about 1½" below yoke seamline and curving around to front leg and down to hem.

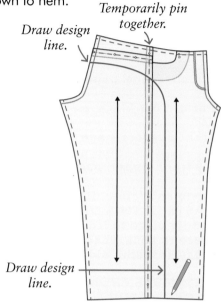

Temporarily pin together.

Draw design line.

Draw design line.

3. Cut on your line. Unpin the side seam. Separate the cut pieces and add seam allowances to both sides of the cut lines. Add some flare to legs.

Original seam allowances. Just unpin.

YOKE

SIDE FRONT

Add seam allowances.

Just unpin.

BACK

FRONT

Add leg flare.

Add seam allowances.

WINDOWPANE LEGS

Lori ran out of denim yardage for full length jeans. She added these sections to fill in the distance. Clever!

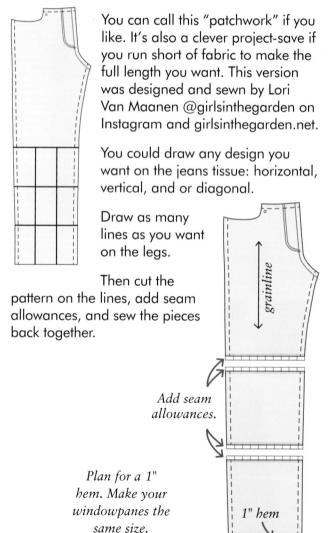

You can call this "patchwork" if you like. It's also a clever project-save if you run short of fabric to make the full length you want. This version was designed and sewn by Lori Van Maanen @girlsinthegarden on Instagram and girlsinthegarden.net.

You could draw any design you want on the jeans tissue: horizontal, vertical, and or diagonal.

Draw as many lines as you want on the legs.

Then cut the pattern on the lines, add seam allowances, and sew the pieces back together.

grainline

Add seam allowances.

Plan for a 1" hem. Make your windowpanes the same size.

1" hem

164

THE PRINCESS-SEAMED JEAN

This technique is more than just a design feature, it can be a great way to get the fit you want in jeans or any pant. You can add princess seams to front, back, or both, and shape the new seams to your body during fabric fitting. It's easier to have a helper pin the princess seams to your body, but you can do it alone.

I show the alteration on the back and front pieces.

Be mindful of your front pockets while doing this alteration. If your princess seam interferes with the inside curve of the pocket, consider drawing your pocket opening a little closer to the side seam or the center front so the princess seam is inside or outside of the curve where it meets the waist.

Prepare your pattern

Add a princess seam to both the back and front pattern pieces.

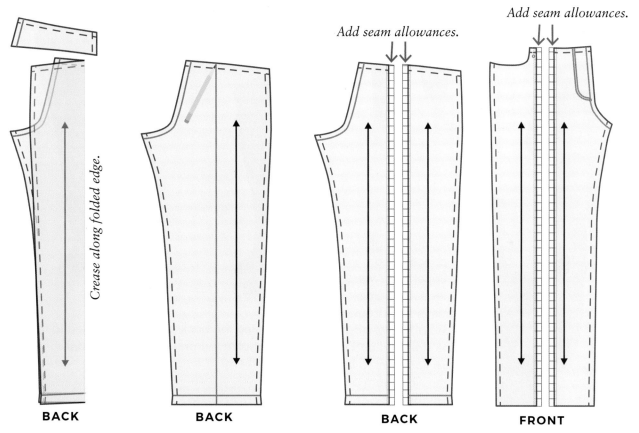

Crease along folded edge.

Add seam allowances.

Add seam allowances.

BACK

BACK

BACK

FRONT

Fold pattern piece in half lengthwise, parallel to the grainline. The cut edges of the leg will match only until about halfway up the leg. Make a good crease with your fingers.

Unfold and draw a line on your foldline. Yes, you could just cut on the creased line. I find a marked line easier to cut on accurately.

Cut on the line to create two leg pieces. Add seam allowances to the cut edges. Draw a grainline parallel to the cut edge on the piece that doesn't already have a marked grainline.

Front Before

Because we started with Julie's altered pattern, the front looks good without any changes.

Back Before

Her fabric is a stretchy denim, so we can shape the back seam to fit tightly and she can still bend over.

To slightly straighten the princess seam in the upper back we will let out the side seams in that area. Place horizontal pins at the start and end of where you want to let out the side seam and take in the back.

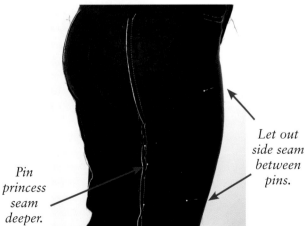

Pin princess seam deeper.

Let out side seam between pins.

JULIE IN PRINCESS JEANS

Julie and her dog, Kelly, are loving the look, fit, and comfort of her princess jeans. The careful fine-tuning was worth it!

Julie wanted the back pockets. I decided to topstitch them to match the princess lines in order to visually continue them.

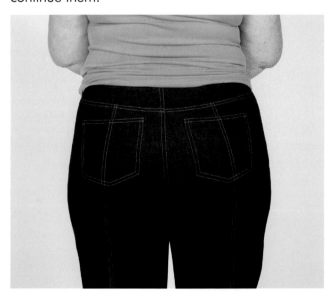

POCKET MODS

POCKET BAG VARIATIONS

Converting Trouser-Style Pocket to Jeans Style

Jeans pockets differ from trouser pockets. Jeans have a short side front attached to a lightweight cotton bag. In trousers, fashion fabric is included in the pocket bag, adding bulk. In a pant with more ease, especially a pleated trouser style, the bulk won't show. In fitted jeans, it could.

JEANS

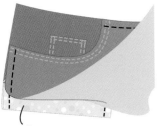

TROUSERS

Pocket Bag

Sometimes pocket pieces are made wider to be included in the fly front. This is nice in pleated trousers because it keeps the pleats flat. But remember that anchoring the front pockets into the fly area has no "tummy flattening" power unless you have a stay that goes all the way around the body! The pocket bag can have the seam at either the inside edge of the bag near the center front or at the bottom of the bag. It will depend on your pattern and your preference.

Yours can be just how you like them for how you use them. Front pockets in jeans are not always just design features. I've had students who want longer, stronger pockets than their pattern calls for. My most-asked-for pocket bag modifications follow.

Most current jeans patterns have the RTW-style jeans pockets with good sewing instructions. If you're digging out a vintage jeans pattern and it has the trouser-style pockets, here's how to modify them to a RTW-style jeans pocket.

The pattern pieces you'll work with are the front, side front, and pocket bag. Look for these shapes, as pattern nomenclature varies.

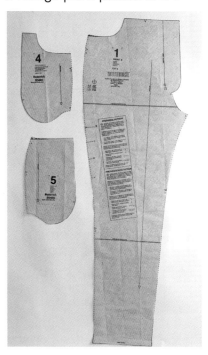

Create New Jeans Side Front

1. Place side front **on top of** the front, lining up pattern markings.

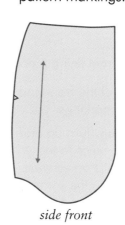

side front

two layers, side front on top of front

2. **Create the shape of the NEW side front.** Draw a curved line from the top inside corner of the side front to the side seam, ending about 2" below the cut edge of the pocket opening. Pocket openings vary in size. This piece can also have a squared bottom. No rules. Go crazy.

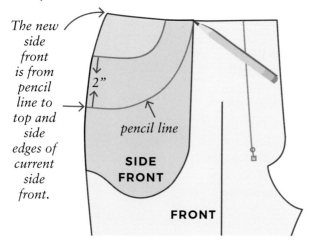

The new side front is from pencil line to top and side edges of current side front.

3. On the side front, cut on your line, discarding the bottom portion. This becomes your new side front for a jeans pocket.

Make a new pocket bag shape from lining piece.

1. Place the pocket bag on top of the front and side front, matching pattern markings.

   Decide on depth of pocket bag. Turn up and crease the bottom of the bag piece to the depth you want your pocket. It's an estimate here. You'll make it all perfect in the coming steps. **Remove the side front and pocket bag** from the front.

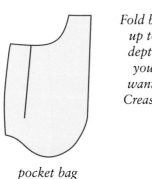

pocket bag

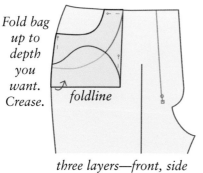

Fold bag up to depth you want. Crease.

three layers—front, side front, and pocket bag

2. Cut a piece of Perfect Pattern Paper at least 4" wider than your pocket lining and at least twice as long as the distance from your estimated foldline to the top of waist.

   Place your side front and pocket bag pieces on top of the Perfect Pattern Paper, matching pattern markings. Pin to anchor the **three layers** together.

3. Place these three layers on top of front, matching pattern markings carefully. Pin through all **four layers** in a couple of places above your estimated foldline.

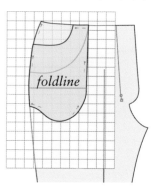

4. Fold all pocket layers up on your foldline. The Perfect Pattern Paper will be higher than the waistline all across the top. The foldline at the bottom of your pocket bag should be perpendicular to the grainline. The Perfect Pattern Paper tissue may not be square. This is fine. You decide how long you want the pocket bag.

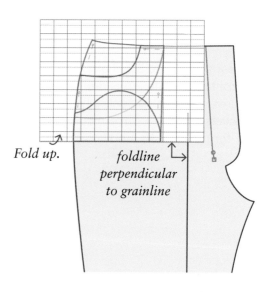

Fold up. *foldline perpendicular to grainline*

5. Anchor all layers together with a pin as shown. Draw a line on the Perfect Pattern Paper for the inner edge of pocket bag at least 3/4" from the original edge. This will become the inner bag seam. Make it wider if you want to do a French seam vs. a serged seam. You can easily see the edge through the Perfect Pattern Paper.

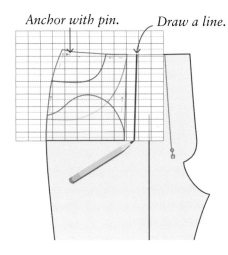

Anchor with pin.   *Draw a line.*

6. Cut the folded Perfect Pattern Paper on the line you just drew and then around the top and side of the folded pocket bag.

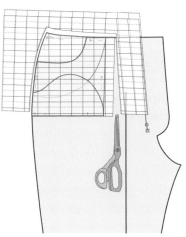

7. Unfold pocket bag. Unpin as necessary to remove front and side front. Leave pocket bags pinned together. Cut away the Perfect Pattern Paper from the pocket opening. Mark the foldline of the crease. Mark notches.

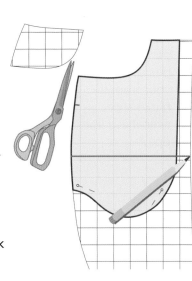

8. Remove the original pocket bag and mark a new grainline on the pocket bag perpendicular to the foldline.

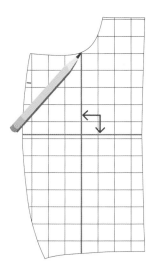

Assemble the pieces for a final check

1. Flip the pocket bag so the opening curve is at the bottom. Place side front on pocket bag, matching notches and top and side edges. Pin. Fold pocket bag up on foldline. Top and side edges should be even.

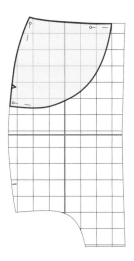

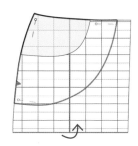

Curved area of lining will be sewn to front pocket opening, then turned to inside. Other end with new side inset attached will come up and finish the top of the front.

2. Place folded bag under front for a final check that all pieces fit together. Sewing instructions for front pockets begin on page 130.

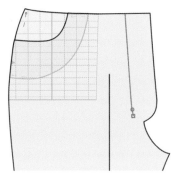

MOVING POCKET BAG SEAM

Some pocket bags have the seam at the bottom of the bag and some are at the inside edge. I feel that there is less bulk on my leg in a snug-fitting pair if the seam is on the inside edge. Here's how to flip them. Sew easy!

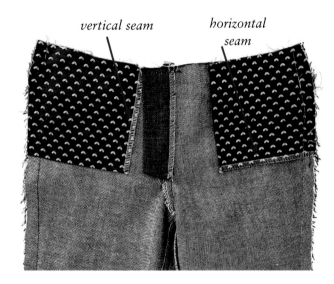

vertical seam *horizontal seam*

This pattern is designed with the pocket bag seam at the bottom.

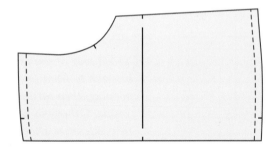

It's just a matter of rotation—let's flip it, like this:

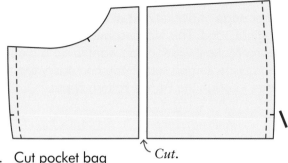

Cut.

1. Cut pocket bag in half along foldline. Leave the shaped piece in place, with the side seam at the side.

2. Rotate the other piece so its side seam lines up with the side seam of the shaped piece. The horizontal line where they meet becomes the new foldline.

3. Tape together at foldline.

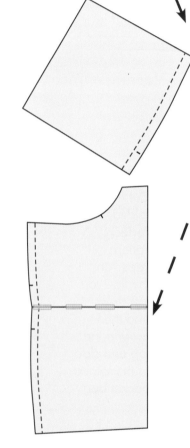

4. Be sure to place all the pieces under your front to make sure everything lines up.

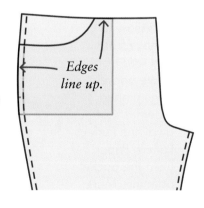

Edges line up.

That's it! Now sew your front pockets exactly as described in Chapter 7 on page 130.

LENGTHENING POCKET BAGS

Long, durable pocket bags in work jeans and hiking pants just make sense. I've included a couple of sewing techniques for front pocket durability in Chapter 7, pages 129 and 132. Here's how to alter your pattern to make a longer pocket bag. You choose the length of the pocket and whether you leave the center front corner angled or more curved.

For these flannel-lined jeans, I wanted a slightly deeper pocket and a French seam at the bottom for more durability.

For this technique you'll need a bottom seam pocket bag. If your pattern has the seam on the inside edge, see page 170 to change seam position.

1. Add Perfect Pattern Paper in your desired amount to the bottom of your of your pocket bag. I added 1¾" here.

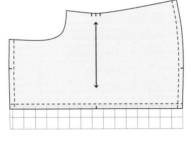

2. Fold the pocket bag on its foldline taking care to line up all markings so your pattern retains its intended shape.

    Draw a curved line from the outer edge of the pocket bag to the inner

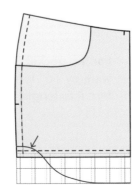

edge as shown. I started this a little higher than the original pattern at the side so there is less pocket bag in the side seam. If you make the pocket the same length all across the bottom when it's longer than about 8" it can constrict leg movement. This again is a personal preference detail. Play around.

3. Use a couple of pins near the bottom edge to keep your edges even. Trim away extra tissue on your line.

4. Be sure to place all the pieces under your front to make sure everything lines up. See below.

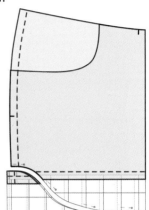

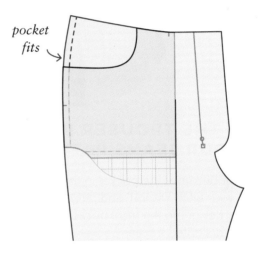

pocket fits ←

Here's how your finished pocket bag pattern will look. When you sew, finish the bottom edge with a French seam. See page 132.

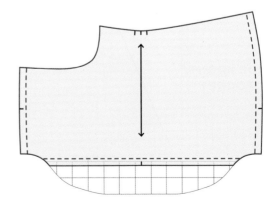

SINGLE-LAYER TOPSTITCHED TROUSER POCKETS

Start with any jeans pattern with a rise to the waist or just below it. You may want to make a copy of your pattern for this pocket version, as you'll be making considerable design changes.

CREATE THE TROUSER POCKET FROM YOUR JEANS PATTERN

The side front becomes the pocket in this technique. You'll need your SIDE FRONT and FRONT pieces. You will be redesigning the front pocket from a jeans style to a slanted trouser pocket and creating a facing for it. The three pieces will look like this when complete. Follow along. You can do it!

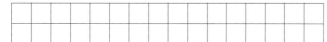

POCKET FACING

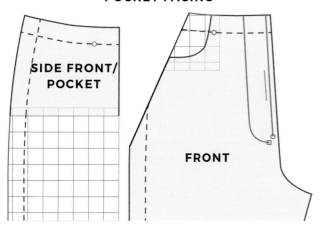

1. Mark your waist and side seamlines on both front and side front with a soft-leaded pencil or a permanent marker so they are clearly visible.

   NOTE: This pattern has 1" side, inseam and waist seam allowances.

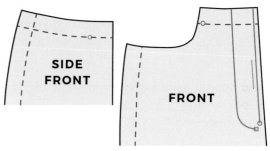

2. **To the side front to make the pocket:** Add a piece of tissue such as Perfect Pattern Paper large enough to make the piece 10"-12" long from waist to bottom and 8" wide across the bottom, as shown. This will accommodate most sizes.

   The length can be adjusted at the end of the process by holding the pattern to your body and seeing if you like the length.

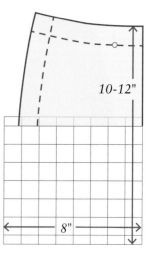

3. **To the front:** Add a piece of PPP that extends 1" above the top front of the pattern piece and 1/2" beyond the side of the pattern piece.

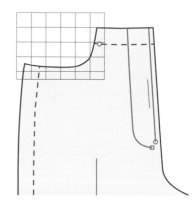

4. **For the pocket facing:** Cut a piece of PPP 2" wide by 16" long. It will be too long, but we will trim it to length later.

POCKET FACING

5. Place the side front under the front, lining up pattern markings, as shown. Be sure grainlines on both pieces are parallel so that the pocket bag will be on grain with the leg.

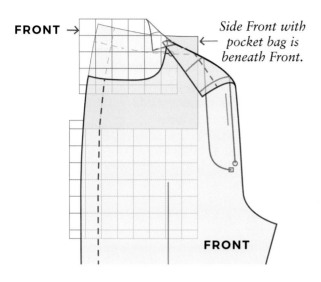

FRONT →

Side Front with pocket bag is ← beneath Front.

FRONT

NOTE: Your side front/pocket markings may not line up because ease is sometimes built in for a person small in the waist and fuller in the hips, allowing space for a hand to go into a pocket. Most of us are pretty flat in this area and don't need the ease. To remove the ease, match the marks at the side seam. Smooth the pocket opening flat and re-mark the waist-matching points.

6. Trace the shape of the side front top onto the front and trace the side front onto the pocket bag side edge.

Trace.

Trace.

7. Separate the pieces and trim away the tissue at the lines you drew. Draw waist and side seamlines onto the tissue you added.

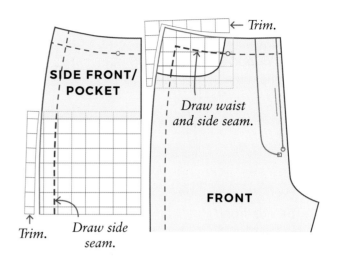

SIDE FRONT/ POCKET

← Trim.

Draw waist and side seam.

FRONT

Trim.

Draw side seam.

8. To create a slanted pocket opening on the front, measure along the waist seamline 1½" from the side seamline and make a mark. Draw a line that measures 5¼" from that mark to the intersection of the side seam, and mark this intersection.

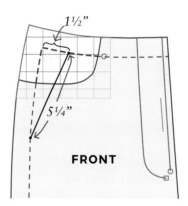

1½"

5¼"

FRONT

9. Draw a line through both marks, extending to the top and side edges, as shown.

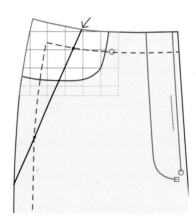

173

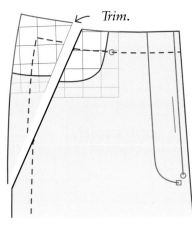

Trim.

10. Cut on your line. Save the piece you cut away so you can use your pattern with a regular pocket another time.

11. The side front/ pocket should measure 6"-6½" from the side seamline to the inner edge. If it is wider, trim some of the width along the vertical inside edge.

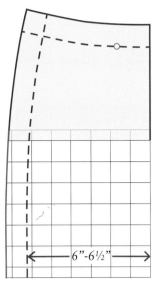

6"-6½"

Here are your three modified pocket pieces.

POCKET FACING

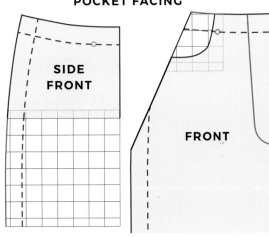

SIDE FRONT

FRONT

SEWING THE TROUSER POCKET

The side front becomes the pocket in this technique.

SIDE FRONT/ POCKET

right side

serged edges →

1. Serge finish the inside and bottom edges on side front. If you serge with the wrong side facing up, the prettier upper looper threads will show on the inside.

2. Turn one long edge of pocket facing 1/4" toward wrong side and press.

POCKET FACING - *wrong side*

3. Pin pocket facing to front, right sides together. Line up the folded edge with the top raw edge of the front as shown. Then line up the long raw edge with the pocket opening.

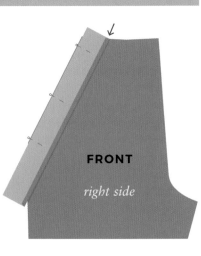

FRONT

right side

4. Stitch facing to pocket with a 3/8" seam allowance.

3/8"

FRONT

right side

174

5. Press seam allowance open.

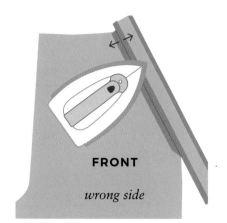

FRONT

wrong side

6. Grade seam allowance to 1/4" on facing side only.

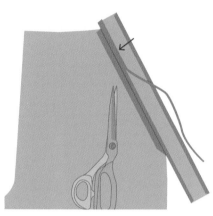

7. Press facing to inside, rolling the seam 1/16" to 1/8" toward the wrong side. Pin.

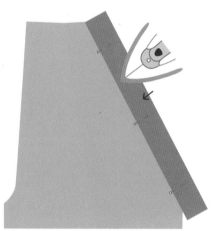

8. From wrong side, trim away facing that extends beyond top and side edges.

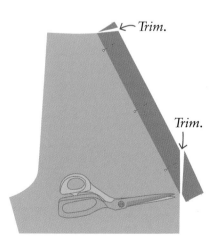

← Trim.

Trim.

9. To keep layers from slipping and make your topstitching accurate, from the wrong side, baste with long machine stitches very close to the folded edge of facing.

10. From the right side, topstitch just to the inside of the basting stitches. If desired, topstitch again 1/4" inside the first row. Edgestitch the facing seam edge. You're the designer here! Remove the basting stitches.

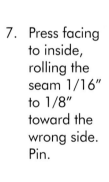

FRONT

right side

11. Place front on side front/pocket, lining up pieces at waistline and side seams. Pin along pocket opening.

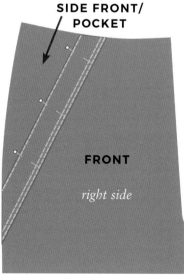

SIDE FRONT/ POCKET

FRONT

right side

12. From wrong side, pin side front/pocket to front.

13. Baste side front/pocket to front at waist and sides. Baste it in place close to its inside and bottom edges, forming a pocket bag.

SIDE FRONT
wrong side

FRONT
wrong side

14. From the right side, topstitch just inside basting stitches along front and bottom pocket edges, and again 1/4" from the first row. Remove only the basting stitches close to topstitching.

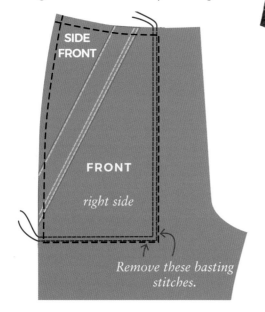

SIDE FRONT

FRONT
right side

Remove these basting stitches.

COIN POCKETS

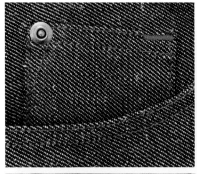
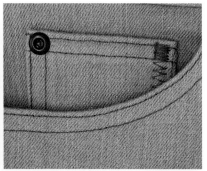
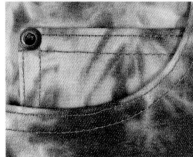
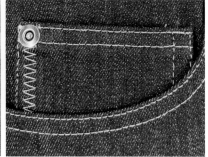

I like to see both top corners of my coin pockets. One style is not better than the other, it's just a personal preference. It's an easy change-up. If your coin pocket pattern is shaped like the one below, cut it out of fabric as designed and then make a hem on the inside edge. Make sure the top opening measures at least 2½". Press, trim excess seam allowance from new hem. Follow directions in Chapter 7 page 128 to complete.

I like to leave the pattern piece intact so I can make either coin pocket style depending on my mood.

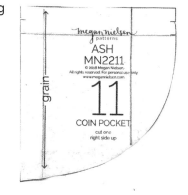

Play around with your topstitching, bartacking, rivets (or not) and see what inspires you. Put it on the left side. Leave it off...WHAT? If you never tuck your shirt in and you don't use the coin pocket, you have permission to skip it. You're the design boss. I like and use my coin pocket to hold an extra guitar pick.

COIN POCKET SHAPE

VS

INDEPENDENT STUDY ASSIGNMENT

The pocket below was applied on the wrong side of the side front and topstitched on the right side. There is no reason for this other than that's what the designer wanted! Of course, I just had to try it. It's similar to the topstitched welt pocket described on page 181. My point here is not really to encourage you to spend half a day sewing a coin pocket, it's to challenge you to look at the jeans in your closet (and online and in stores and on other people) and see if you can figure out how to create the RTW techniques that interest you. Thank me silently for not writing the instructions for this pocket!

BACK POCKETS

POCKET PLAY!

It's fun to design your own custom back pockets. Diana Stanley, one of our Portland jeans workshop attendees, turned out pocket designs for our entire class one year. Tips for topstitching and bartacking success are found in Chapter 6, starting on page 115.

Katarina and Pati stylized their initials.

Pati decided her two P's could stand for Pati Palmer or Palmer/Pletsch, or even Portland!

There are a few of my designs sprinkled in too. Use them, vary them, get creative! It's also okay to just topstitch your pockets on and leave them plain, or do a more understated tone-on-tone design, highlighting texture more than color.

Try using your sewing machine's triple stretch stitch, satin stitch, or other decorative stitches for variety in the thickness and texture of the stitches. Most importantly, have fun! If nothing inspires you here, a quick visit to sewists on social media will give you unlimited ideas.

Your back pocket design can be as simple as waving the topstitching somewhere on the pocket hem or when you sew it on to the jeans.

I call this design Diamonds and Dungarees. Sew the little diamond shape of the design before the pocket is attached. Leave threads long, pull them to the wrong side and tie with a square knot.

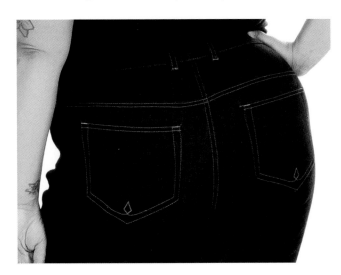

Stitching pocket to jeans:

1. Edgestitch all around first.

2. Sew a second line of stitching ¼" from the first. Start at the top right corner, carefully connect stitching to the bottom of the diamond, and continue up the second side to the top. Leave threads long, pull through to the wrong side, tie off and bury.

pocket design by Bini Leach

BACK POCKET DESIGN TEMPLATE

On the next page are a few designs for inspiration. Most of them will look good with the perspective flipped on the other back pocket, but the choice is yours. You also don't have to match pockets. The Vortex design might be a bit much on both sides of your bum. Maybe its pocket-mate is just topstitched on with no other design.

Below is a blank pocket template, so you can come up with your own design. Enlarge this at 200% on your copier so each pocket is 7¼" tall. Top foldline should be ¾", all side seam allowances are 5/8".

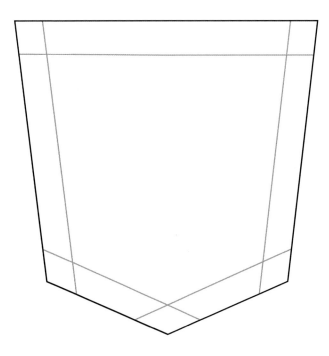

BACK POCKET DESIGN IDEAS

Rerouting by Diana Stanley

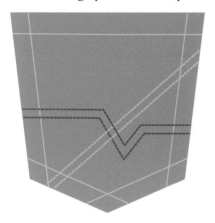

Cardio by Diana Stanley

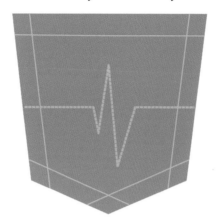

Butterfly by Jeannette Schilling

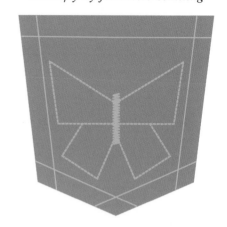

The Vortex by Diana Stanley

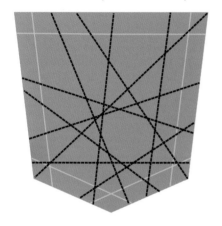

Kitty by Bini Leach

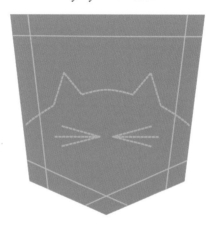

Wanderlust

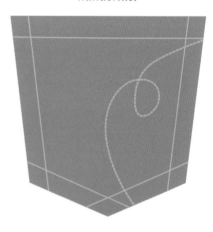

Initials, P for Pati

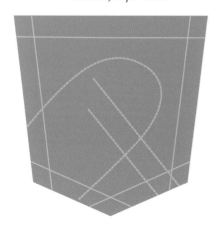

Initials, K for Katarina

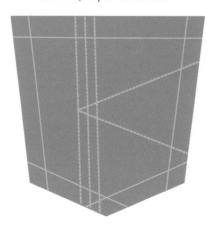

Diamonds and Dungarees

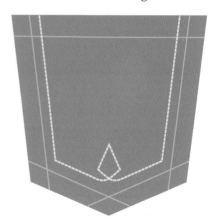

SINGLE-LAYER TOPSTITCHED WELT POCKETS

Lynne Smart, a workshop attendee from San Jose, CA, sent me a catalogue photo of cropped jeans with a trouser pocket (page 172) and these topstitched back welt pockets. The price was $440.00! Eek! She Said, "I want to make these!" Lynne came to my home for private lessons and made a pair which we dubbed the $440 jeans. I love it when I can incorporate designer details into my basic patterns for a fraction of the cost of RTW. These jeans cost me $32.

This pocket is fun to make and changes things up a bit. It is an inside patch pocket with a single welt for the opening. At first glance, it looks complicated, but it's really just a few more steps than a patch pocket. Read the instructions all the way through before starting and maybe even make a sample pocket with scraps to boost your confidence. Determine pocket placement in your fitting steps in Chapter 7, page 142.

WELT POCKET TEMPLATE

The templates for the pocket and welt are found in actual size on page 233. They will make a pocket that is 6" wide by 5¼" high with a welt 5" wide by 1/2" high. If you want a larger pocket, enlarge the templates before beginning.

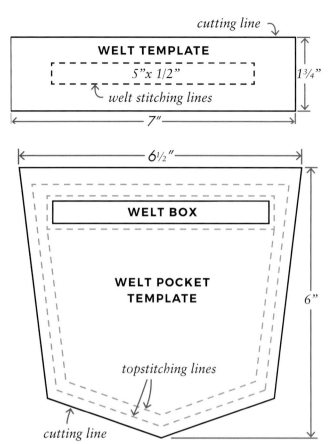

1. Trace or photocopy the templates for the welt and pocket pattern pieces on page 233.

HAZEL SAYS...

Make two copies of your pocket template: one cut out on outside cutting line for a pattern and one cut out along the inner topstitching line to use for pocket placement while you fit and sew your jeans. See Chapter 7, page 142 for determining your best pocket placement.

- From your denim: Cut two of each piece to make two pockets.

- From a lightweight nonwoven sew-in stabilizer, cut two WELT pieces using your welt template. If you have only fusible nonwoven interfacing in your stash, such as fusible Pellon, fuse two pieces, fusible sides together. This will make a stable welt stitching piece.

2. Mark your pieces carefully.

These are your marked pieces. Let's go through each one individually.

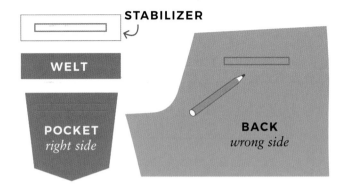

- **Pocket:** Mark the welt placement lines from the pocket template on the right side of your pocket piece.

- **Backs:** Mark welt placement lines on the wrong side of the fabric. Placement for welt pockets is individual. In general, you'll want the inside corner of welt at least 1¼" down from the yoke/back seamline (remember, this seam gets pressed toward the pant back and topstitched) and the top corner of welt about 2" from the back crotch seam.

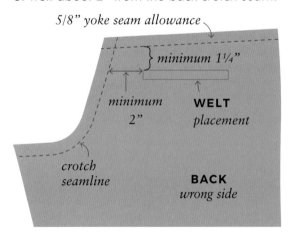

- **Stabilizer:** Using a fine-tip marker or sharp pencil, draw a box in the center of the stabilizer that measures 5" long by 1/2" high. This will become your stitching line.

Draw a line 1/2" under the box spanning the length of the stabilizer.

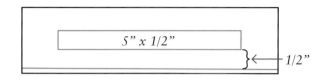

HAZEL SAYS...

Transfer welt box lines to pocket and jean backs by putting straight pins through box corners, lifting up template and marking pins with chalk. Connect the dots using a ruler.

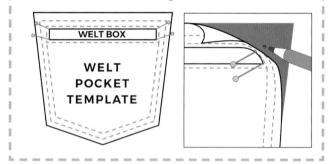

3. Serge or zigzag finish:

- The long edges of the welt piece.

- All five sides of the pocket. (Serge wrong side up so the prettier upper looper threads show on the inside of your jeans.)

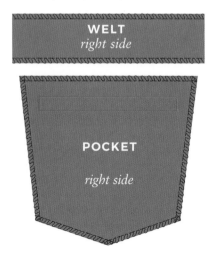

NOTE: You can sew the welt before or after sewing the yoke on. Here I have sewn, pressed, serged and topstitched the yoke seam first.

4. On the wrong side of jeans back, place the stabilizer piece over the pocket placement lines. Secure with pins.

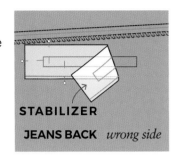

STABILIZER

JEANS BACK *wrong side*

HAZEL SAYS...

Use temporary spray adhesive on the wrong side of the stabilizer piece to help secure it to jeans back and eliminate the need for pins.

5. Beginning in the middle, stitch around the box using a 2mm stitch length. Stitch corners accurately.

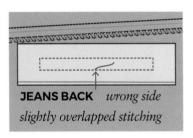

JEANS BACK *wrong side*
slightly overlapped stitching

6. On **right side**, center right side of welt over stitched box, lining up bottom of serger threads (needle stitching line) over the lower box line. Pin.

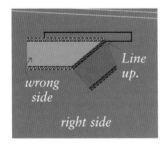

Line up.
wrong side
right side

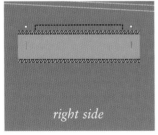

right side

7. From the stabilizer side (wrong side), stitch on the bottom line of the box.

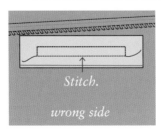

Stitch.
wrong side

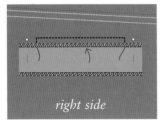

right side

8. On stabilizer side, baste 1/2" below the bottom line.

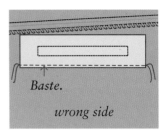

Baste.
wrong side

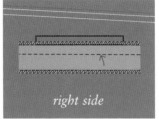

right side

9. On **right side**, fold the welt up over basting. Press and pin in place.

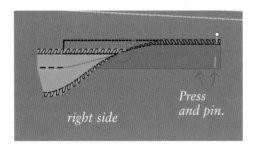

right side
Press and pin.

10. On **wrong side**, stitch again on the lower long side of the box.

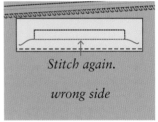

Stitch again.
wrong side

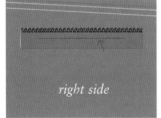

right side

11. Carefully fold the welt back so you won't stitch through it when you sew on the top line in the next step.

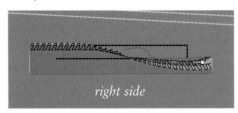

right side

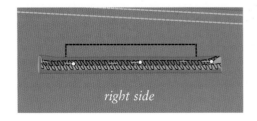

right side

183

12. With **right sides** together, place pocket piece on right side of back upside down, lining up top lines of each box, with the bottom of the pocket toward the waist.

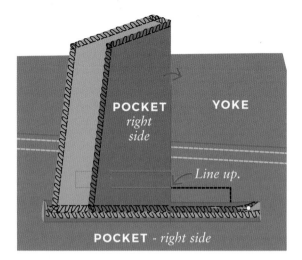

Pin as shown.

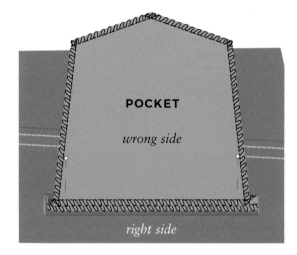

13. Stitch carefully from **wrong side** of jeans along top line of box.

14. Remove basting.

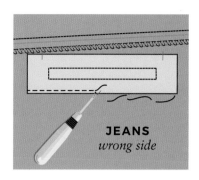

15. So that you don't cut through the pocket in the next step, fold pocket up away from stitching and pin.

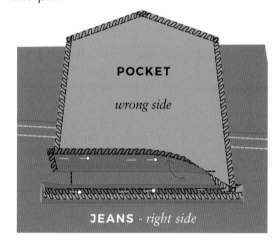

16. Slash through stabilizer and jeans, cutting to corners.

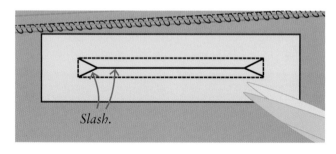

17. Pull pocket and welt through opening to wrong side. Press.

18. From the wrong side, fold back pocket edges and press welt area well.

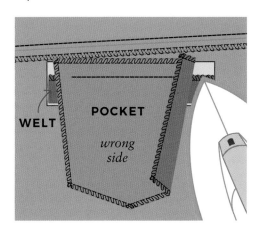

19. Look at jeans from the right side. Fold back welt fabric and stabilizer. Sew triangles at ends to **welt only**. Stitch through triangle on original stitching line and a few more times to flatten and stabilize.

20. On wrong side, trim away welt and stabilizer from sides so they're 1/8" shorter than pocket and are hidden underneath the pocket.

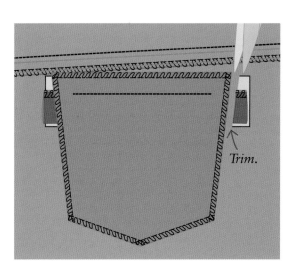

Trim.

21. Trim the pocket template as shown. Place it below the welt and draw the inner topstitching lines around the edges.

    Then draw the outer topstitching lines 1/4" away as shown.

inner topstitching lines

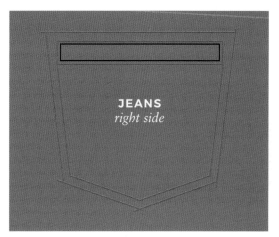

HAZEL SAYS...

Taking the time to draw clear stitching lines will make the topstitching much more accurate and much easier to sew than "eyeballing" it.

22. Fold pocket away and using **topstitching** thread edge-stitch jeans just below bottom of welt, extending stitching line to **inner** topstitching line on both sides of welt. Keep threads long and pull through to wrong side and tie off.

Fold pocket up and out of the way.

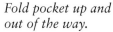

Edgestitch.

23. Fold pocket down. Pin through both layers so pocket does not shift while topstitching.

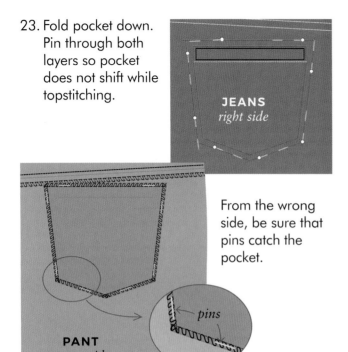

JEANS *right side*

PANT *wrong side*

pins

From the wrong side, be sure that pins catch the pocket.

24. Topstitch around welt on chalk lines starting at bottom right corner of welt. Sew another line of topstitching 1/4" from the first line. Leave threads long. Pull to wrong side and tie off.

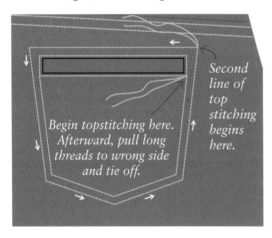

Begin topstitching here. Afterward, pull long threads to wrong side and tie off.

Second line of top stitching begins here.

Admire your work and repeat for the other side. Great job!

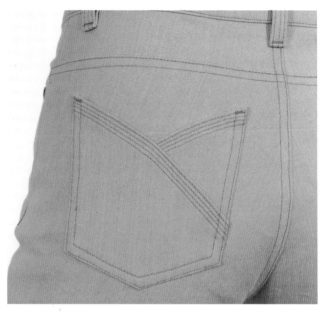

TULIP POCKET

This pocket looks great when paired with the tulip hem or all on its own. Try a colored denim and bold topstitching thread to spice things up.

For the matching tulip hem, see page 216.

TULIP POCKET TEMPLATE

This template is found in actual size on page 234. It will make a pocket that is 5½" wide by 6" high. If you want a larger pocket, enlarge the template before beginning. All seam allowances are 1/2".

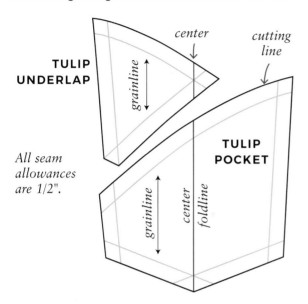

1. Trace or copy the tulip pocket template from page 234. Cut two of each piece from your denim for two pockets. Your fabric pieces will look like this.

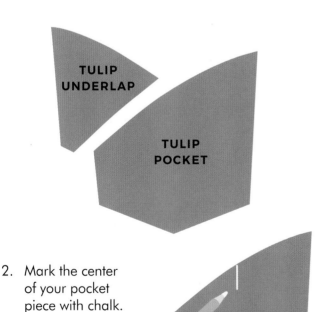

2. Mark the center of your pocket piece with chalk.

3. Turn curved top edges of each piece 1/2" toward wrong side. Press.

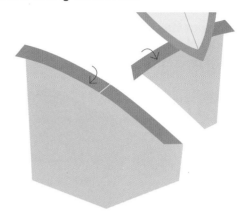

4. Unfold curved edge of underlap and serge or zigzag finish.

5. Re-press curved edge and topstitch with as many rows as you like. We started 1/16" from the top edge and sewed four rows 1/8" apart. The final row catches the bottom of the serged edge. Mark with chalk the center where the underlap folding intersects with the folded edge.

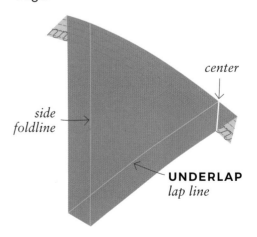

6. Fold open pressed edge of pocket. Place underlap on pocket, right sides together, lining up side edges and center markings. Serge or zigzag together along raw edges as shown. Continue the stitches along the entire curved edge of pocket.

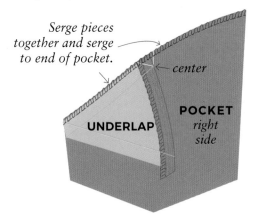

Serge pieces together and serge to end of pocket.

center

UNDERLAP **POCKET** *right side*

7. Fold underlap up with seam allowances pressed toward the pocket as shown. Pin pocket to underlap.

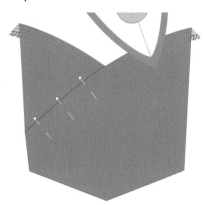

8. Check for symmetry by folding pocket in half and making sure both sides are the same length. If not, adjust and re-pin. OR make them asymmetrical. You're the designer!

9. Topstitch the top of the pocket 1/16" from the folded edge and 1/8" between rows to match the underlap stitching.

10. Serge or zigzag finish the pocket sides.

11. Press seam allowances under 1/2".

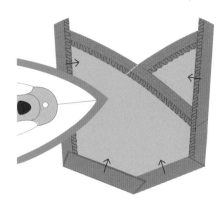

12. Fold top corner edges under as shown and press well.

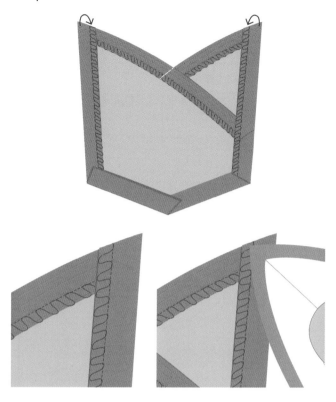

13. Topstitch pockets to jean backs. Add bartacks at the top corners to keep them secure.

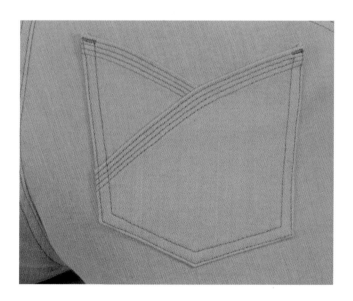

DARTED CARGO POCKET WITH FLAP

I am an avid hiker and have collected all my favorite hiking pant features into the jeans you see here. I prefer long pants to shorts to keep my legs protected from brush, so leg features are paramount. I like a low-profile leg pocket that has a little extra volume but doesn't expand, tempting me to load them up too much or causing them to hang up on branches. I also love a waist-high style so my backpack and my waistband are not at the same level on my body. Here's where being your own designer makes sewing even more rewarding.

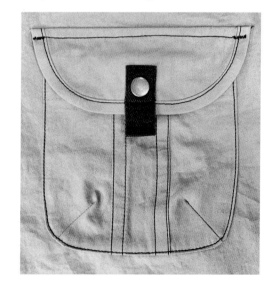

This is a loose-fitting, straight-legged jeans pattern with an articulated knee (page 159), and these great pockets make the ultimate hiking, camping and travel pant. The darts make the pockets just roomy enough, and flap bindings and snap tabs help them hold up to heavy use. The leg pocket is the perfect size for your smartphone, keeping it handy for photo ops.

Design your own pockets or copy the templates on page 234 and use as pattern pieces to make the pockets I feature on this hiking pant. The leg pockets are longer and wider than the back pockets. Construction is the same for both.

FABRIC

Fabric for your hikers should be a fast-drying, tightly woven technical fabric designed for outdoor wear. Some are cotton (treated and fast-drying) and others are nylon or polyester. It should also have breathable qualities. Wovens with a little stretch can make great hiking pants too. For good suppliers of technical fabrics and notions see page 235.

NOTIONS

- 3/4" twill tape for the snap pull tabs.
- 1/2" to 5/8" spring snaps.

These leg pocket templates are shown here for reference. Templates for both leg and back pockets are on page 234, with instructions for copying.

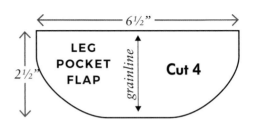

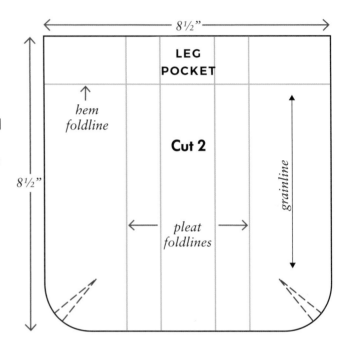

For each pocket you will cut:

- 1 pocket piece
- 2 flap pieces
- 1 bias strip, 1¼"x10", of your fabric for flap binding.
- 1 piece of 3/4" twill tape, 3½" long, for snap pulls.

CONSTRUCTION ORDER

If you choose to add leg pockets, you'll sew your side seams before the inseams and crotch so you can sew the leg pockets on flat over the finished side seams. You may choose not to topstitch your inseams for ease of construction. It can be done, it's just a little tricky. Here is your Snap-View construction order for pants with leg pockets.

Snap-VIEW
CARGO POCKET
CONSTRUCTION ORDER

☐ **Cut out jeans, page 112**

☐ **Pattern markings, page 113**

☐ **Front pockets, page 128**

☐ **Fly front zipper, page 133**

☐ **Baste and fabric fit, page 139**

☐ **Yokes, page 143**

☐ **Back pockets, page 144 style OR make small cargo pockets using template and this technique.**

☐ **Side seams, page 147**

☐ **LEG CARGO POCKETS**

☐ **Complete jeans from "inseams," page 144 to the end.**

1. Snip-mark pleat and hem foldline marks and dart ends with 1/4" snips. Mark darts with pen or chalk.

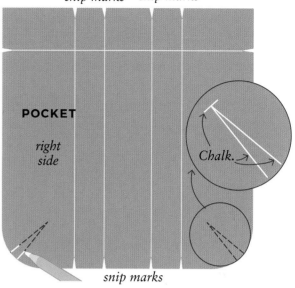

2. To make the pleats: Press inside foldlines as shown, wrong sides together.

Press inside foldlines separately to crease.

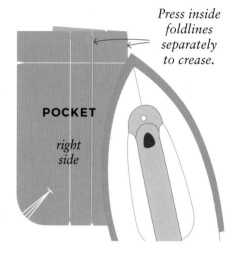

Inside and outside lines meet.

3. Bring inside foldlines to outside foldlines, matching snip marks. Press.

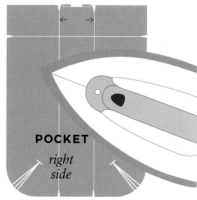

4. With **topstitching** thread, edgestitch along fold and then topstitch 1/4" from first row of stitching. If you prefer expanding pleats, omit the topstitching, or edge-stitch the pleat only, not stitching it to pocket.

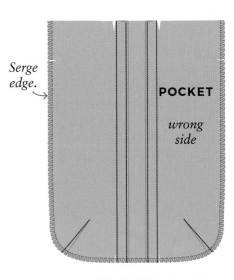

7. Serge or zigzag finish the side and bottom edges.

Serge edge.

5. Sew darts, right sides together. Leave threads long and tie off with a square knot.

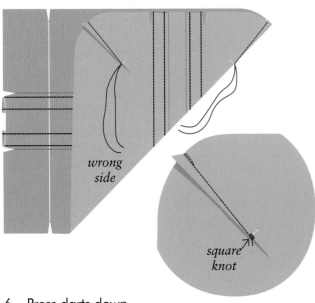

wrong side

square knot

8. Press top edge under 1/4" toward the wrong side.

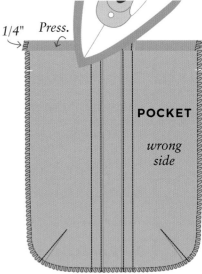

1/4" Press.

6. Press darts down.

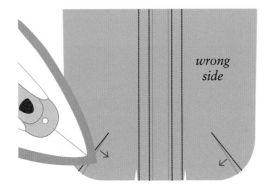

wrong side

9. Fold down hem on upper edge of pocket at snips, right sides together. Pin in place. Stitch around the curved edge of the pocket 3/8" from the serged edge.

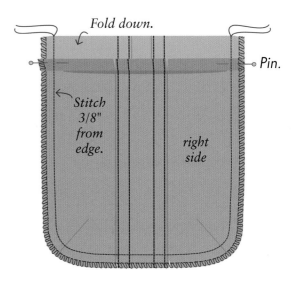

Fold down.

Pin.

Stitch 3/8" from edge.

right side

10. Trim the corners diagonally.

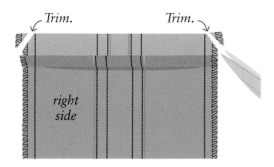

11. Turn the hem right side out. Use a point turner to sharpen corners. Press.

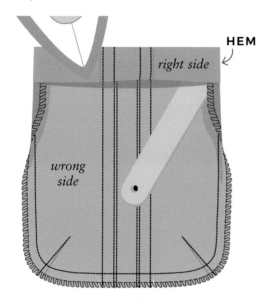

12. Pin and press the side and bottom serged edges under along your stitching line.

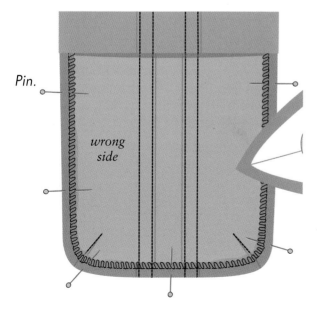

13. Stitch the hem in place.

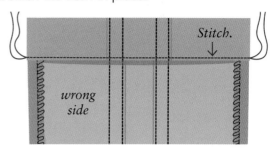

POCKET FLAPS

1. Make the pocket flaps: Place the flap pieces wrong sides together and stick with basting glue or spray or baste together close to edges.

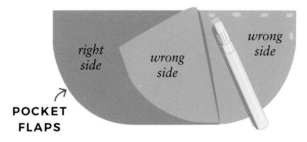

2. To bind the flap curved edge, pin 1¼" bias strip to pocket flap, right sides together.

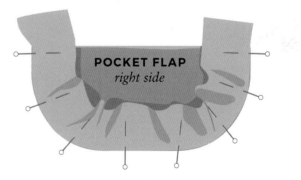

3. Sew bias strip to pocket edge with a 1/4" seam allowance.

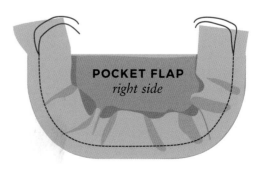

4. Press binding over seam.

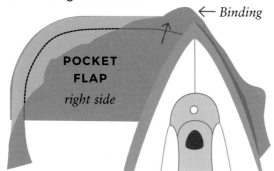

5. Wrap binding over seam allowance toward back side of flap. Press.

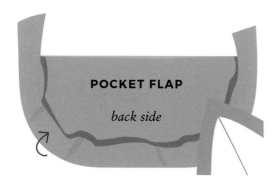

6. On back side of flap, turn raw edge under 1/4" and press. Fold should reach to stitching line or just past.

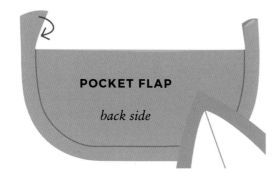

7. Trim excess binding even with flap top.

8. From front side of flap, using **topstitching** thread, stitch binding 1/16"-1/8" from seam. Be sure folded edge of binding is caught in the stitching on the back side.

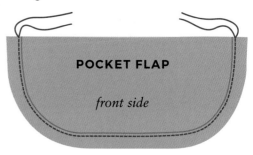

POCKET SNAPS

1. For each pocket snap pull, cut 3½" of 3/4" twill tape.

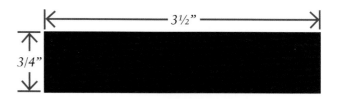

2. Fold ends in to meet in the center. Press.

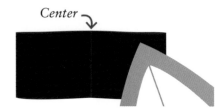

3. Fold flap in half and mark center of curve with a pin.

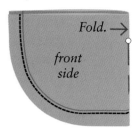

4. Stitch tape to center of pocket flap as shown. Reinforce by stitching again on top of first stitches. Snap pull will extend 1/2" below bottom of flap. The lower edge of stitching can be anywhere on lower flap as long as you catch under layer of tape.

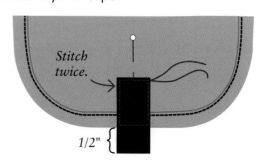

5. Center pocket over side seam. Using **topstitching** thread, edgestitch to pant. Bartack at pocket tops if desired. Test your bartack stitches on a scrap first. Try a 1.8mm width and .8mm length zigzag stitch and adjust from there.

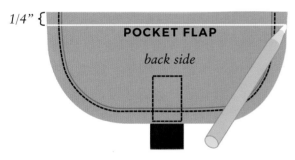

6. Draw a stitching line with chalk 1/4" from flap top on the **back** side.

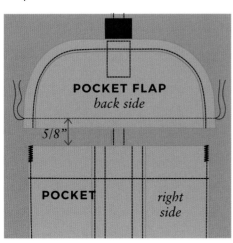

7. Sew flap to pant with stitching line 5/8" from top of pocket.

8. Trim seam allowance to 1/8".

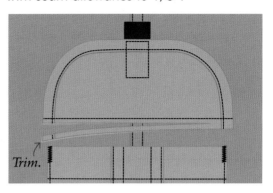

9. Fold flap down over pocket. Topstitch in place 1/4" from seam. Bartack at each end for durability.

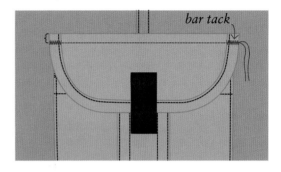

10. Add spring snap closure.

HAZEL SAYS...

Spring snaps have a little slider on the female side to capture the other half securely. The strong twill tab will make it easy and safe to unsnap without tearing the fabric.

Return to the Snap-view construction order on page 191 and complete your jeans. You'll be ready to hit the trail!

FRONT CLOSURES

BUTTON FLY FRONTS

These are the original front closures for jeans because zippers weren't invented when jeans first arrived on the scene. A button fly is actually easier to construct than a zipper fly and I love wearing both styles.

HIDDEN VS. EXPOSED BUTTON FLY

Gosh, the names are pretty darned descriptive!

A hidden button fly looks the same as a zipper fly when fastened and commonly has a 17mm button at the waist, and three, four, or five 14mm buttons fastened to the fly protector. A hidden placket holds the buttonholes.

An exposed button fly usually sports buttons uniform in size. The buttonholes are sewn through the faced front and fasten to the buttons attached to the fly protector. The simplest closure of all. The shorts above are obviously well-loved because they are well-worn!

Several pattern companies have jeans patterns designed for button fly closures. You can use the pieces from any pattern and do the construction as described here. You can also use a jeans pattern with a regular fly front by making a couple of changes.

You can follow the instructions in your pattern, but don't finish the crotch seam until you fit.

Now for the how-tos for both hidden and exposed button fly fronts.

HIDDEN BUTTON FLY

*Hidden buttonhole placket
sewn to left fly facing.*

You can use a jeans pattern with a regular fly by **adding a hidden placket** and sewing it to the fly facing before it gets sewn to the front. Follow the sewing order for jeans in Chapter 7, but when you get to the fly front zipper, follow these instructions instead.

To create the hidden placket cut a piece of fabric the length of the fly facing and almost twice the width with both sides of the bottom rounded. Use my dimensions for all the pieces for now. They will make sense as you go.

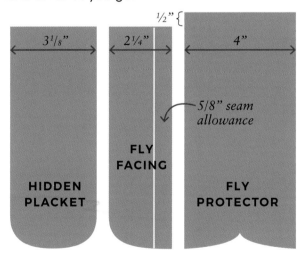

Your fly protector will be 1/2" longer than the other pieces (1/4" for bottom seam + 1/4" to cover the other pieces so the inside is pretty).

There is no seam allowance on the hidden placket because it will be serged to the fly facing, which has a 5/8" seam allowance on the straight edge for sewing it to the left front. The fly protector has a 3/8" seam allowance on the long edge that will be sewn to the right front.

You don't have to remember all of this right now, because seam allowances are specified at each step.

Mark and interface the fly pieces

1. Mark the foldline and the buttonholes on your hidden placket as shown. I use 14mm tack buttons on this fly, so my buttonholes are 3/4" long. Start them 1/4" from the foldline. The lowest buttonhole should be about 2¼" from the bottom edge to leave room for topstitching the crotch later on.

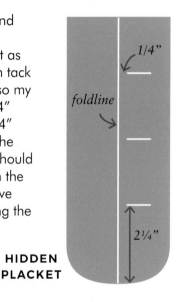

2. Interface all three pieces with PerfectFuse Sheer interfacing. No interfacing is needed on the jeans fronts. (If you cut interfacing a little smaller than your fabric, it won't stick to your ironing board.)

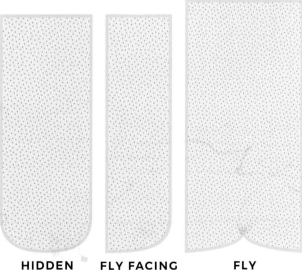

Left Front—The Hidden Placket

Prepare hidden placket.

1. Fold hidden placket on foldline. Press. Sew buttonholes. Cut open.

Fold and press.

2. Place hidden placket on fly facing right sides together, with the folded edge of placket 1/8" from the fly facing seamline. This is very important so that your hidden placket stays hidden on your center front. Pin. Baste the long curved edges together.

Fly facing

Placket on top of fly facing

Baste.

Place placket 1/8" from seamline toward curved edge.

3. Press well after basting.

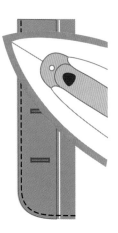

4. Serge finish the long curved edge through all layers.

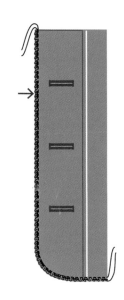

Sew placket/facing to left front.

1. Pin placket/facing to left front, right sides together. Sew with a precise 5/8" seam to avoid catching hidden placket in stitches. You can do it!

HIDDEN PLACKET FACING

LEFT FRONT *right side*

5/8"

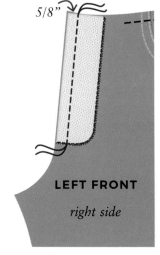

LEFT FRONT *right side*

2. Press seam open.

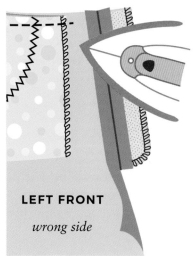

LEFT FRONT *wrong side*

3. Grade seam. Trim facing seam allowance to 1/4". Trim front seam allowance to 1/2" all the way to the inseam. The right front seam allowance will be trimmed in the next section.

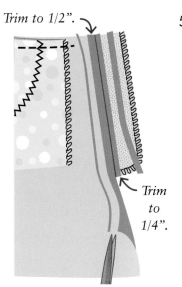

Trim to 1/2".

Trim to 1/4".

5. From the right side, with **topstitching** thread, edgestitch, being careful not to catch the hidden placket in stitches. Sew as far down toward the crotch as your presser foot will allow. When you sew and topstitch the crotch seam later in construction, the stitching will meet and extend over this. Back-stitch. No need to bury threads.

Here's how it looks when you open up the placket.

LEFT FRONT

right side

4. Press placket/facing to wrong side of left front. Notice that the hidden placket sits just inside the center front edge.

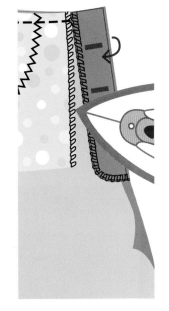

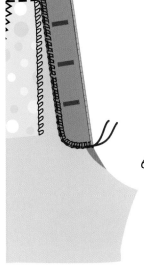

6. From the wrong side baste through hidden placket and left front, close to edge of hidden placket as shown.

7. From the right side, with **topstitching** thread, sew just inside the basting and another row 1/4" from the first. Remove basting.

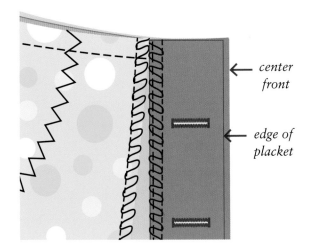

← *center front*

← *edge of placket*

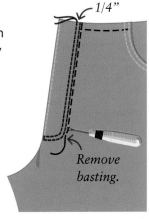

1/4"

Remove basting.

8. From the wrong side, clip crotch seam allowance at bottom of serging to the seamline so it lies flat and makes it easier to sew the crotch seam.

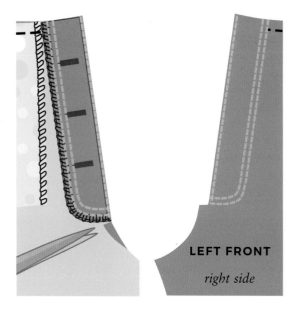

LEFT FRONT
right side

Right Front—Fly Protector

Prepare fly protector.

You will be creating the underlap onto which you will eventually sew your buttons.

Fold fly protector in half right sides together. Sew bottom edge of fly protector with a 1/4" seam allowance. Trim curved edges with pinking shears because they also notch. Turn right side out, press. Leave long edges raw.

Sew fly protector to right front.

1. Baste fly protector to right front, right sides together, with a 3/8" seam allowance creating a 1/4" underlap. The basting holds all the layers together and serves as a guide for serging in the next step.

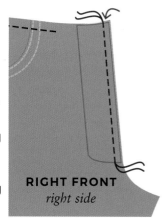

RIGHT FRONT
right side

2. Serge fly protector to right front using basting line as a guide and continuing down crotch seam to inseam. If you accurately follow your basting line, you will remove 1/8" of fabric with the serger knife.

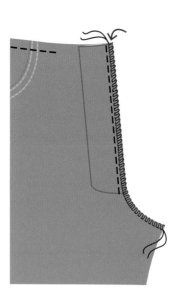

HAZEL SAYS...

Did you know that the grooves or ridges on your serger presser foot line up with the needles? Use the right needle mark on the foot to follow your basting line with accuracy.

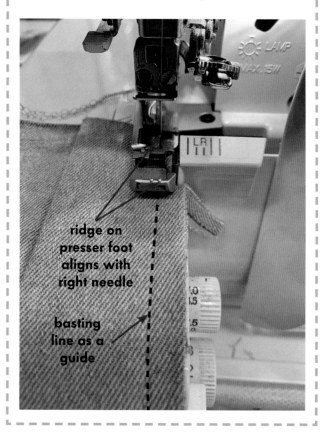

ridge on presser foot aligns with right needle

basting line as a guide

3. From the wrong side, carefully clip 1/4" into seam allowance at bottom of fly protector. This is a tiny snip so your seam will lie flat for the next step. Press seam flat.

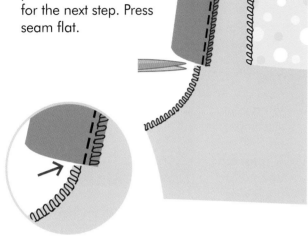

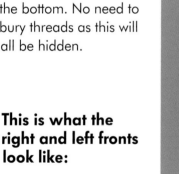

4. From right side, using **topstitching** thread, edgestitch, being sure to catch the serged seam underneath. Backstitch at the bottom. No need to bury threads as this will all be hidden.

This is what the right and left fronts look like:

Sew crotch seam

1. Pin left and right fronts together at crotch seam. Edges should be even. Sew crotch seam from bottom of fly protector to 1½" from inseam. Backstitch at both ends.

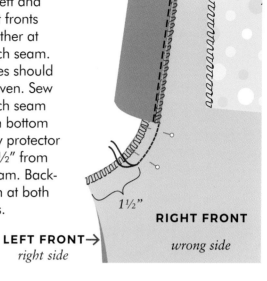

2. Trim 1/8" off the left front crotch seam. When you topstitch the crotch seam you will press it toward the left front, and the serging on the right front will cover it.

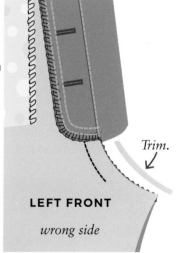

The view from the right side:

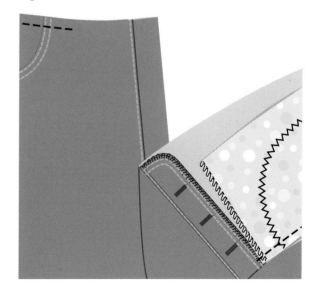

The view from the wrong side:

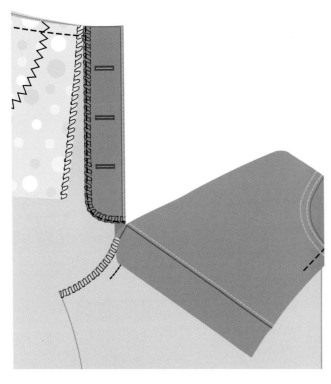

Now complete your jeans following the order in Chapter 7, page 124. When you get to the point where you are sewing and topstitching the crotch, page 134, follow these steps.

1. Carefully lay overlap onto hidden placket, lining up center fronts. The hidden placket will be flush with the center front seam. Make sure all layers are flat. Pin in place.

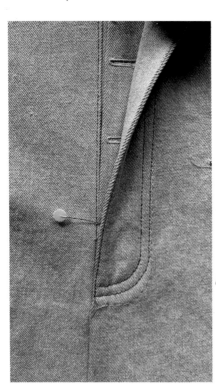

2. Using **topstitching** thread, edgestitch and topstitch the complete crotch seam starting at the back waist. See page 146.

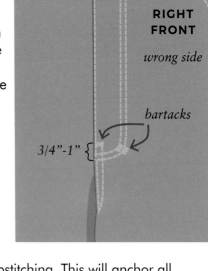

RIGHT FRONT

wrong side

bartacks

3/4"-1"

3. Bring your stitching up 3/4" to 1" past the bottom of the lowest row of fly topstitching. This will anchor all layers together and close up the fly area. Add bartacks now or later.

Buttons

Install your fly buttons to the fly protector when you do your waistband button. Tips for marking and installing tack buttons are on page 157.

EXPOSED BUTTON FLY

It's fun to bling up your jeans a bit with exposed buttons. Buttonholes can pop with contrast thread or disappear into the fly with matching thread. You choose.

Construction order is important here to maximize the fit-as-you-sew results.

Snap-VIEW
CONSTRUCTION ORDER FOR JEANS WITH EXPOSED BUTTON FLY

- [ ] **Before cutting out jeans see step 1, page 204, for fly facing and fly protector mods.**
- [ ] **Cut out jeans, page 112.**
- [ ] **Pattern markings, page 113.**
- [ ] **Front pockets now or after fly, page 128.**
- [ ] **SEW EXPOSED BUTTON FLY through page 207 step 4.**
- [ ] **Baste & fabric fit, page 139.**
- [ ] **Yokes, page 143.**
- [ ] **Back pockets, page 144.**
- [ ] **Inseams, page 144.**
- [ ] **SEW BUTTONHOLES.**
- [ ] **Sew, finish, topstitch crotch seam, page 146.**
- [ ] **BARTACKS IN FLY AREA** can be done anytime now.
- [ ] **Complete jeans from side seams, page 147 to the end.**

Prepare pattern pieces.

You'll need both fronts, a fly facing, and fly protector cut from your fabric in the following dimensions.

Cut your fly facing 2" wide plus a 5/8" seam allowance. The curved edge has no seam allowance. It will be serged.

Cut your fly protector 4" wide and 1/2" longer than your fly facing (1/4" for bottom seam + 1/4" to extend just past fly extension bottom to cover it so the insides are pretty).

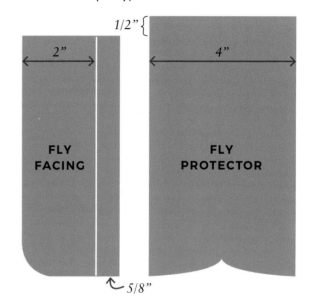

Seam allowances at each step are specified.

On fronts, snip-mark center fronts.

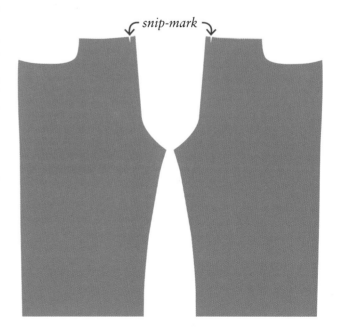

snip-mark

203

Prepare the fly facing and protector.

1. Interface both pieces with PerfectFuse Sheer interfacing. No interfacing is needed on the front pieces.

2. Fold fly protector in half right sides together. Sew bottom edge with a 1/4" seam allowance. Trim curved edges with pinking shears because they also notch. Turn right side out, press. Leave long edges raw.

3. Serge finish curved side of fly facing.

Sew fly facing to left front.

1. Sew fly facing to LEFT front, right sides together with a 5/8" seam allowance. Sew all the way to the bottom of the serging.

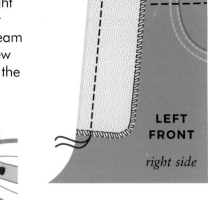

2. Press seam open.

3. Grade seam. Trim facing seam allowance to 1/4". Trim front seam allowance to 1/2" all the way to the inseam. The right front seam allowance will be trimmed in the next section.

4. Press fly facing to wrong side of left front.

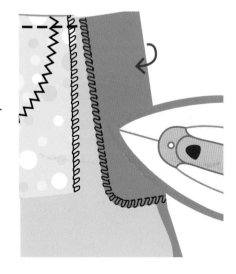

5. From the right side, edgestitch the overlap edge with **topstitching** thread, stopping at the bottom of the fly facing, leaving long thread tail at the bottom. Pull thread to wrong side, tie a square knot. Clip threads close to knot. This whole area is covered up. No need to bury threads.

2. With a 3-thread stitch, serge fly protector to right front using basting line as a guide and continuing down crotch seam to inseam. If you accurately follow your basting line, you will remove 1/8" of fabric with the serger knife. See page 134-136 for serger tips for this area.

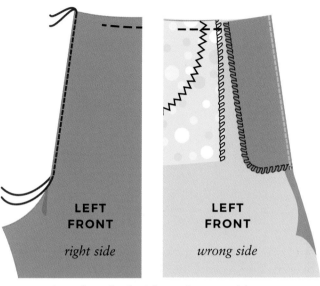

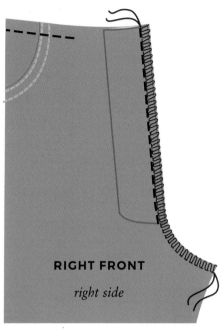

views from both right and wrong sides

Sew fly protector to right front.

You will be creating the underlap as you sew this part.

1. Baste fly protector (prepared earlier) to right front, right sides together, with a 3/8" seam allowance creating a 1/4"-wide underlap. The basting holds all the layers together and serves as a guide for serging in the next step.

3. From the wrong side, carefully clip 1/4" into seam allowance at bottom of fly protector. This is a tiny snip so your seam will lie flat for the next step. Press seam flat.

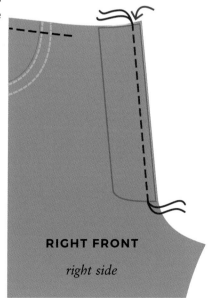

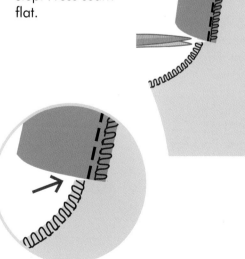

4. From right side, using **topstitching** thread, edge-stitch, being sure to catch the serged seam underneath. Backstitch at the bottom. No need to bury threads as this will all be hidden.

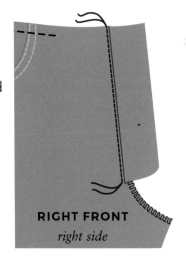

RIGHT FRONT
right side

Finish the crotch.

First, complete your jeans following the order in Chapter 7, page 139. When you get to the point where you are sewing and topstitching the crotch, page 146, follow these steps. So far your fronts look like this from the wrong sides:

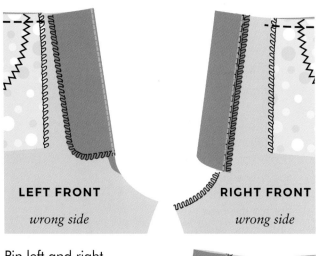

LEFT FRONT
wrong side

RIGHT FRONT
wrong side

Pin left and right fronts together at crotch seam. Edges should be even. Sew crotch seam from bottom of fly protector to 1½" from inseam. Backstitch at both ends.

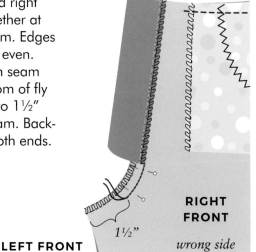

1½"

LEFT FRONT
right side →

RIGHT FRONT
wrong side

The crotch topstitching will close up the bottom securely. This is how it looks now.

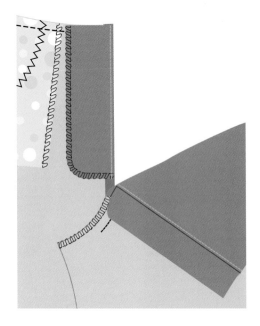

From the right side, make sure your left front (the overlap side) covers the 1/4" underlap and comes to the center front.

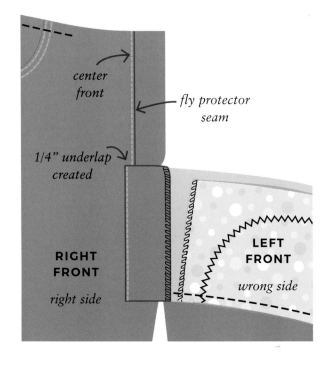

center front

fly protector seam

1/4" underlap created

RIGHT FRONT
right side

LEFT FRONT
wrong side

Topstitching fly front.

1. From the wrong side baste through fly facing and left front, close to long, curved edge as shown.

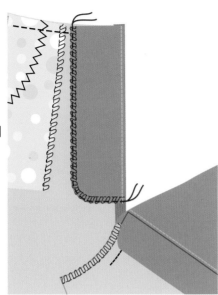

3. Fold right front down so you don't topstitch through the fly protector. Using **topstitching** thread, sew one row of topstitching inside the basting line. If you sew a second row it needs to be at least 1/8" from the buttonhole. You can use one of my topstitching templates on page 232 or make up your own. This topstitching will anchor the fly facing to the left front.

4. Remove basting.

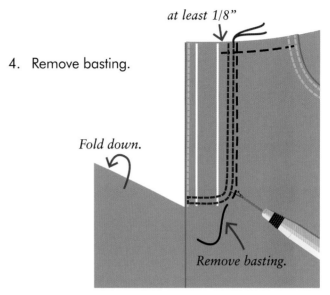

2. To topstitch outside of the future buttonholes, you need to know their width and placement. Draw two lines with chalk as shown—one 1/4" to 3/8" from the center front edge and another 7/8" from the first. This will accommodate a 17mm tack button.

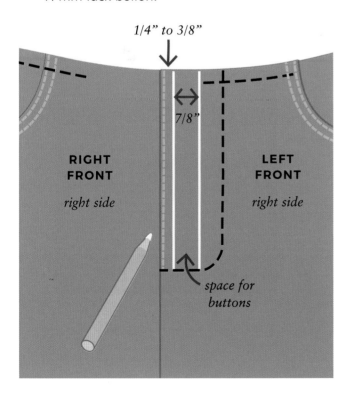

BUTTONHOLES (DON'T DO THEM NOW!)

You are finished with the fly for now. Buttonholes will be sewn after fabric fitting, when you are sure about waist level. This way you'll know the proper spacing.

Do them before you sew, serge, and topstitch the crotch so access to the area is easy. After attaching waistband sew the waistband buttonhole.

Refer to the Snap-View at the beginning of this section for easy sewing order.

BUTTONS

Install your fly buttons when you do your waistband button.

1. Place jeans on a pinnable surface like your ironing board. Close fly, lining up top of waistband and waistband seam and making sure fly is straight. Place straight pins through buttonholes and into press board about 1/4" from the center front edges (this allows for the width of the button shank).

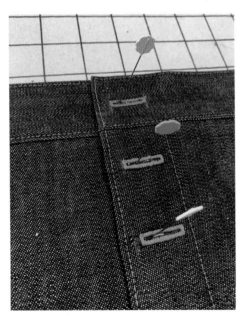

2. Lift fly and mark pins with a chalk pencil.

3. Install your buttons onto the fly protector. See Chapter 3, page 19 and Chapter 7, page 157 for button tips.

208

SEWING REALITY

Sometimes you mess up. It's disheartening to make mistakes in visible places. Find comfort in knowing that not only does everyone slip up but that most things can be fixed. And with jeans, a little rugged repair can add character.

Case in point: The spacing on these buttonholes was wonky and I didn't like them. Too bad I didn't notice until after I cut them open.

I decided to see if I could hide a cut buttonhole and sew a new one close by.

BEFORE   **AFTER**

too low

The smeary pink chalk at the bottom of the fly is a whole other subject. Uh, test your markers on scrap fabric. Yeah, yeah, do it. I really hope this comes out!

I pulled out the stitches and pressed two layers of fusible web under the opening between the layers of the fly. Then I used a darning stitch on my machine to mend the cut. You could use a zigzag stitch too. Key to success here is matching thread to your fabric.

I sewed a new buttonhole 1/4" higher than the first one. Wouldn't want it on the front of my interview suit, but hey, it worked here! And the button will cover most of this.

MOCK FLY FRONT

This is a great modification if you love the ease and comfort of a pull-on style. You can use this technique on any pant that you can get up over your hips without a front opening. It usually requires an elastic waistband. In a stretch denim this can look smooth like a regular waistband with zipper front. We'll cover the mock fly here and the elastic waistband on page 213.

I got to sew a pair of jeans for THE Pati Palmer! What an honor. I was so tickled to make these jeans. Pati wanted a pair of jeans similar to a pair of cropped pull-on RTW jeans she likes. She wanted them to be super-stretchy and full-length instead of cropped.

PREPARE YOUR PATTERN

To strengthen the center front and prevent a seam allowance from showing through, your pattern should have a fold-over fly facing. If your pattern has the sewn-on style, simply overlap the center fronts on the seamlines and cut both sides with the fly facing. You can use the facing that comes with your pattern. Make sure it measures 1¾" from the center front.

Place fly facing over front, aligning center front seams and crotch seam stop mark. Pin in place. Cut both fronts with the fly facing.

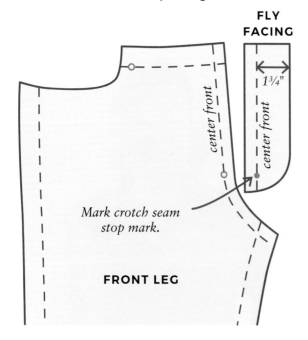

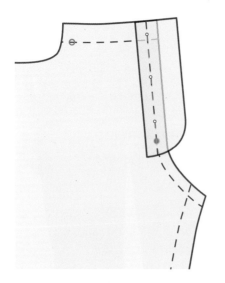

SEWING A MOCK FLY

1. Mark the crotch seam stop mark with chalk on the right and wrong sides of both fronts. Draw a chalk stitching line on the center front of both right and left side fronts.

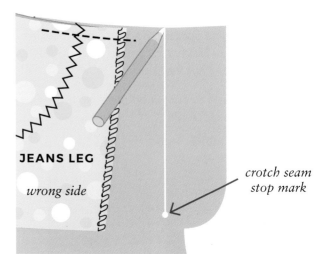

2. Serge finish the raw edge of the **right** side only. Serge with the right side facing up so the prettier upper looper threads show.

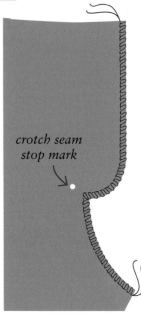

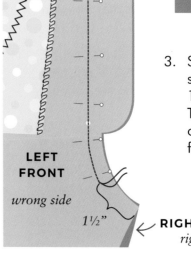

3. Sew center front seam from waist to 1½" from inseam. This last 1½" is left open to make fabric fitting easier.

4. Press the seam open, stopping when you reach the crotch curve.

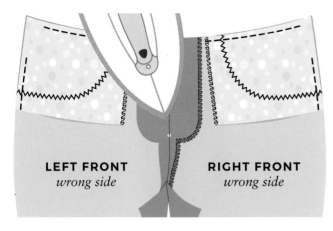

LEFT FRONT *wrong side*   **RIGHT FRONT** *wrong side*

5. Press both fly facings toward the **left** front. Your serged stitches on the **right** front will be facing up.

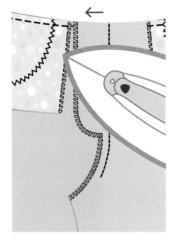

6. Trim the left fly facing so the raw edge will be enclosed with the fly topstitching. Flip the fly facing toward the right front side and trim raw edge of left facing 1/8", continuing down two-thirds of crotch curve. Fold facing to left front.

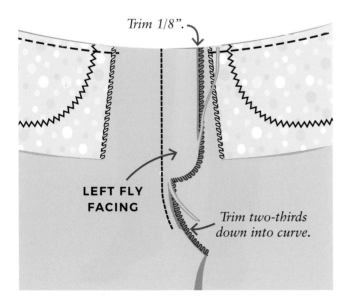

Trim 1/8".

LEFT FLY FACING

Trim two-thirds down into curve.

7. From the right side, to prevent slippage while topstitching, pin the facing to the left front as shown.

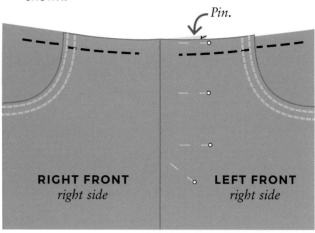

Pin.

RIGHT FRONT *right side*   **LEFT FRONT** *right side*

8. Using **topstitching** thread, edgestitch 1/16" toward the facing side of the center front seam (left front on this sample) from the waist to the crotch seam stop mark. Pull threads to wrong side, tie a knot, and bury threads.

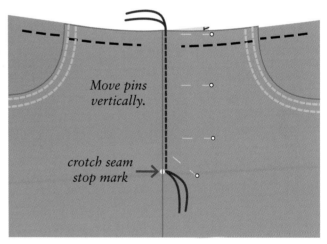

Move pins vertically.

crotch seam stop mark

9. On the right side, place two strips of 1/2" Scotch Magic tape as a topstitching guide.

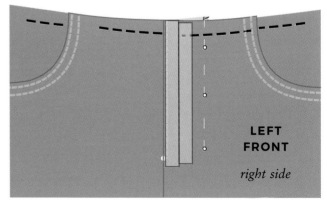

LEFT FRONT *right side*

10. Draw a curve on your tape.

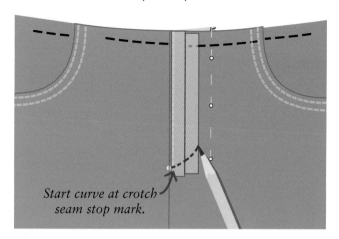

Start curve at crotch seam seam stop mark.

Carry on with sewing your jeans! Basting yokes, inseams and side seams for fabric fitting is next! Go back to page 139 to continue.

Here's Pati looking awesome in her jeans!

11. Using a regular foot and **topstitching** thread, topstitch front to fly facings with two rows 1/4" apart. Start at the top along the edge of the tape and stitch to the center front. With the needle down, pivot and stitch for 1/4", pivot again and stitch up to top.

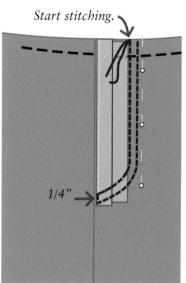

Start stitching.

1/4"

12. Here's how it looks from the back.

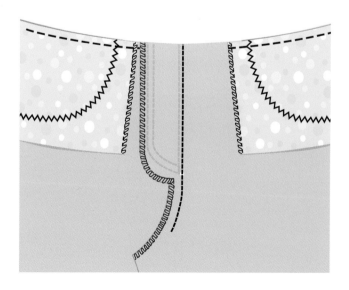

WAISTBANDS

ELASTIC WAISTBAND

This waistband technique pairs perfectly with a pull-on jean (mock fly or plain front) and is oh, so comfy. This is the method I used for Pati's jeans. If you fit your waist snugly to your body, making sure the jeans will pull down past your hips, you should not see a lot of gathers before sewing on the waistband—just a small amount that will gently stretch to fit the body. Here is what the jeans look like off the body.

If you want to add an elastic waistband in a zippered jean, see page 110 in the Palmer/Pletsch *Pants for Real People* book for Marta Alto's genius method. Love!

YOUR ELASTIC

Use a quality elastic. I like 1½" wide for maximum comfort, but you can use 1" too. Be sure it's not too stiff. I'm a big fan of Pamela's Fantastic Elastic, see Resources page 235.

PREPARE THE WAISTBAND AND PIN TO JEANS

1. Cut the length of the waistband to fit the circumference of the top of the jeans plus 1" for two seam allowances. Cut the width twice as wide as your elastic plus two seam allowances. For 1½" elastic the waistband will be 4¼" wide. Do not interface the waistband when using elastic.

HAZEL SAYS...

Using a rotary cutter and ruler makes waistband cutting super easy and accurate. Purrrfect.

2. Serge finish one long edge.

WAISTBAND
right side

Serge.

3. Pin waistband to waist, right sides together, lapping ends at center back. Snip waistband ends where they cross the center back seam at the top and bottom edges.

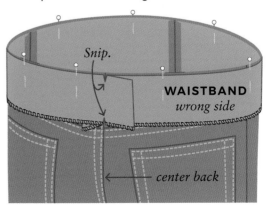

Snip.

WAISTBAND
wrong side

center back

4. Unpin waistband from jeans just enough to sew center back seam. Match snips and sew center back seam, right sides together. Trim seam to 1/4" and press open.

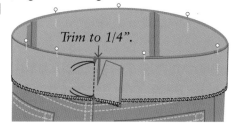

Trim to 1/4".

SEW WAISTBAND TO JEANS

Re-pin the center back to waist. Sew waistband to jeans right sides together, with a 5/8" seam allowance.

Trim waist seam allowance to 3/8". Leave waistband seam allowance 5/8".

ADD ELASTIC

Cut a piece of elastic the same length as the waistband plus 4". You will sew your casing OVER the elastic, eliminating slack in the casing. This makes topstitching easier and gives it a more RTW look.

1. Pin one end of elastic on waistband seam allowance at center back with lower edge on seamline.

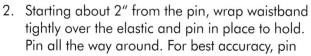

2. Starting about 2" from the pin, wrap waistband tightly over the elastic and pin in place to hold. Pin all the way around. For best accuracy, pin on the right side in the well of the seam with pins pointing toward the center back.

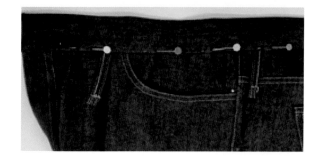

3. From the right side, stitch in the well of the seam, catching the underside of the waistband. Start and stop 2" from each side of the center back.

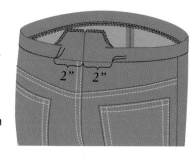

4. Try on jeans. Pull on elastic to tighten it until comfortable. Pin elastic with a safety pin to mark seam overlap. Take off jeans.

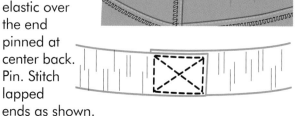

5. Lap 1" of elastic over the end pinned at center back. Pin. Stitch lapped ends as shown.

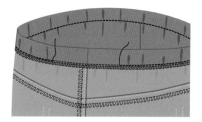

6. Wrap band over center back and finish stitching casing without catching elastic in stitching.

EDGESTITCH TO FINISH

Edgestitching is optional! Before you edgestitch, spend a minute smoothing out your elastic and spreading out any gathers as evenly as possible.

Using **topstitching** thread and starting just before the side seam on right back, edgestitch through all layers of waistband and elastic, gently stretching flat as you go. When stitching lines meet, keep threads long, pull through to back, tie a square knot and bury threads. Now edge-stitch the waistband top edge, through both denim and elastic, stretching elastic as necessary to lie flat.

HEMS + THE BOTTOM LINE

TO HEM OR NOT TO HEM?

A basic jeans hem is described in detail on pages 154 and 155. I'll show you a few other fun ways to finish off the hems of your jeans.

RAW EDGE

There are plenty of raw edges at the hemline in ready-to-wear. If you choose to let your hems fray a bit, run a line of tiny zigzag stitches around at the level you want the fray to stop. Consider your thread color and the potential fading of your jeans. Polyester thread will retain its color longer than the cotton fabric.

You can also hem your jeans and leave the stitching in through a few washings, then remove it to get this look.

FRINGED RAW EDGE

Denim usually has a blue warp yarn or thread and a white weft yarn. If your jeans are cut out on the lenthwise grain, the bottom fringe will be blue.

I cut the black jeans pictured here on the crosswise grain so that I could have contrasting fringe.

Create the fringe by pulling out the crosswise threads at the bottom of your jeans, one or two at a time, working in a circle all the way around. You'll need to work at getting the threads loose at the

Typically the weft threads are undyed and the warp are dyed.

seams, so go slowly. When you've got the amount of fringe you want you can trim and reshape the bottom edge or you can just leave it funky.

For the little notch at the center of the fringe, I made 3/8" clips into the denim above the fringe line and then pulled the crosswise threads out to the end of the clips. It made these little fringy bangs. Play around. Remember to break the rules…

Sew a line of tiny zigzag stitches around at the top of the fringe to stop more fraying. I did no stitching here and may regret it, but I didn't want the thread to show.

Your finished pattern pieces will look like this:

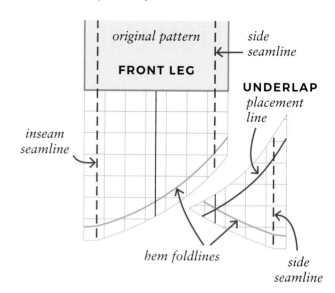

TULIP HEM

The tulip hem adds a little fun to your jeans hemline. You'll need to plan ahead for this finish because your pattern front is redesigned at the hem before you cut out your fabric and the sewing is done with the side seam and inseam sewing.

You must also know the finished length before you begin. It's a great technique to use on jeans that you have already fit and sewn with confidence. If you're the renegade sewing type, you could fit, adjust the length of your jeans, and then recut the bottom of the front to make the tulip hem.

I suggest that you read through the instructions to the end so you'll know what's coming!

CREATING THE TULIP SHAPE ON YOUR PATTERN

All seam allowances on our sample are 5/8". The raw edges are serge finished to reduce the bulk caused by a traditional hem. You can change the measurements to whatever works best for your pattern and your sewing preferences.

Be sure you know the finished length of your jeans before you make the tulip hem pattern! You'll need the front leg pattern piece and pattern paper to create the new leg bottom. We've used Perfect Pattern Paper in our sample.

1. Measure 7" up from the bottom of the front leg and draw a horizontal line. Trace the bottom 7" of your front leg onto your PPP. Make two copies and cut them out. One will be attached to your front leg and one will become the tulip underlap. Where you've drawn your line 7" from the bottom, you will fold the pattern back and attach the new bottom later.

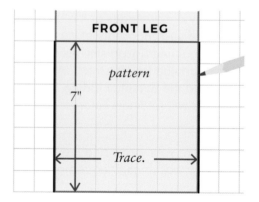

2. Mark the centers of each piece. Label them "front leg" and "underlap."

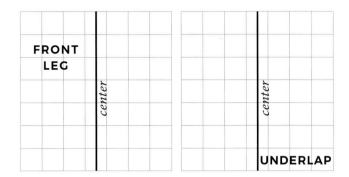

3. On the front leg, draw a curve from the bottom of the inseam seamline to the side seam edge 4" from the bottom. Trim on your line and discard bottom piece.

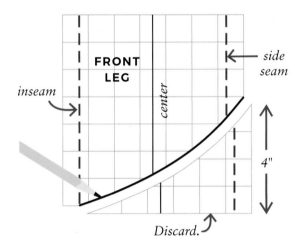

4. Place front leg on top of the underlap, matching center lines. Trace the bottom curve of front leg onto the underlap.

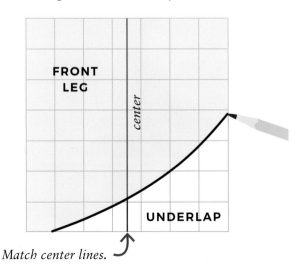

Match center lines.

5. Flip front leg over, center on underlap and trace the bottom curve again. Your lines will intersect at the center.

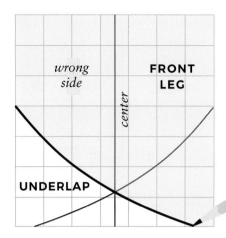

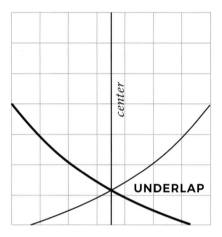

6. The underlap will need a 5/8" seam allowance at the top edge for lapping and 5/8" at the bottom for a hem. To accommodate, draw a curved line 1¼" from the first curved line. The pink lines become the cutting line for the underlap pattern piece.

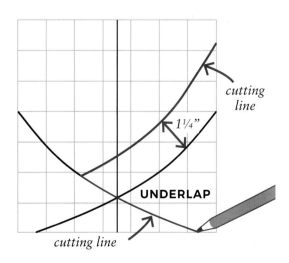

cutting line

217

7. Cut on the pink lines as shown. The triangular piece becomes your underlap. Discard the larger piece.

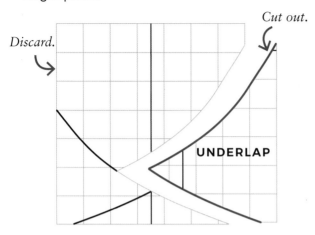

8. Tape the new front leg to the bottom of your orginal pattern front leg. Be sure that you tape at the line that is 7" from the bottom, so your jeans are the length you intended. You may want to label your foldlines and seamlines for clarity while sewing. All seam allowances and hems are 5/8".

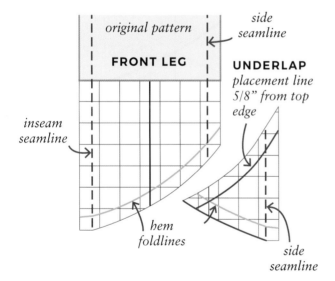

After cutting, your leg pieces look like this:

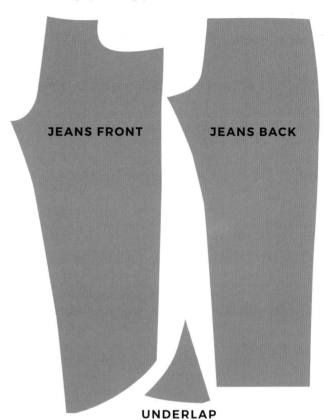

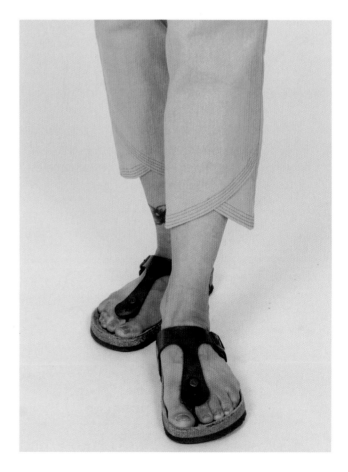

Here is your construction order at a glance. You must sew in this order to have a final hem topstitched "in the round" resulting in the prettiest finish.

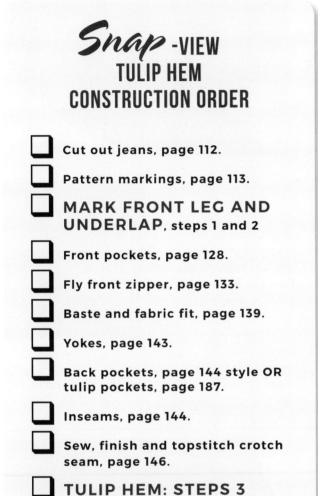

Snap-VIEW
TULIP HEM
CONSTRUCTION ORDER

- [ ] **Cut out jeans, page 112.**
- [ ] **Pattern markings, page 113.**
- [ ] **MARK FRONT LEG AND UNDERLAP, steps 1 and 2**
- [ ] **Front pockets, page 128.**
- [ ] **Fly front zipper, page 133.**
- [ ] **Baste and fabric fit, page 139.**
- [ ] **Yokes, page 143.**
- [ ] **Back pockets, page 144 style OR tulip pockets, page 187.**
- [ ] **Inseams, page 144.**
- [ ] **Sew, finish and topstitch crotch seam, page 146.**
- [ ] **TULIP HEM: STEPS 3 THROUGH 13**
- [ ] **Complete jeans from "side seams," page 147.**

1. **Marking your front leg:** Fold your front pattern piece in half lengthwise. With jeans front legs wrong sides together, place folded pattern piece on fabric as shown and mark the center on the fabric with chalk.

2. **Marking the underlap:** On the **right** side of underlap, mark a 5/8" underlap placement line with chalk. This will ensure a perfect overlap of the front piece later.

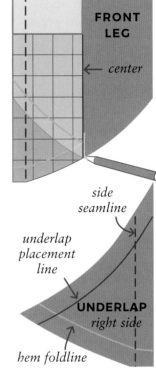

IMPORTANT: Sew your jeans through the crotch seam step on your at-a-glance order in this section. Your jeans will look like this:

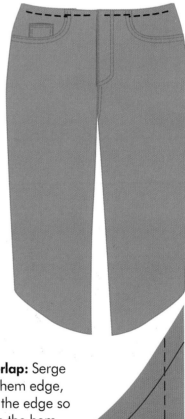

3. **Prepare the underlap:** Serge finish the curved hem edge, barely skimming the edge so you won't shorten the hem.

Serge.

4. Fold hem edge up 5/8" to wrong side. Press.

5. To make the tulip peak tidy on the inside, serge finish the underlap seamline edge, catching the hem in the folded position. Bury the serger chain tail under the stitches on the **right** side of underlap.

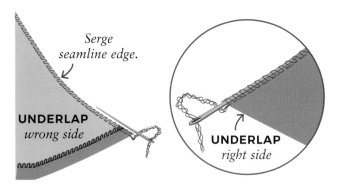

Serge seamline edge.

UNDERLAP *wrong side*

UNDERLAP *right side*

This is how the underlap will look when completed, showing the placement of this corner.

COMPLETED UNDERLAP *wrong side*

6. Fold underlap hem open. Place underlap on back, right sides together, lining up bottom edges and sides. Stitch from the bottom for 2½" and stop. Press seam open and then toward the **back**.

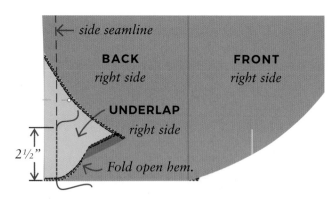

← *side seamline*

BACK *right side*

FRONT *right side*

UNDERLAP *right side*

2½"

← *Fold open hem.*

7. Serge finish seam, serging off at the top of stitching as shown. The rest of the side seam will be completed later.

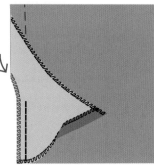

8. Serge finish remaining bottom edge of hem, carefully sewing over some of the stitches on underlap. Bury chain tail through stitches on the wrong side.

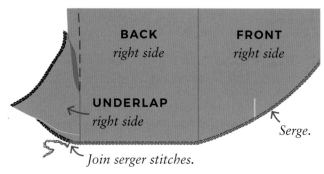

BACK *right side*

FRONT *right side*

UNDERLAP *right side*

Serge.

Join serger stitches.

9. Turn hem up 5/8" to wrong side, joining underlap hem. Press.

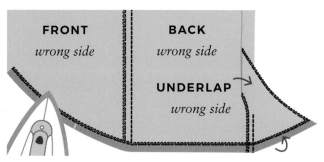

FRONT *wrong side*

BACK *wrong side*

UNDERLAP *wrong side*

10. This hem will have four rows of topstitching, starting 1/16″ from the fold. Sew three rows 1/16″ apart. Wait to sew the last row, which catches the serger hem edge, until you pin the overlap to the underlap.

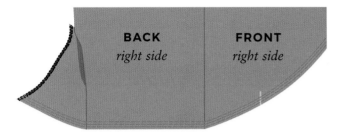

11. **Attach front to underlap with your final row of topstitching.** Working from the right side, line up the center front lines and barely cover the placement line as shown. Pin.

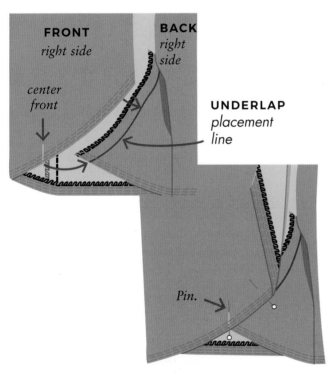

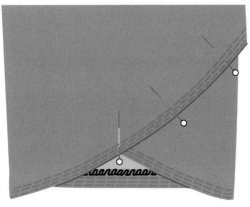

12. Begin topstitching at side seam 1/16″ from previous row, stitching through **front and underlap only**. *You will need to keep the back leg out of the way so you don't stitch through it.* Stitch in a circle passing center front, and continuing around the back returning to the center front. Lift front edge. Sew a couple of stitches underneath the front edge. Leave long thread tails when you remove from the machine.

START	FINISH

13. Pull threads through to the wrong side. Tie off and bury thread ends.

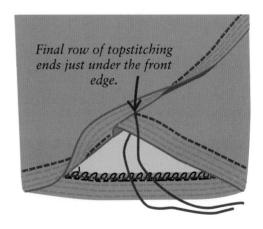

Final row of topstitching ends just under the front edge.

14. Pin side seams together. Start stitching at the bottom, overlapping side seam stitches on inset. Hold the layers taut as you sew to the top. If you get slippage, you will see a bubble in the top layer before each pin. Remove stitches, re-pin, and hold the layers more tautly as you stitch. Or use a walking foot. Press open, then to the back.

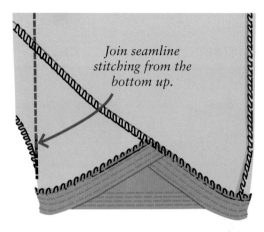

Join seamline stitching from the bottom up.

15. Serge finish the side seam allowance, carefully joining serger stitches near bottom.

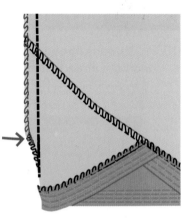

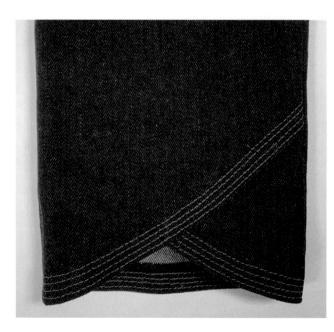

Ooo-la-la! Your finished tulip hem! Great work! Now continue your jeans construction, moving on to the belt loops and waistband.

tightly and yet they were oh so comfy! Without the zipper at the ankle it would have been impossible to get them on over my foot. If they were to be worn for a night out, they were put on fresh from the dryer to maximize the snug fit. They stretched out significantly in the seat and knees and had to be washed after each wearing. I loved the feel and fit of these jeans so much that I wore them until the knees turned white and the seat turned to dust. Here is my ankle zip tutorial and tribute to this special garment.

The ankle zippers in vintage '80s jeans were centered and hidden in the seam. I think if you're going to go to the effort of adding a zipper, then you ought to be able to see it!

This zipper is positioned just to the front of the side seam. It's much easier to sew the zipper while the seam is flat, so you'll sew the zipper and part of the side seam before you sew your inseams. Keep the rest of the side seam at least two-thirds unsewn until after the crotch is completely finished and topstitched.

ANKLE ZIPPERS

EXPOSED ANKLE ZIPPER

In the mid-1980s I bought a pair of Guess jeans at a San Diego mall. They were an investment for a college student, $79, but I just had to have them, and I remember their details vividly. They were waist-high with tapered legs and 6" zippers in the side seams at the ankle. The denim was a hefty indigo and white narrow herringbone stripe. The indigo bled into the white making the stripe very subtle after several washings. The denim was non-stretch aside from a slight mechanical crosswise stretch of the twill. We wore these jeans

Here is your at-a-glance sewing order.

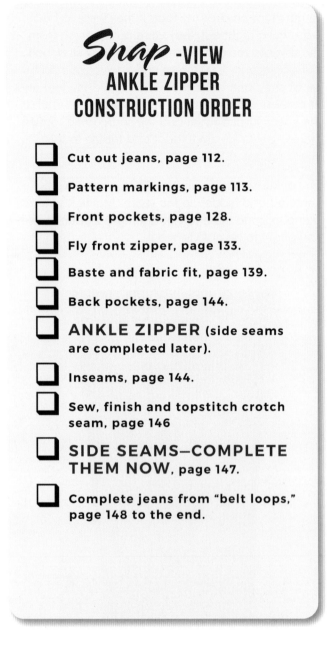

Snap-VIEW ANKLE ZIPPER CONSTRUCTION ORDER

- ☐ Cut out jeans, page 112.
- ☐ Pattern markings, page 113.
- ☐ Front pockets, page 128.
- ☐ Fly front zipper, page 133.
- ☐ Baste and fabric fit, page 139.
- ☐ Back pockets, page 144.
- ☐ ANKLE ZIPPER (side seams are completed later).
- ☐ Inseams, page 144.
- ☐ Sew, finish and topstitch crotch seam, page 146
- ☐ SIDE SEAMS—COMPLETE THEM NOW, page 147.
- ☐ Complete jeans from "belt loops," page 148 to the end.

This sample uses a 6" metal zipper. You can get many lengths and colors with a quick online search. If desired, shorten your zipper from the bottom for this technique. See Resources page 235.

1. **Markings:** Draw the following lines clearly on the wrong side of your front and back legs.

   - **Side seams:** Draw the bottom 12" of your side seam stitching lines. Our example is a 5/8" seam.

   - **Hem foldlines:** 1" from bottoms.

   - **Side seam stop mark:** Measure your zipper from bottom stop to top stop and add 1". Measure this distance from the bottom and make a mark. Our sample is 7".

   - **Zipper stitching box:** 3/8" wide and 7" long in our example. (Measure your zipper and add 1" for box length.)

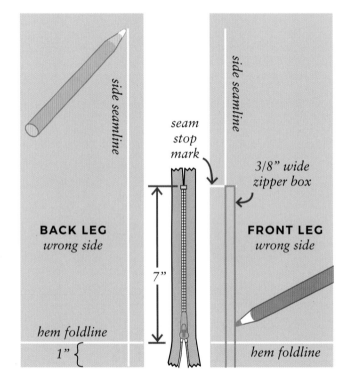

2. Fuse a 1" x 2" piece of PerfectFuse Sheer interfacing over the top of stitching box to stabilize. Redraw stitching lines if you can't see them clearly through interfacing.

3. On the front leg, using a 1.5mm stitch length, sew the top and long side of your stitching box. The other side of your box will be formed by the folded edge of back leg seam allowance.

Stitch.

FRONT LEG
wrong side

4. Sew side seams, right sides together. Starting at seam stop mark, backstitch, and sew upward for 4". Remember, we are leaving the rest of the side seam open to make finishing your jeans easier later.

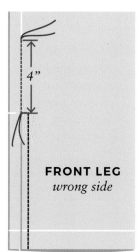

4"

FRONT LEG
wrong side

5. Press seam open, including unstitched seam allowances to bottom of hem.

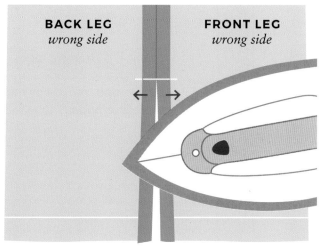

BACK LEG
wrong side

FRONT LEG
wrong side

6. Make a diagonal clip in the front leg seam allowance ending at the stop stitching mark.

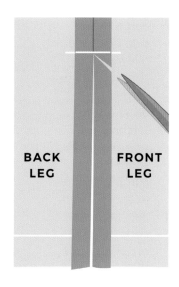

BACK LEG   **FRONT LEG**

7. Trim away front leg seam allowance from bottom to clip as shown.

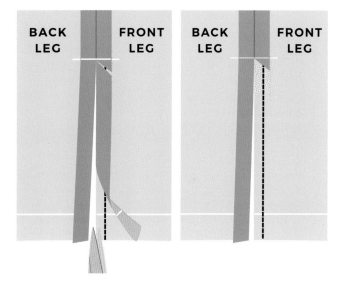

BACK LEG   **FRONT LEG**   **BACK LEG**   **FRONT LEG**

8. Press seam allowance above clip toward back.

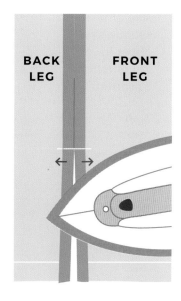

BACK LEG   **FRONT LEG**

225

9. Serge finish side back seam allowance as shown. We have serged off the edge above stitching on side seam. This seam will be completed later in construction. See snap-view construction order on page 223.

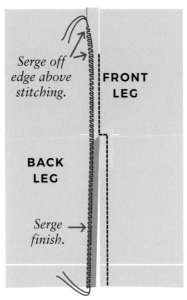

Serge off edge above stitching.

FRONT LEG

BACK LEG

Serge finish.

10. To open stitching box, slash through front leg only to corner as shown.

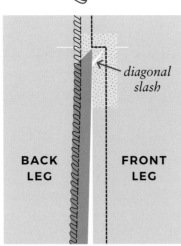

diagonal slash

BACK LEG

FRONT LEG

11. Press top and side of box seam allowances toward top and front as shown.

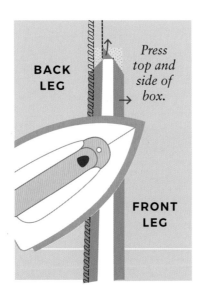

BACK LEG

Press top and side of box.

FRONT LEG

12. Serge finish the long raw edge.

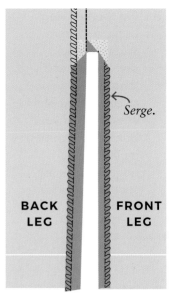

Serge.

BACK LEG

FRONT LEG

13. Here is your completed zipper box shown from the right side.

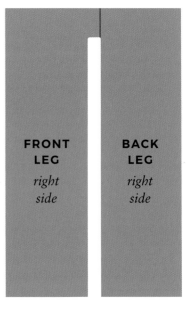

FRONT LEG
right side

BACK LEG
right side

14. Apply 1/8" basting tape very close to the edge of zipper tape. Peel away the protective paper.

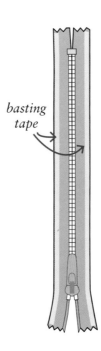

basting tape

15. From right side, center zipper in box, having bottom stop flush with top edge of box. The top stops should be just above your hem foldline.

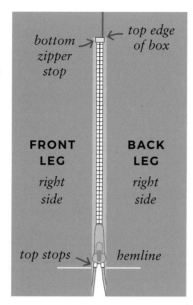

16. Using a zipper foot and **topstitching** thread, edge-stitch around box.

Now resume construction of your jeans beginning with the inseams through the hem. See Snap-view construction order on page 224.

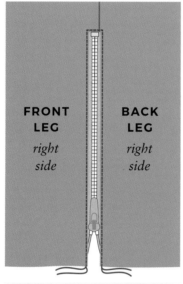

You will make a 1" hem so that the teeth of your zipper will just clear the fold, as shown. Press the bottom up 1", turn under the raw edge 3/8"-1/2" and stitch.

You can go on and finish your jeans now, or make your bartacks now, over the hemline on both sides of zipper and on topstitching at top of box.

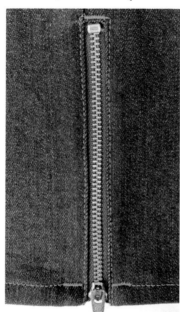

SIDE SLIT AT ANKLE

You'll want to plan for this slit before you sew your side seams. Here is your Snap-View Order for the easiest way to incorporate this technique.

Snap-VIEW SIDE SLIT CONSTRUCTION ORDER

- [ ] **Cut out jeans, page 112.**
- [ ] **Pattern markings, page 113.**
- [ ] **Fit and sew jeans from pages 125-146.**
- [ ] **Baste side seams.**
- [ ] **TRY ON JEANS AND MARK HEM, ALLOWING FOR A 1¼" HEM. INCORPORATE SIDE SLIT AND HEM INTO SIDE SEAM.**
- [ ] **Complete jeans from "belt loops," page 148 to the end.**

1. Mark the depth of your slit on the edge of the outseam with chalk. On this sample I allowed a 1¼" hem + 3/8" to turn under. The slit opening itself is 5⅜". I made my chalk mark 7" from the bottom edge, but you can make the slit any length.

2. Sew side seam, stopping at your mark. Backstitch.

3. Make a diagonal clip from outer edge of side seam to end of stitching on the FRONT only. A clip on the bias won't fray.

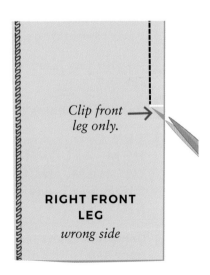

4. Press seam above clip to BACK. Press slit edges below stitching even with seam allowance. Here it is 5/8".

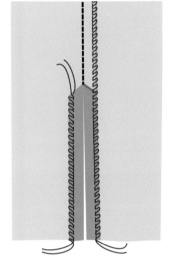

5. Serge finish slit seam allowance on back, continuing above clip to serge seam allowances together. Serge finish the other side of slit.

6. Bury serger tail under the serged edge on the wrong side.

7. Press bottom edge under 3/8" to the wrong side of the fabric.

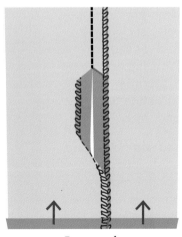

Press under.

8. Turn up 1¼" to right side and stitch seam. Cut corners diagonally to reduce bulk.

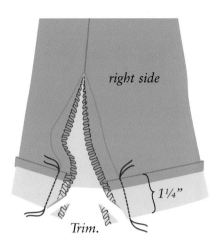

right side

1¼"

Trim.

9. Turn to right side and press.

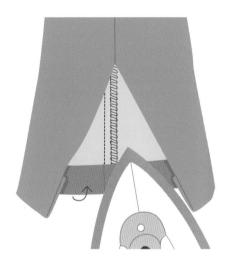

10. Trim away inseam seam allowance at an angle from fold to raw edge to reduce bulk.

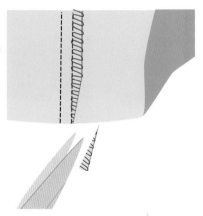

11. Using **topstitching** thread, topstitch 1" from lower edge, beginning just before the inseam, pivoting at corners and stitch 3/8" from opening edges, squaring stitches above slit. Stitch until you meet your starting point. Leave threads long. Pull top threads to wrong side, tie a square knot, and bury the threads.

THAT'S ALL FOR NOW

I have oh so many more ideas for design modifications floating around my imagination, but this chapter must come to an end. I hope that something here has inspired you to take your sewing beyond the pattern and into the realm of your own creativity. Wear your art.

CHAPTER 9

CARE & FEEDING OF JEANS

LAUNDERING

Wash your jeans. Yes! Wash them with cold water and mild detergent. For longest life, hang them to dry. Any stiffness disappears after a few minutes of wearing.

Not washing denim goes in and out of vogue in certain circles, but whether it's in style or not, it's disgusting. There. I said it. Moreover, freezing your jeans so the bacteria dies does not remove the oils left from your skin or any other dirt that happens with wearing. That grime actually breaks down the cotton fibers of your denim and, without laundering, shortens its life. Once again, wash your jeans!

It may also interest you to know that professional denim menders generally won't accept dirty garments for repairs because, yuck. For more on laundering denim, see page 109.

At right, raw materials donated by my dear friend, fellow guitarist, and Dye, Hippie, Dye bandmate, Steve. His uniform since we met in 1984 has been Levi's 501's, T-shirt, and Converse high-tops. He stopped by my sewing lounge with these "worn past perfection" gems. Notice the similar wear pattern on the right thigh. Only a guitar player.

MENDING

You may love your new jeans so much that you wear them to the point of needing a repair. Several books and blogs cover the topic of visible mending. Sashiko embroidery is featured in the book Hazel is reading, *Mending Matters: Stitch, Patch, and Repair Your Favorite Denim & More* by Katrina Rodabaugh. Take a look around on social media too.

A SECOND CHANCE (OR THIRD, OR FOURTH)

After you sew your jeans and get them worn in well, that little (or big!) tear or blowout can be restored to undetectable perfection by a talented darning-machine artist like Rain Delisle of Indigo Proof Denim Repair in Portland, Oregon.

She uses mid-20th century darning machines, once relegated to quick repairs for factory workers' clothing, to create flawless jean rejuvenation. This is an example of her work. Check out her truly jaw-dropping talents at indigoproof.com

Indigo Proof Denim Repair in Portland, Oregon.

THE ART OF WEARING JEANS

Keep a wearing, washing, and mending diary on your pocket bags? One can easily spend upwards of $300 on a pair of RTW jeans or many hours sewing a handmade pair. Maybe they do deserve a historian.

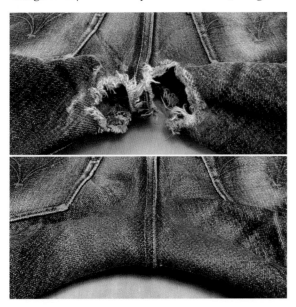

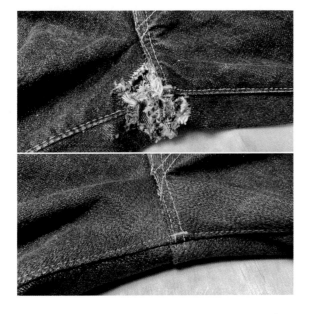

Lastly, you don't need to churn out multiple pairs of jeans. I've done it as research for this book and to use as samples for my workshop attendees.

This book was written to encourage the thoughtful creation of a comfortable, long-wearing garment. If they don't turn out the way you'd hoped the first time around, please complete them anyway and donate them to a reputable clothing charity so someone else can use them. I hope you sew slowly and enjoy the process.

With endless love, hugs & stitches,

Helen Bartley

CHAPTER 10
TEMPLATES

Here are some stitching and pocket templates that you can copy or trace. Please be sure to color outside the lines. Follow your sewing heart whenever and to wherever your imagination takes you. These are just guidelines.

FLY TOPSTITCHING TEMPLATES

Instructions start on page 133. These are exact size. Copy without enlarging.

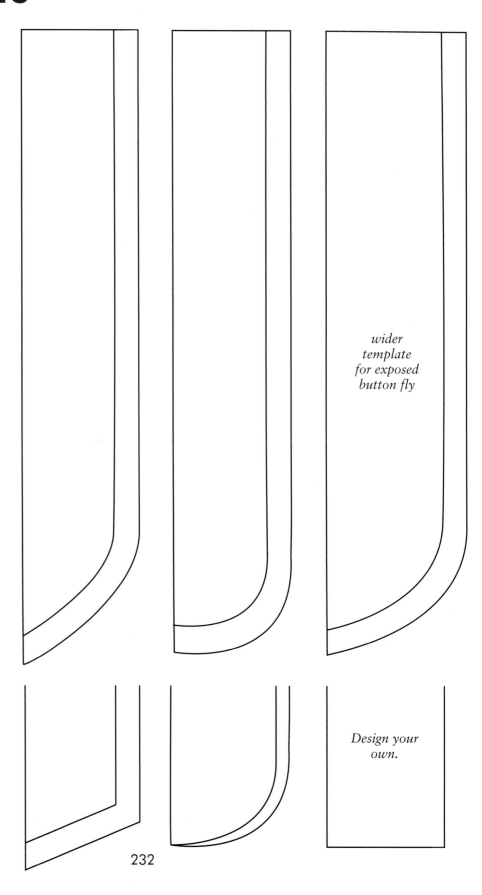

wider template for exposed button fly

Design your own.

POCKET TEMPLATES

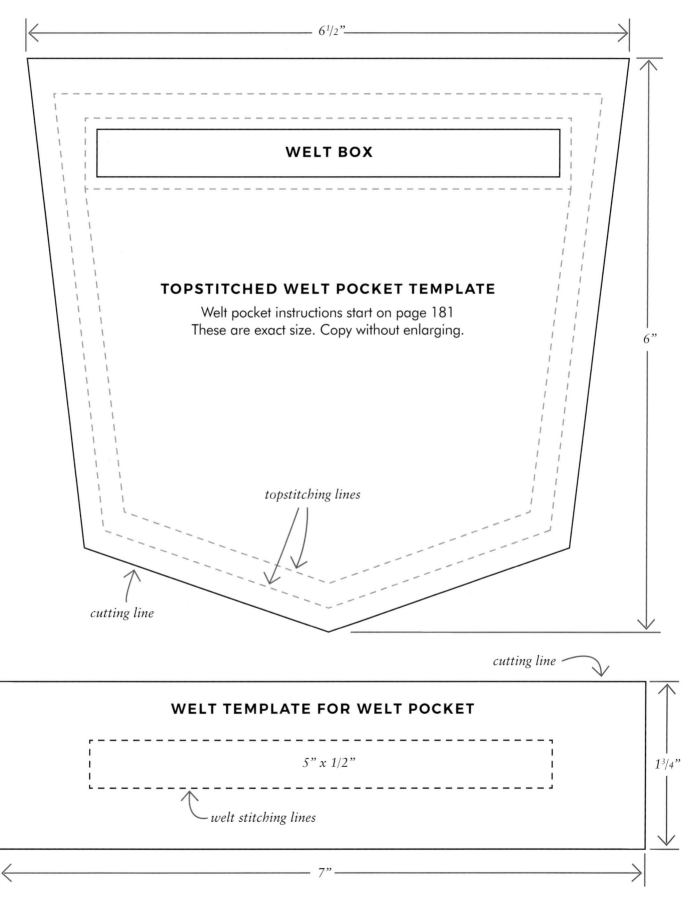

6½"

6"

WELT BOX

TOPSTITCHED WELT POCKET TEMPLATE

Welt pocket instructions start on page 181
These are exact size. Copy without enlarging.

topstitching lines

cutting line

cutting line

WELT TEMPLATE FOR WELT POCKET

5" x 1/2"

1¾"

welt stitching lines

7"

TEMPLATES

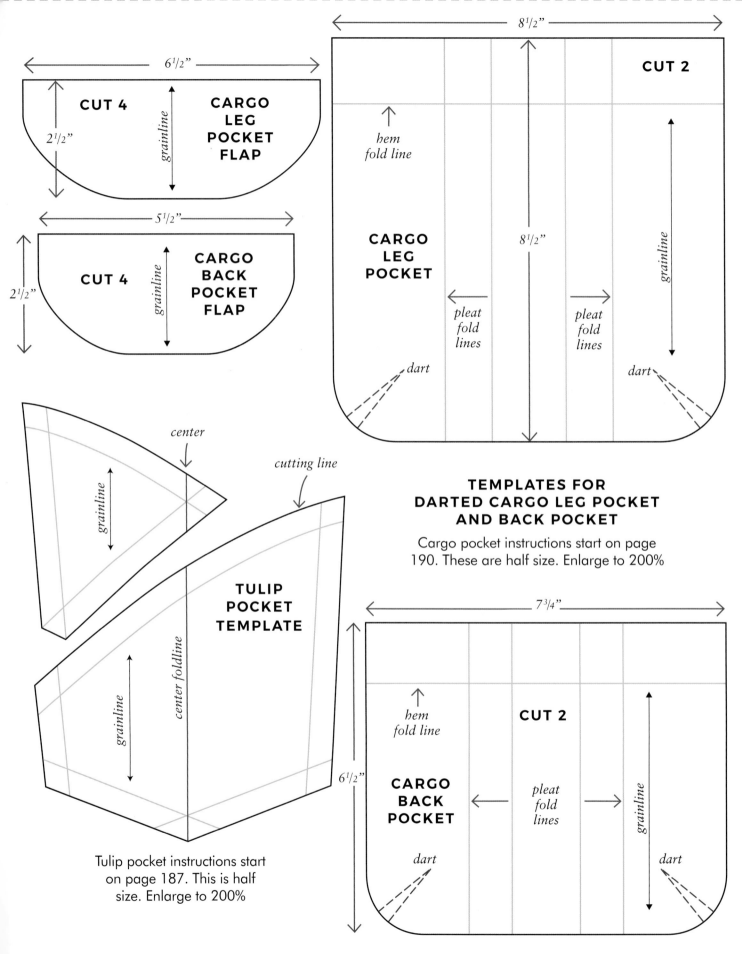

CUT 4

6¹/₂"

2¹/₂"

grainline

CARGO LEG POCKET FLAP

CUT 4

5¹/₂"

2¹/₂"

grainline

CARGO BACK POCKET FLAP

8¹/₂"

CUT 2

hem fold line

CARGO LEG POCKET

8¹/₂"

grainline

pleat fold lines

pleat fold lines

dart

dart

center

cutting line

grainline

TULIP POCKET TEMPLATE

grainline

center foldline

Tulip pocket instructions start on page 187. This is half size. Enlarge to 200%

TEMPLATES FOR DARTED CARGO LEG POCKET AND BACK POCKET

Cargo pocket instructions start on page 190. These are half size. Enlarge to 200%

7³/₄"

CUT 2

hem fold line

6¹/₂"

CARGO BACK POCKET

pleat fold lines

grainline

dart

dart

RESOURCES

DENIM WEBSITES

- Denim Hunters, denimhunters.com

- Heddel's, heddels.com (education tab)

JEANS HISTORY, STORIES, AND SEWING BOOKS

- *Jeans: A Cultural History of an American Icon* by James Sullivan

- *The Blue Jean Book: The Story Behind the Seams* by Tanya Lloyd Kyi. This book is filled with fabulous images of early jean manufacturer advertisements and it also touches on the impact of RTW jeans manufacturing on a social and ecological level.

- *A Denim Story: Inspirations from Bellbottoms to Boyfriends* by Emily Current, Meritt Elliot and Hilary Walsh. A pictorial jeans love story.

- *Denim: Street Style, Vintage, Obsession* and *Denim Dudes* by Amy Leverton

- *Denim Branded: Jeanswear's Evolving Design Details* by Nick Williams with Jenny Corpuz

- *Mending Matters: Stitch, Patch, and Repair Your Favorite Denim & More* by Katrina Rodabaugh

- *Sewing Jeans: The complete step-by-step guide* by Johanna Lundström

JEANS-MAKING PRODUCTS AND RESOURCES

Anytime you can shop your local fabric store—please, please do. Check with them first. If enough folks request an item, they will want to carry it.

Every day a new resource for denim fabric and sewing gear pops up. Use the headings below in your favorite internet search engine and see what appears.

- **Custom-made sewing hams and sleeve rolls:** Stitch Nerd Custom Shop: stitchnerdcustomshop.com

- **Denim:** Far, far too many to list. Again, try your local shop first.

- **Elastic:** Pamela's Fantastic Elastic, pamelaspatterns.com

- **Fabric reuse and recycling:** SCRAP Creative Reuse, scrapecreativeresuse.org; fabric scrap reuse—free "pouf" ottoman pattern at closetcorepatterns.com/fabric-floor-pouf-free-sewing-pattern

- **Jeans hardware—rivets, tack buttons, and setting tools:** Tandy leather, tandyleather.com; Prym kits available on Etsy and Amazon; Micron America, micronamerica.com; Pacific Trimmings, pacifictrimmings.com

- **Jeans-making kits (denim, thread, hardware):** Closet Core, closetcore.com; Cashmerette, cashmerette.com; Megan Nielsen Patterns, meganneilsen.com; Thread theory, threadtheory.ca

- **Jeans sewing patterns:** Butterick, Butterickpatterns.com; Cashmerette, cashmerette.com; Closet Core, closetcore.com; Jalie Patterns, jalie.com; McCall's, McCallpatterns.com; Megan Nielsen Patterns, meganneilsen.com; Pamela's Patterns, pamelaspatterns.com (pattern coming in 2022); Simplicity, simplicity.com; Thread theory, threadtheory.ca; Vogue, voguepatterns.com; Workroom Social, workroomsocial.com

- **Perfect Pattern Paper** (see page 240)

- **Rivet removal tool:** leathercrafttools.com

- **Technical fabrics:** Rockywoods, rockywoods.com; The Rain Shed, rainshed.com; Discovery Fabrics, discoveryfabrics.com (Canada).

TEACHER RESOURCES & HANDOUTS

INDEX

SNAP VIEWS

REAL PEOPLE MODELS:

PRO VIEWS:

METRIC CONVERSIONS:

1/8" = .3cm
1/4" = .6cm
3/8" = 1cm
1/2" = 1.3cm
5/8" = 1.5cm
3/4" = 2cm
7/8" = 2.2cm
1" = 2.5cm
1 1/2" = 3.8cm
2" = 5cm
36" = 91.44cm
39" = 1 meter (100cm)
45" = 1.14 meters (114 cm)
54" = 1.37 meters (137 cm)
60" = 1.52 meters (152 cm)

Note: Due to rounding, some conversions are not exact. Use the ruler at right to measure.

COMMON ABREVIATIONS

CF—Center Front

CB—Center Back

FGM—Finished Garment Measurements

RTW—Ready-to-Wear

METRIC RULER (CENTIMETERS)

LOOK FOR THESE PRODUCTS FROM PALMER/PLETSCH

BOOKS ON FIT, FASHION & FABRIC

OUR BOOKS, WRITTEN FROM DECADES OF EXPERIENCE, ARE FILLED WITH COLOR PHOTOS AND ILLUSTRATED, EASY-TO-FOLLOW HOW-TOS.

 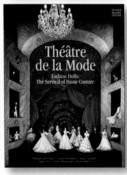   

BOOKS FOR THE HOME...AND SERGING

 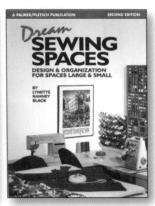

FROM BASICS TO CREATIVE POSSIBILITIES

AND A COOKBOOK

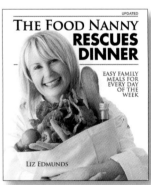

It all started with the book "Pants for Any Body" in 1973. We still have some of our "great value" small-format titles, which have been updated.
~ Pati

WE ALSO HAVE A "MASTER YOUR SERGER AT HOME" PROGRAM

238

VIDEOS

THE STYLES AND TECHNIQUES IN OUR BOOKS ARE BROUGHT TO LIFE AND EXPANDED ON BY MARTA ALTO, PATI PALMER, AND OTHERS IN THESE VIDEOS. AVAILABLE AS DVDS OR AT **PALMERPLETSCHDIGITAL.COM** FOR STREAMING AND DOWNLOAD

LEARN TO SEW PROGRAM

Janet Corzatt's Learn to Sew home study program includes four DVDs plus worksheet PDFs, templates, and two patterns.

CHILDREN LOVE TO SEW...

My First Sewing Books and Kits, by Winky Cherry
Along with a teaching manual and DVD, these offer a complete, thoroughly tested sewing program for children ages 5 to 11.

PATTERNS

Palmer/Pletsch for McCall's and Butterick are among The McCall Pattern Company's top-selling patterns.

USER-FRIENDLY INTERFACINGS & NOTIONS

PERFECT FUSE

- Developed BY sewers FOR sewers.

- These four distinctly different products cover 90% of interfacing needs.

- Come in convenient 1-yard and 3-yard packages.

- Extra wide for cutting larger pattern pieces.

- Each interfacing has its own separate use and care instructions.

- All four weights available in charcoal-black and ecru-white.

PERFECT SEW NEEDLE THREADER

Now thread both machine and hand needles with ease. On one end of this tool is the specially designed hook that makes threading easy. The other end is an integrated needle inserter for both conventional and serger machine needles.

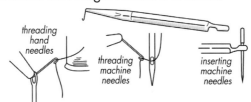

threading hand needles

threading machine needles

inserting machine needles

PERFECT SEW

Liquid wash-away fabric stabilizer

PERFECT PATTERN PAPER

two 84" x 48" sheets

BUSINESS & TEACHING TOOLS

PALMER/PLETSCH WORKSHOPS

Our "Sewing Vacations" are offered on a variety of sewing and fit topics. Workshops are held in Portland, Oregon, and at satellite locations around the country.

Teacher training sessions available on some topics include practice teaching sessions, digital slides and teaching script, camera-ready workbook handouts, and marketing information.

Visit www.palmerplesch.com for a complete schedule.

SEMINARS FOR TEACHERS

provided as downloads or CDs

For more details on these and other products, workshops, and teacher training, please visit our website:

PALMERPLETSCH.COM
PALMERPLETSCHDIGITAL.COM

info@palmerpletsch.com